EU and CARICOM

Investigating the unique EU-CARICOM legal relationship, this book explores the major theme of globalisation, which shapes inter-regional organisations individually and determines their relationship to one another. It evaluates how EU-CARICOM relations have fostered trade, security and other development measures, reflecting on the past, future and present of the Caribbean states that are active in the EU-CARICOM framework.

Providing case studies on key issues such as immigration, tax and energy, it examines the impact that the EU-CARICOM has on the slave trade and the deportation of millions of people. Such bitter experiences still indirectly shape culture, hopes and the economic framework of possibilities today; therefore, the focus of the volume is on the issues which the constant stream of globalisation creates. The book assesses many potential impacts that the agenda of the EU and Brexit pending will have upon the EU-CARICOM relationship, given the potential for these to create instability.

Overall, it highlights how the EU and CARICOM are representations for multilateralism and serve as models that provide the basis for many successful initiatives and agreements. In all new agreements and negotiations, the will to accept the Sustainable Development Goals and thus to make inequality, climate change and other goals of the SDGs the basis of an order that puts people at the centre, are evaluated, and the global agenda 2030 and its impact on EU-CARICOM.

Alicia Elias-Roberts is Deputy Dean and Lecturer in law, Faculty of Law, the University of the West Indies, St Augustine campus, Trinidad and Tobago.

Stephen Hardy is Professor of Law and a scholar in employment law. He is currently Head of the Coventry Law School, Coventry University, UK.

Winfried Huck is Professor of International and European Economic Law and Dean at the Brunswick European Law School, Ostfalia University of Applied Sciences, Wolfenbüttel, Germany.

Transnational Law and Governance

Series Editor: Paolo Davide Farah

West Virginia University, USA and gLAWcal – Global Law Initiatives for Sustainable Development, UK

In recent years the concepts of "transnational law" and "governance" have been explored by both scholars and practitioners with the terms taking on new meaning and significance, particularly in light of the ongoing economic crisis and a corresponding critical reappraisal of global institutional structures and governance. This multidisciplinary series aims to provide a home for research exploring these issues.

Transnational law covers a broad theoretical definition which includes studies emerging from disciplines such as international law, comparative law, international economic law and administrative law undertaken by legal scholars but also features extensive research undertaken by scholars from other disciplines, including but not limited to, political sciences, international relations, public administration, sociology, history, philosophy and geography. Governance in particular is now seen as important when we refer to the general stability of the markets, to good faith and other key principles which are fundamental to the notion of a fair market which is responsive to the needs of governments and citizens as well as businesses.

This series features cutting-edge works which critically analyse the relationship between governance, institutions and law from a variety of disciplinary perspectives.

Available titles in this series include:

EU and CARICOM
Dilemmas versus Opportunities on Development, Law and Economics
Edited by Alicia Elias-Roberts, Stephen Hardy and Winfried Huck

Business and Human Rights in Europe
International Law Challenges
Angelica Bonfanti

Forthcoming titles:

Administrative Appeals in EU Law
Giacomo Gattinara and Alessandro Di Mario

What Money Can't Buy, What Business Can't Sell
International Trade and Non-Trade Values
Csongor István Nagy

The Transnationalization of Anti-Corruption Law
Regis Bismuth, Jan Dunin-Wasowicz, Phils Nichols

Technocracy, Expertise and Multilevel Governance
What Role for Accountability?
Alessandra Arcuri and Florin Coman Kund

For more information about this series, please visit: www.routledge.com/Transnational-Law-and-Governance/book-series/TRANSGOVLAW

EU and CARICOM

Dilemmas versus Opportunities on Development, Law and Economics

Edited by Alicia Elias-Roberts, Stephen Hardy and Winfried Huck

Routledge
Taylor & Francis Group
LONDON AND NEW YORK

First published 2021
by Routledge
2 Park Square, Milton Park, Abingdon, Oxon OX14 4RN

and by Routledge
52 Vanderbilt Avenue, New York, NY 10017

Routledge is an imprint of the Taylor & Francis Group, an informa business

British Library Cataloguing-in-Publication Data
A catalogue record for this book is available from the British Library

Library of Congress Cataloging-in-Publication Data
A catalog record for this book has been requested

ISBN: 978-0-367-85776-9 (hbk)
ISBN: 978-0-367-56233-5 (pbk)
ISBN: 978-1-003-09686-3 (ebk)

Typeset in Galliard
by Apex CoVantage, LLC

Contents

Contributors

Aschille Clarke-Mendes is a graduate with an LLM from Queen's University, Canada.

Alicia Elias-Roberts is Deputy Dean and Lecturer in law, Faculty of Law, the University of the West Indies, St Augustine campus, Trinidad and Tobago.

Cherisse Francis is an attorney-at-law and graduate with an LLM from the University of Aberdeen, UK.

Anthony Gafoor is a PhD candidate, the University of the West Indies, St Augustine campus, Trinidad and Tobago and Chief Judge of the Tax Appeal Court of Trinidad and Tobago.

Stephen Hardy is Professor of Law and scholar in employment law. He is currently Head of the Coventry Law School, Coventry University, UK.

Winfried Huck is Professor of International and European Economic Law and Dean at the Brunswick European Law School, Ostfalia University of Applied Sciences, Wolfenbüttel, Germany.

Claudia Kurkin is Research Associate, Brunswick European Law School, Ostfalia University of Applied Sciences, Wolfenbüttel, Germany, and PhD candidate, Faculty of Law, Leibniz University of Hanover, Germany.

Margaret Liu is Senior Lecturer in Law, Coventry Law School, Coventry University, UK.

Stuart MacLennan is Senior Lecturer in Law, Coventry Law School, Coventry University, UK, and an associate member, Centre for Financial and Corporate Integrity.

Hannes Prochno is Research Assistant for European, Trade and Customs Law at Brunswick European Law School, Ostfalia University of Applied Sciences, Wolfenbüttel, Germany.

Achim Rogmann is Professor of European and International Business Law at the Brunswick European Law School (BELS), Ostfalia University of Applied Sciences, Wolfenbüttel, Germany.

Fabian Stancke is Professor of Civil Law, Insurance and Competition Law at the Brunswick European Law School, Ostfalia University of Applied Sciences, Wolfenbüttel, Germany.

Foreword from the President of the Caribbean Court of Justice

The Honourable Justice Mr Adrian Saunders

It has been just over ten years since the signing of the CARIFORUM-EU Economic Partnership Agreement (the EPA). One readily recalls that, in the lead-up to the execution of the EPA, and for some time afterwards, there was significant public discourse in the region about the advantages and disadvantages of the agreement. The EPA was, after all, the first of its kind to be negotiated between the European Union and any of the African Caribbean and Pacific (ACP) states. Moreover, after the United States of America, the EU is CARIFORUM's second largest trading partner.

While some regarded the EPA favourably as the dawn of a new era of relations between CARIFORUM and the EU, sceptics saw the principle of having these separate agreements as a weakening of the bargaining strength of ACP states. Certainly, a feature of the EPA is to introduce the reciprocal grant of preferences instead of the more favourable non-reciprocal duty-free market access ACP states enjoyed in the past.

In examining the relationship between the EU and CARICOM, it is always tempting to compare the process of integration in Europe with that which obtains among the Member States of the Caribbean Community. The reality is that, as the authors remind us, these processes have only so much in common. For a start, deeply political motivations impelled war-weary states in Europe to take pro-active steps to integrate, to pool and to surrender aspects of their national sovereignty. Closer to home, on the other hand, it may well have been the emerging threats posed by globalisation (especially the end of preferences) and the influence of international power-brokers that pressured regional leaders, jealous of and revelling in their sovereignty, to implement the Revised Treaty of Chaguaramas Establishing the Caribbean Community Including the CARICOM Single Market and Economy and to establish CARIFORUM. One obvious consequence to all this is that, on the one hand, there is *the European **Union***, while in this region there is *a Community of **Sovereign** States.*

Built into the EPA was a requirement for five yearly reviews of the progress in implementing the agreement. A study dated September 2014[1] provided a basis for discussion between the parties, and, in July 2015, a Joint Working

1 Monitoring the Implementation & Results of the CARIFORUM–EU EPA Agreement, Final Report – Executive Summary, September 2014.

and inequality. For this reason, we need the country at a national level, supported by other actors and integrated governance frameworks at the international level. In this regard, the role of the judiciary is also of great importance, as it cannot only guarantee that law is respected, but it can also set milestones with the potential to greatly impact the course of the society. The comparative analysis of the roles of the Court of Justice of the European Union and the Caribbean Court of Justice is of interest in this respect.

While looking at globalisation through a historical lens, the authors were careful not to overlook signals of modern drivers shaping the face of the world and potentially influencing the nature of globalisation in the future. The share of digital economy on GDP worldwide is growing and the disruptive character of digital technologies has a potential to significantly shape the nature of (not only) international trade. Big data and blockchain technology are already household names, and the trade between the European Union and the CARICOM region does not ignore these developments. On the contrary, various actors worldwide are looking for ways to implement them in an appropriate and effective manner. Vessels are still important to overcome geographical and physical distances, especially when it comes to trade in the context of the CARICOM region. However, the increased use of technologies facilitates the trade in this regard to a great extent. What is notable is the way the authors shed light on the potential of digital technologies and digital economy to contribute to the realisation of SDGs in a manner that balances economic growth and improves the situation of developing countries. Digitalisation, in a similar manner as automatisation, has a potential to make the work of value chains and businesses more efficient.[8] In this way, it has the potential to create more spare time and resources for steps benefiting the society and common good. Such integration of SDGs in daily business is crucial to examine their applicability in practice.

One needs to be reminded that the realisation of SDGs needs to be done in a manner respecting the intricate relationship among all the different SDGs. Hence, in an ideal case scenario, the realisation of one SDG should not be done to the detriment of others. They need to be seen and realised in a mutually supportive, non-conflicting manner. This book and case study of the CARICOM region illustrates how to achieve it in specific geographical and sectoral contexts.

Professor Paolo Davide Farah

Editor-in-Chief for the gLAWcal Book Series "Transnational Law and Governance" published by Routledge (New York/London).
West Virginia University, USA and gLAWcal – Global Law Initiatives for Sustainable Development, UK

8 Angelica Bonfanti, *Business and Human Rights in Europe: International Law Challenges* (gLAWcal Book Series, Transnational Law and Governance Series, Routledge Publishing 2018), Hardback, ISBN 9781138484672, pp. 1–264.

as the origins of the CARICOM integration are rooted in the United Kingdom's effort to empower its colonies economically and to strengthen their competitiveness through their economic integration. Hence, even though it is possible to detect parallels between the integration leading to the creation of the European Union and CARICOM region, the observer should pay attention to the fact that the motives behind it demonstrate certain differences.

The common phrase 'intercultural competence' presupposes also the ability to look at certain prior events and developments through a certain cultural lens. The variety of authors involved in the present volume guarantees that the book meets this condition. For this reason, readers – and eventually stakeholders from other regions with professional or commercial interest in the CARICOM region – will not get lost in translation and will get the understanding of collective memory and complex context of the CARICOM countries.

As noted previously, in order to achieve a level and form of globalisation capable of bringing benefits to the people from all layers of society, it is necessary to take active steps towards the realisation of Sustainable Development Goals enshrined in the Agenda 2030. Hence, it is necessary to shape the governance frameworks in the light of these goals and integrate them therein. The European Union is a formidable model in this regard. The European Union set the stage for the adoption of the Paris Agreement, and the new generation of free trade agreements is set to make ecological and sustainable development concerns stable pillars of global trade relations. The process of the adoption of the MERCOSUR agreement and the role of the Amazonian forest is a point of contention between the European Union and Brazil under the leadership of current President Bolsonaro. It represents a valuable example by reminding us of the possibility to place environmental concerns and other NTCs[7] at the same level as trade-related matters, and difficulties related therewith. At the same time, this conflict is also a reminder of the fact that to make it happen, it is necessary to overcome and challenge certain dogma ingrained in the nature of global trade. In fact, such development is indispensable, considering that the future of global trade and the market economy itself will depend more and more on our ability to address climate change-related risks.

At the same time, the world of business should not be spared of efforts to contribute to the fulfilment of corresponding obligations and objectives. The idea of sustainability should be embraced by businesses around the world and translated in business strategies and business models, as well as in global value and supply chains. If sustainability is to ever become more than a buzzword, this implementation is crucial. Sustainable Development Goals (SDGs) represent a prospective tool and frame of reference for establishing balance between the pursuit of profits and wealth and NTCs. We need the market economy to generate wealth and prosperity, but an unregulated market economy does not care for ecological costs

7 Paolo Davide Farah, 'Trade and Progress: The Case of China' (2016) 30 Columbia Journal of Asian Law 97–107.

At the core of meaning of NTCs, there is the assertion that it is not really possible to have economic growth in the long term without a real geographical and geological balance between human activities and the Earth's habitat. In general, we need to have an effective paradigm shift in the idea of industrialisation and particularly in the cities' development. Any further expansion of the human race must happen with much more consideration to the protection and respect of the forests, the flora and fauna. Otherwise, nature might continue to show us more and more visible negative effects on our human society, with unpredictable spillover effects[5] like what has been occurring for COVID-19. Security, trade, investment, economic growth and environmental protection are so far separated components of national policy that should now be balanced and reconciled with a holistic and more naturally oriented vision.

These topics are constitutive and pivotal of the gLAWcal book series on "Global Law and Sustainable Development" and "Transnational Law and Governance", both published by Routledge Publishing (New York/London).

It is possible to observe a shift in environmental governance towards participatory and inclusive approaches, as well as a more polycentric, multi-scalar and multi-level governance,[6] which has both positive and negative consequences. Moreover, the model of the European integration, with all its shortcomings, has the potential to serve as a model for the CARICOM region as well.

Any meaningful attempts to create a bright future – or at least a hope for it – presuppose the ability to learn from the past. Even though one needs to be aware of the profound truth of the disclaimer known to investors – past profits are not a guarantee of future returns – the past has undoubtedly a quality to powerfully shape our perception of the present and our understanding and vision for the future. The notion of mental slavery, known in the narratives of the Afro-Caribbean region as one of the symptoms that needs to be overcome to achieve emancipation from the bondages of the past, is one of the preconditions for reaching full potential of the CARICOM region. Hence, the authors rightly point out the often-horrific nature of globalisation in the past: slave trade, representing a trade scheme that led to the genocide of indigenous people living in the CARICOM countries. When one wants to build a societal consensus about the benefits of present-day globalisation and integration related therein, one inevitably needs to show a formidable degree of cultural sensitivity and empathy. Europe´s prosperity and wealth accumulated in the course of the centuries are only one side of a coin. Europe´s historical wealth is to a great extent owed to the profits stemming from a darker variety of globalisation represented by the slave trade. The role of the United Kingdom is particularly illuminative in this regard,

5 David Quammen, *Spillover: Animal Infections and the Next Human Pandemic* (W. W. Norton & Company 2013).

6 PD Farah and P Rossi, 'National Energy Policies and Energy Security in the Context of Climate Change and Global Environmental Risks: A Theoretical Framework for Reconciling Domestic and International Law through a Multiscalar and Multilevel Approach' (2011) 20(6) European Energy and Environmental Law Review 232–244.

Foreword from the Editor-in-Chief for the gLAWcal Book Series "Transnational Law and Governance", Routledge Publishing – Professor Paolo Davide Farah

Paolo Davide Farah[1]

EU and CARICOM: Dilemmas versus Opportunities on Development, Law and Economics, edited by Alicia Elias-Roberts, Stephen Hardy and Winfried Huck, represents a relevant collection of chapters and authors, and in the light of its various facets shows one of the pieces in the complex puzzle of globalisation.

Globalisation is a phenomenon of inherent complexity. As such, it is defined by a number of positive, as well as negative, traits. The seemingly inextricable links between countries – created by international trade and membership in a variety of international organisations – are seen as a guarantee and precondition of (relative) international security and peace. However, they are being questioned by various forms of nationalism, disguised in the forms of trade protectionism or feverish defence of state sovereignty. Even though globalisation has managed to create unprecedented links between countries across the world, it has also made the divisions in society more visible. Events such as Brexit – a prominent example of profound political miscalculation and risk of applying instruments of direct democracy to questions of great complexity – depict a picture of the British society divided between the so-called anywheres and somewheres. It seems that our hunter-gatherer mind-set still needs to cope with the evolution of a globalised world that is constantly outpacing the ability of the human mind to

1 Paolo Davide Farah, West Virginia University, John D. Rockefeller IV, School of Policy and Politics, Department of Public Administration and College of Law; West Virginia University, Energy Institute and Center for Innovation in Gas Research and Utilization (CIGRU); West Virginia University, Institute of Water Security and Science (IWSS). Founder, President, Director, Principal Investigator and Senior Research Fellow at gLAWcal – Global Law Initiatives for Sustainable Development. Senior Fellow at the IIEL – Institute of International Economic Law, Georgetown University Law Center. Editor-in-Chief for the gLAWcal Book Series 'Global Law and Sustainable Development' and for the gLAWcal Book Series 'Transnational Law and Governance' published by Routledge (New York/London).

manage change. Brexit is a step into the unknown for the British society as well as for the European Union – it is one of the first steps backwords in the story of the European integration. Even though this observation is not positive, this event can undoubtedly serve as a catalyst in a chain of unforeseen consequences. Considering the special relationship and ties between the United Kingdom and CARICOM, the authors of the present volume wrote a book that might potentially be a starting point for a highly topical research line in the near future. Brexit has wide-ranging ramifications, with a potential impact on the relationship between the United Kingdom and the CARICOM countries as well. As the authors note in the beginning of their book, the consequences of Brexit are not limited to the mutual relationship between the European Union and the United Kingdom – and the matters within the United Kingdom, which might even have an impact on the independence of the British judiciary – but can be felt on the other side of the world. As such, it is an example of the so-called butterfly affect, in which the movement of a butterfly´s wings can cause a storm on the other side of the world.

The present book does not shy away to name the shortcomings of globalisation in the field of institutional and legal frameworks. However, the motive of this form of diagnosis is inherently positive, articulating the inevitability of globalisation – naturally respecting and promoting the importance of sustainable development – as it lacks any meaningful alternative capable of improving our lives. Even though states remain relevant actors, their role is balanced with the increasingly relevant role of non-state actors, ranging from individuals to companies and non-governmental organisations. Thus, the spirit and notion of collaborative governance[2] penetrates the book as a red line and an underlying precondition for realisation of the idea of sustainable development in a globalised world.

Due to COVID-19,[3] the necessity to balance sustainable development and globalisation has become even more important with the recent events, which the world is currently witnessing, and perfectly fits into the broader discussions related to the necessary changes and improvements of the international legal norms and systems of governance towards the protection of Non-Trade Concerns (NTCs).[4]

2 Margaret Stout and Jeannine M. Love, *A Radically Democratic Response to Global Governance. Dystopian Utopias* (gLAWcal Book Series, Transnational Law and Governance Series, Routledge Publishing 2016), Hardback, ISBN 9781138654051, pp. 1–242. See also Paolo Davide Farah, 'Foreword' in Margaret Stout and Jeannine M. Love (eds), *Integrative Governance: Generating Sustainable Responses to Global Crises* (gLAWcal Book Series, Global Law and Sustainable Development Series, Routledge Publishing 2019), Hardback, ISBN 9781138695733, 2018, pp. 1–260.

3 Ruiyun Li et al., 'Substantial Undocumented Infection Facilitates the Rapid Dissemination of Novel Coronavirus (SARS-CoV2)' (2020) Science 1.

4 Paolo Davide Farah, 'Trade and Progress: The Case of China' (2016) 30 *Columbia Journal of Asian Law* 97–107; Paolo Davide Farah and Elena Cima (eds), *China's Influence on Non-Trade Concerns in International Economic Law* (gLAWcal Book Series Global Law and Sustainable Development Book Series, Routledge Publishing September 2016), ISBN 978-1-4094-4848-8, pp. 1–584.

Document[2] was issued reflecting the five-year review. The review noted the inauspicious timing of the coming into force of the EPA as the latter coincided with the onset of a major global financial and economic crisis that naturally had 'a profound impact on economic development generally and on the ability of the Parties to take advantage of the market access opportunities available under the Agreement'.[3] The global crisis severely exacerbated the peculiar challenges faced by CARIFORUM States, all of which, in the best of times, are seriously burdened by their extreme vulnerability to external shocks and weak international competitiveness.

As to trade in goods, the review did not evince any material changes favourable to the region over the five-year period. Indeed, there was a significant decline in trade between the Organisation of Eastern Caribbean States (OECS) and the EU with the value of OECS exports into Europe declining as compared to the five years before the signing of the agreement. The review of trade in services was affected by the limited availability of relevant data. Paragraph 15 of the Working Document bears repetition in full. It states:

> According to the review study, estimates for revenue losses of CARIFORUM States range from € 74 million to € 159 m for the period 2009–2013, and from € 353 m to € 498 m for the period 2009–2033. This projection does not take into account any trade divergence resulting from lower tariffs being applied to EU goods over the period of liberalisation nor the elimination of other duties and charges as provided for under Article 16. The projections also do not take into account any fiscal adjustment measures implemented by CARIFORUM States.

Into this maelstrom there looms all the uncertainties attendant upon the United Kingdom's separation from the EU. What shape will that humongous divorce take? How will it affect the EU and also the UK? What would be the consequences for EU – CARICOM and too CARICOM – UK relations? As this book goes to press, it is impossible to answer these questions with any degree of certainty. But, as is attempted by Stephen Hardy, one can posit the possibilities that exist within certain parameters.

The authors of this book are to be complimented for an extensive analysis of and commentary on disparate aspects of the relationship between Europe and the Caribbean in the context of the EPA. Reviews of the EPA must not be left only to the Joint CARIFORUM-EU Council and the EPA institutions. There needs to be as well far more discussion among members of the region's academic community. This book makes a welcome contribution to this endeavour.

The Honourable Justice Mr Adrian Saunders
The President of the Caribbean Court of Justice

2 Five Year Review of the CARIFORUM–EU Economic Partnership Agreement, Joint Working Document, 14 July 2015.

3 ibid.

Abbreviations

AAAA	Addis Ababa Action Agenda
AB	Appellate Body
ACP	African Caribbean and Pacific
AfCFTA	African Continental Free Trade Agreement
AG	Advocate General
BEPS	Base Erosion and Profit Sharing
Brexit	Britain Exiting the EU
CARICOM	Caribbean Community
CARIFORUM	Caribbean Forum
CARIFTA	Caribbean Free Trade Agreement
CCC	Caribbean Competition Commission
CCJ	Caribbean Court of Justice
CCP	Common Commercial Policy
CCCTB	Common Consolidated Corporate Tax Base
CCREEE	Caribbean Centre for Renewable Energy and Energy Efficiency
CEO	Chief Executive Officer
CEFACT	Centre for Trade Facilitation ad Electronic Business
CELAC	Community of Latin America and Caribbean States
CETA	Comprehensive Economic and Trade Agreement
CIPS	Citizenship by Investment Programme
CJEU	Court of Justice of the European Union
COFCOR	Council for Foreign and Community Relations
COM	Commission
CPAS	Cotonou Partnership Agreement
CRC	Controlled Foreign Companies
CSR	Corporate Social Responsibility
CSME	CARICOM Single Market and Economy
DSB	Dispute Settlement Body
EBA	'*Everything But Arms*' Agreement
EC	European Community
ECCB	Eastern Caribbean Central Bank
ECJ	European Court of Justice
EEA	European Economic Area

EEC	European Economic Community
ECOFIN	European Committee on Finance
EFTA	European Free Trade Agreement
EPA	European Political Agreement
EU	European Union
FTA	Free Trade Agreement
GATT	General Agreement on Tariffs and Trade
GATS	General Agreement on Trade in Services
GDP	Gross Domestic Product
GR	Generic Resources
GSP	General System of Preferences
HE	Her/His Excellency
HOGS	Heads of Government(s)
ICJ	International Court of Justice
ICSID	International Centre for the Settlement of Investment Disputes
IGBA	Illegal Gambling Business Act
ILA	International Law Association
ILC	International Law Commission
IMF	International Monetary Fund
IMO	International Maritime Organisation
IPR	Intellectual Property Rights
ISPS	International Ship and Port Facility Security
JEFTA	Japan Economic Partnership Agreement
LDC	Least Developed Countries
MAR	Market Access Regulation
MFN	Most Favoured Nation
MDG	Millennium Development Goals
MS	Member State
NAFTA	North American Free Trade Agreement
NEC	New European Consensus
NT	National Treatment
NYC	New York Convention
OCTS	Overseas Countries and Territories
OECD	Organization of Economic Cooperation and Development
OECS	Organization of Eastern Caribbean States
PEPS	Politically Exposed Persons
REFIT	Regulatory Fitness and Performance Programme
RoO	Rules of Origin
RKC	Revised Kyoto Convention
RTC	Revised Treaty of Chaguaramas
SCC	Stockholm Chamber of Commerce
SDGS	Sustainable Development Goals
SIAS	Sustainability Impact Assessment
SOLAS	Safety of Life at Sea
SW	Single Window

TEI	Trade and Economic Integration
TFA	Trade Facilitation Agreement
TFEU	Treaty on the Functioning of the EU
UK	United Kingdom
UKPC	United Kingdom Privy Council
UN	United Nations
UNCTAD	UN Conference on Trade and Development
UNCITRAL	UN Convention on International Trade and Arbitration Law
US	United States of America
VCLT	Vienna Convention on the Law of Treaties
WBG	World Bank Group
WCO	World Customs Organisation
WTO	World Trade Organisation

Introduction

1 The EU-CARICOM in context

Alicia Elias-Roberts, Stephen Hardy and Winfried Huck

In October 2008 Antigua and Barbuda, The Bahamas, Barbados, Belize, Dominica, Grenada, Guyana, Jamaica, Saint Lucia, Saint Vincent and the Grenadines, Saint Kitts and Nevis, Suriname, Trinidad and Tobago, and the Dominican Republic signed the CARIFORUM-EU Economic Partnership Agreement. CARICOM is the official bastion of the Caribbean's regional integration. It represents the culmination of long-standing struggles often precipitated by progressions in European integration. Though CARICOM and the EU both emerged from post-World War II conditions, their objectives influenced very different paths to development.[1] Europe's integration was spearheaded by independent nations guided by the 'safeguarding of peace through economic integration'.[2] The emphasis on equality reduced the struggle for political power,[3] resulting in increased and improved trade as a fortunate by-product. On the other hand, Caribbean integration was initiated by the United Kingdom on behalf of its colonies and became primarily focused on economic growth, competitiveness in the global marketplace and trade from an early stage.[4] Today, the two entities are mainly linked as trading partners, with the EU providing significant development aid.

In the first instance, the United Kingdom proposed a federal model for Caribbean integration. It proposed that ten former colonies would form a single state, which remained financially and institutionally controlled by Britain.[5] This federation was intended to function similarly to the Australian Commonwealth or the

1 David S Berry, *Caribbean Integration Law* (OUP 2014) ch 2, 30.
2 Miroslav N Jovanovic, 'Was European Integration Nice while It Lasted? (2013) 28(1) Journal of Economic Integration 1, 2.
3 ibid.
4 Consolidated Version of the Treaty on the Functioning of the European Union [2016] OJ C 202/59, Preamble; RTC (n 19) art 6.
5 The West Indies Federation existed from 3 January 1958 until 31 May 1962, and the countries which were members of the Federation are Barbados, Trinidad and Tobago, Jamaica, St. Lucia, Grenada, Antigua and Barbuda, Guyana, Dominica, St. Kitts and Nevis, St. Vincent and the Grenadines. *See* Elisabeth Wallace, 'The West Indies Federation: Decline and Fall' (1962) 17(3) International Journal 269, 269.

Canadian Confederation with the ultimate political goal of independence.[6] This model was inherently colonial and was criticised by islands such as Jamaica and Trinidad and Tobago who at the time held controlling interest in the region. These territories supported the federation to the extent that it 'offered an escape from colonialism and a gateway to independence'.[7] However, expectantly their leaders remained concerned about the financial implications of this system.

Eventually, both Jamaica and Trinidad and Tobago withdrew from the Federation in favour of independence. This led to its dissolution and a secondary attempt with the remaining eight territories, which ended unsuccessfully in 1965 due to a lack of resources and a small population.[8] These failures revealed that the region's political and social climate, plagued by internal 'divisions by history, geography and local attachments' was unready for this type of integration.[9]

Simultaneously, the independent nations in Europe were forging ahead with indigenous integration initiatives, which reflected their circumstances and remained culturally relevant.[10] One of the manifestations of these efforts was the 1960 Stockholm Convention.[11] Five years later, the region once again followed in European footsteps, shifting the focus of their integration from a political focus to an economically driven free trade model. The result, the first Caribbean Free Trade Association (CARIFTA) Agreement,[12] like many before it contained provisions which were verbatim to European conventions.[13] Yet this agreement quickly suffered from a lack of capacity to form a political or economic union[14] and a deficit in benefits when compared to the involved risks. The second, more widely adopted CARIFTA Agreement,[15] diverged from the European model and represented the Caribbean's political and economic conditions more thoroughly.[16] In the 1970s Caribbean integration began its continuous evolution into the

6 'Centrifugal Force: Caribbean Integration' *The Economist* (London, 2 June 2012) <www.economist.com/node/21556277>.

7 Wallace (n 5) 270.

8 Trinidad and Jamaica accounted for three-quarters of the wealth within the Member States and made up seven-eighths of the population. See Elisabeth Wallace, 'The West Indies Federation: Decline and Fall' (1962) 17(3) International Journal 269, 270.

9 Wallace (n 5) 270.

10 Richard L Abbott, 'The Caribbean Free Trade Association' (1969) 1(3) Lawyer of the Americas 1, 12.

11 Convention Establishing the European Free Trade Association (signed 4 January 1960, entered into force 3 May 1960) 370 UNTS 3 (Stockholm Convention).

12 Dickenson Bay Agreement establishing the Caribbean Free Trade Association (adopted 15 December 1965, entered into force 1 May 1968) 772 UNTS 3.

13 Abbott (n 10) 1. EFTA now competes with the EU and most of the founding members of EFTA have left EFTA and joined the EU.

14 ibid. 6.

15 The Agreement establishing CARIFTA was signed by Barbados, Guyana, Trinidad and Tobago and Antigua, Dominica, Montserrat, St. Vincent, St. Kitts, Nevis, Anguilla, St. Lucia, Grenada and Jamaica. See Richard L Abbott, 'The Caribbean Free Trade Association' (1969) 1(3) Lawyer of the Americas 1, 1.

16 Abbott (n 10) 1,9,12.

current CARICOM system.[17] Reformations continued at the dawn of the millennium when Europe was redefining its integration process and treaties.[18] CARICOM was influenced by this and overhauled its institutional and legal structures. This aided the expansion of regional markets and the creation of an economic community.[19]

Consequently, this book investigates this first decade of this unique EU-CARICOM legal relationship. The thread running through the volume can be seen in the major theme of globalisation, which shapes inter-regional organisations individually and determines their relationship to one another in a way that is open to the future, given that the drivers of globalisation are trade, tax, investment and SDGs which provide the substantive framework of this material pouring into the present. Therefore, this contemporary subject matter found within this volume reflects on the past, future and present of the Caribbean states that are active in the EU-CARICOM framework. To that end, this book evaluates how EU-CARICOM relations have fostered trade and security and other development measures. Further, it provides case studies on key issues such as immigration, tax and energy. The impact that the EU-CARICOM has on the slave trade and the deportation of millions of people will be examined. Such bitter experiences are woven into the genetic code of Caribbean culture and still indirectly shape culture, hopes and the economic framework of possibilities today. The focus of the volume is therefore on the issues which the constant stream of globalisation creates, notably with the agenda of the EU and the pending Brexit of the UK which also affects CARICOM, due to the numerous relations of the Member States with the UK and the EU. Consequently, any relapse into nationalism does not create answers, but instead it invokes instability. Any potential impact upon the EU-CARICOM relationship will be assessed.

Overall, this book highlights how the EU and CARICOM show that multilateralism in particular is a model that provides the basis for many successful initiatives and agreements; for example, the currently negotiated Post-Cotonou Agreement with 79 African, Caribbean and Pacific countries, with CARIFORUM, CELAC and numerous other agreements that create and stabilise further links. In all these new agreements and negotiations, the will to accept the SDGs and thus to make inequality, climate change and other goals of the SDGs the basis of an order that puts people at the centre will be evaluated, as will the global agenda 2030 and its impact on EU-CARICOM, as the authors seek to reshape and even redefine the EU-CARICOM as an alternative framework for transnational trade and economic and social relations.

17 Treaty Establishing the Caribbean Community (adopted 4 July 1973, entered into force 1 August 1973) 949 UNTS 17 [Treaty of Chaguaramas].

18 Treaty on European Union (adopted 7 February 1992, entered into force 1 November 1993) (The Maastricht Treaty) (TEU).

19 In 2001 the 1973 treaty establishing the Caribbean Community and the Annex to the treaty merged with the Revised Treaty of Chaguaramas, establishing the Caribbean Community including the CARICOM Single Market and Economy (adopted 5 July 2001, entered into force 1 January 2006) 2259 UNTS 293 (RTC).

Accordingly, this monograph, comprising four parts, is borne out of a partnership between the University of the West Indies (Trinidad and Tobago), Coventry (UK) and Brunswick European Law School of Ostfalia University (Germany), and a conference convened in Trinidad in September 2018 seeks to critically evaluate the challenges of the past and in the future facing sustainable development within the context of transnational law and governance. To that extent this monograph explores such an emerging contemporary context, whilst acknowledging the potential impact of Brexit, and will assess its impact on a diverse range of issues including trade, tax, environment, sustainable development and migration. Accordingly, the collective intellectual thought assesses these thematic issues and questions the challenges to overcome and those facing the EU-CARICOM in the future. Given these emerging trends, this text seeks to analyse how these challenges will be met and/or resolved. All of these objectives will be explored throughout the proposed monograph. Moreover, its discourse will not only detail transnational law but also will explore new approaches. Consequently, such comparative evidence in this monograph will offer insightful lessons and highlight a new pursuit of a new strategic approach to EU-CARICOM issues.

The first chapter is written by Alicia Elias-Roberts, Stephen Hardy and Winfried Huck and provides a preview of the entire text. It introduces the reader to general and specific issues covered in the various parts of the book and sets the context for the EU-CARICOM dialogue which follows in the various chapters. In Part I, the impact of Brexit is considered. In Chapter 2 Stephen Hardy surveys how Brexit joined our lexicon following the United Kingdom's Referendum on its then prospective withdrawal of the European Union on 23 June 2016. Following that Referendum, with 51.9% of the participating UK electorate voting to leave the EU, 'Brexit' the term, concept and legal withdrawal method was born. It is a short and simple and now widely acknowledged term with pervasive implications. However, how will the UK cope when it returns to its pre-EU legal order? To that end, what challenges exist both at present and in the future for the UK, EU and other nations? Arguably, the UK is in search of a new legal order. But what will that be? And, how will it interact with the rest of the world, alongside other alternative and sometimes competing legal orders? Within such a contemporary and controversial ongoing debate, this chapter therefore canvasses the potential impact areas post-Brexit. Having identified such impact, an assessment of what Brexit means for the UK's engagement, in legal terms, globally will be evaluated. Navigating through the new Brexit terrain, is the UK in search of a new legal order? If so, what will influence that? Overall, this chapter will review how Brexit impact can be a positive and not just a negative experience and posits a progress report on the state of 'global law' today.

Similarly, in Chapter 3 Margaret Liu considers the impact of Brexit on anti-suit injunctions since, as a result of a Brexit referendum in 2016, the UK is currently negotiating its existence from the EU, and this will have a significant effect on arbitration in London. Anti-suit injunctions are often sought in the English courts to exercise their supervisory role over arbitration and restrain foreign proceedings in favour of arbitration. The impact of Brexit on anti-suit injunctions of arbitration will depend almost entirely on the terms of the Brexit negotiations. To this end, this book will critically analyse the jurisdictions advanced by the UK courts for issuance of anti-suit injunctions and the effect of the decisions of the European Court of Justice in *Turner v Grovit*, *West Tankers* and *Gazprom*. It then examines whether the UK courts will revert back to the full practice of anti-suit injunctions and depart from the ECJ decision in the *West Tankers* case and how this will affect the arbitration of dispute after Brexit and the possible options available for the UK regarding the scope of the ECJ decision in the UK.

In Part II, Chapter 4 Achim Rogmann places the EU-CARICOM relationship in its central trade context. The main focus of this chapter is on trade in goods and relevant instruments for trade liberalisation. This contribution examines EU's market access provisions and their compatibility with WTO commitments. The contribution evaluation also addresses the trade facilitation aspect by canvassing those elements of the EPA dealing with measures governing trade facilitation, especially in comparison with other international tools in terms of this objective. Hereby it will be demonstrated that various standards of the EPA already form part of other multilateral instruments in the area of customs legislation, hence with lack of capability to introduce new standards for promoting trade and development. Taking care about current developments consequences of the Brexit have been integrated into the contribution.

Hannes Prochno further develops the EU-CARICOM trade theme in Chapter 5, assessing how digitalisation impacts upon maritime trade. Notably, Member States of the Caribbean Community and the European Union share a long tradition of maritime trade with each other as well as with the rest of the world. Due to recent trends of digitalisation, policymakers of both economic regions are and will be confronted with legal issues with regard to the interchange of electronic data. Two major chances, but also challenges, in this context have been put on the agenda under the context of trade facilitation: First, there is the implementation of a so-called Single Window concept, which has been dealt with by legal scholars and legislators for some time. Second, there is the recent approach of introducing blockchain technology into the digital infrastructure of shipping, discovering its potential beyond crypto currency. This contribution will evaluate both innovations and point out how they are captured and connected on a legal basis under the scope of sustainable development.

In Chapter 6 Claudia Kurkin suggests that the energy and investment sector is the sphere of legal significance in terms of sustainability with a focus on implementing the Sustainable Development Goals in the Energy and Investment sector. It deals with current developments in international investment law respectively the lack of sustainable development and with the concept, legal grounds and current challenges for the newly formed European Energy Union. It becomes clear that there are various EU interactions in the context of transnational law-making. And the following problems are discussed in particular: is a new WTO Agreement on Trade in Energy needed? Does the European Commission have a new right to issue intergovernmental agreements? How could the concept of sustainability effectively be integrated in international investment law?

The existing possibilities are examined, and the following thesis is developed: the sustainability concept and thus the Sustainable Development Goals can be integrated into international investment law, in particular by means of a modified proportionality test which leads to thoroughly balanced, reasonable and transparent results for all parties involved.

In Part III, the key issues of taxation and immigration and their regulation in the EU-CARICOM are critically evaluated. Anthony Gafoor sets the scene in Chapter 7 and examines the development and evolution of the relationship between EU-CARICOM in relation to trade and development. This chapter examines the initial history of trade relations between the two groupings, including preferential access to EU Member States by way of multilateral treaties by CARICOM and the move towards a Caribbean single market and economy. It also discusses the case law which has emanated from the two trading blocs. These speak to emerging developments in regional integration and the extent to which there has been the application and importation of trade-related principles through case law from both the Court of Justice of the European Communities as well as the Caribbean Court of Justice in relation to treaty interpretation.

However, of global significance and of importance to EU-CARICOM relations is cooperation on tax avoidance. To that end, in Chapter 8 Stuart MacLennan considers the role of Caribbean states and territories in facilitating tax avoidance. For almost 20 years, institutions including the OECD, the EU, and, more recently, the G20 have sought to develop measures to curtail tax avoidance. An increasingly globalised economy and the relative ease with which capital flows internationally, however, means that national or even regional solutions to the problems of tax avoidance have proved insufficient. These institutions have, therefore, sought to bring outside actors, in particular those in the Caribbean, into line with what are increasingly broadly accepted international standards on taxation. Although sometimes grudgingly, most countries and territories that are conventionally regarded as tax havens are gradually moving towards compliance with these international norms. Attempts at imposing new tax rules on tax havens, in particular by the EU, have not been without controversy, and it is arguable that without the United Kingdom as a moderating influence within the EU, coordinated action against tax havens will become stricter still, which will affect the Caribbean more than any other region in the world. This chapter considers these issues in three sections. First, this chapter examines previous and current efforts at tackling tax avoidance, in particular in the EU, with particular reference to the Caribbean. Second, this chapter outlines the shifting and, at times, diverging approaches to taxation between the UK and EU. Third, this chapter considers the relationship between Caribbean countries and territories and the EU, and the UK, and the effect that the UK's exit from the EU will have on the latter's approach to Caribbean tax havens. This chapter concludes that while the UK's exit from the EU will result in a diminution of the influence of Caribbean countries and territories within the EU with respect to tax policy, the prevailing global trend is towards stricter rules on tax avoidance and that further action against tax havens, including those in the Caribbean, may be inevitable.

The final chapter in this part discusses social challenges such as immigration and citizenship. Chapter 9 by Aschille Clarke-Mendes evaluates the new concept of self-deportation within the CARICOM region which offers lessons for EU and wider-ranging reforms. For instance, the Republic of Trinidad and Tobago's Immigration Act contains problematic provisions which give unfettered discretion to executive bodies. Furthermore, it guarantees scarce rights to non-citizens. This resultant confusion has caused severe deprivation of liberties, arbitrary arrests, prolonged detention, and a state of limbo for those without the rights of "membership" guaranteed to citizens. Amending this legislation is paramount for Trinidad and Tobago to apply the principles of non-discrimination and equal opportunity to everyone within its jurisdiction. The challenge must be met most pertinently if the State is to address the continuing fallout of the Venezuelan Refugee Crisis with a humanitarian, universalistic agenda.

Further, in Part IV of this monograph, the CARICOM as an offshore region is scrutinised. The contributing editor Alicia Elias-Roberts in Chapter 10 considers the challenges to maritime law. She explains that the Caribbean Community established the CARICOM regional organisation by virtue of the Revised Treaty of Chaguaramas (RTC) to provide an opportunity for all of its Member States to benefit from regional integration. With the development of new frontiers in the oil and gas industry in countries like Guyana, the role of CARICOM to support regional integration and provide a coordinated and uniform regional response to issues surrounding maritime delimitation and energy security in the region is being put to the test. However, challenges regarding maritime delimitation and the concept of absolute sovereignty can hinder stronger regional integration. In this chapter particular attention is paid to Guyana managing its petroleum exploration and production and the international legal litigation concerning its borders in the *Guyana v Venezuela* dispute. The delusion or myth of absolute sovereignty to which some Member States of CARICOM appear to adhere is examined in the context of maritime delimitation. The response of CARICOM to the *Guyana v Venezuela* border controversy is analysed, and recommendations on the way forward are highlighted.

Yet, Winfried Huck, as contributing editor, in chapter 11 assesses the impact of globalisation and how it embraces soft law as opposed to well-established hard law approaches. Therefore, in this chapter, globalisation in its present form is critically reviewed. The impact of globalisation upon EU-CARICOM relations is subject to political, economic and legal forces that are constantly evolving. The history has not been completed; it underlies the collective memory also of the Caribbean people and determines the current political and legal agenda regarding historical injustice and inequality (Ten Points/CARICOM Reparations Commission). The progressing open and hidden agenda of the political and economic power fields (3000 FTAs reshaping the field of trade and investment, OBOR, RCEP, Influence of China, Made in China 2025, AB of the WTO) requires an acknowledgement and improvement of the legal position of an individual also in international law in the interest of fairness and equality. Further, the UN resolution on Global Agenda 2030 and the 17 SDGs and 169 sub-goals are not legally binding as soft law. However, this does not neutralise the effect of the SDGs through conviction. The tasks of states and of the private sector (through CSR) is to integrate the three dimensions of sustainable development (social, economic, and environmental) based on the Human Rights Treaties and by advancing a universal approach (UN Global Compact). Therefore, there are beginnings in international law for the development of legal principles of sustainable development. The content and scope of the principles have demonstrable effects; however, the crystallisation process is not yet complete. Sustainable development is not yet confirmed as customary law by the ILC.

Accordingly, numerous effects of SDGs through adoption in international, inter-regional, European, national and transnational law are clearly visible. The EU has incorporated the SDGs into its internal and external policies and integrates them in many ways. This transforms the SDGs into directly applicable law and has a legally binding effect between the parties involved. Consequently, the new European consensus on development is a cornerstone of the new EU's global challenges and opportunities in the light of the United Nations' Sustainable Development Goals and Global Agenda 2030. The EU and its Member States have to implement a human rights-based approach to development cooperation covering all human rights. For instance, the Cotonou Partnership Agreement expires in 2020 and therefore has to be renegotiated starting in 2018. It is the legal framework ruling relations between the EU and 79 countries in Africa, the Caribbean and the Pacific (ACP). The achievement of the Sustainable Development Goals and the implementation of Agenda 2030 are universally seen as key priorities which are to be integrated. It can be observed that there is a shift from the ACP States to China and a reluctant approach regarding the EU caused by Brexit and other dissensions internally. The CARIFORUM-EU Political Agreement (EPA) is the first and the only comprehensive EPA concluded by the ACP States. The Parties of EPA agree that the Cotonou Agreement and this Agreement shall be implemented in a complementary and mutually reinforcing manner. To CARICOM the SDGs and related questions of inequality are in the centre of such interest.

However, Fabian Stancke in chapter 12 further elaborates upon the impact of the UN's Sustainable Development Goals (SDGs) and focuses on trade policy in the form of tariffs and regulation. However, more indirect policies like the formation and preservation of National Champions through political support must not be forgotten because they may also have significant impacts on trade, trade policy and thus on SDGs. The formation and preservation of National Champions is an important tool for industrial politics, which means the potential for (ideally) elected bodies to exercise decisive influence on the way the undertakings and markets work. However, sustainable development can be significantly influenced by National Champions, leading to less competition in a region resulting in economic injustice, lower quality of goods for consumers and higher prices. If governments decide to take measures to favour individual companies, this should only be temporary. Such support has to be consistent with long-term goals and should not lay the basis for future structural problems. Only in markets that remain vulnerable can consumers be protected from excessive prices and inappropriate terms, as well as benefit from quality products, new ideas and services.

The trade context is further evaluated by Cherisse Francis, in Chapter 13, where she explores the viability of CARICOM's current approach to development in light of recent global challenges. It will consider the current regime, modelled after the European Union (EU) to determine whether it should continue or whether a new approach is necessary. Reference is made to the relationship between the two sub-regions to provide examples and assess the success of this relationship. It examines the Sustainable Development Goals (SDGs) and the 2030 Agenda for Sustainable Development as a possible framework. The option of creating a totally indigenous proposal is also highlighted. This chapter argues that a home-grown structure would require extensive understanding of our shared histories, limitations and contemporary realities. This approach though revolutionary could also encounter several challenges at the implementation level, such as maintaining CARICOM's competitiveness without foreign aid. The implications of these options are considered and expanded upon to suitably address current and future challenges.

Finally, this important survey of the EU-CARICOM is concluded by forward-looking reflections by the authors. In its variant parts, the text first addresses the key topical issues related to EU-CARICOM legal relations, including the impact of Brexit. The second part addresses trade and security issues and will include a chapter on how to improve electronic data exchange in maritime, with its third part tackling fiscal issues and implications and its fourth and penultimate part assessing environmental development and sustainability. The final part engages with the key challenges in the region. This final chapter offers concluding remarks and outlines some forward-thinking views to strengthen the future of transnational law and governance and sustainable development. Such a wealth of knowledge will enable evidence-based solutions to the future problems.

Part I

Brexit and EU-CARICOM relations

2 The impact of Brexit

In search of a new legal order?

Stephen Hardy

On 23 June 2016, the UK voted to leave the EU, or Brexit as it has become known. That new dawn brought the start of the search for a new order. But post-Brexit: what will it be?

In 1951 the founding six European countries signed the Treaty of Paris establishing the European Coal and Steel Community, followed shortly by the 1957 Treaty of Rome establishing the then European Economic Community (EEC), later the European Community (1986) and now better known as the European Union (EU). However, the UK belatedly joined on 1 January 1973, having had its original membership vetoed in 1963, following a Referendum in 1967.

The UK's withdrawal from the EU, more commonly termed Brexit, is governed by Article 50 of the Treaty on European Union. Under Article 50, the invocation procedure required the UK to notify the European Council of its withdrawal, and thereafter the EU is required to negotiate and conclude an agreement with the UK, as a leaving State, setting out the arrangements for its withdrawal, taking account of the framework for its future relationship with the EU. The negotiation period is limited to two years unless extended, after which the Treaties cease to apply. Accordingly, British Prime Minister Theresa May notified the EU on 29 March 2017, invoking Article 50, and therefore, the UK had until 29 March 2019 to negotiate its withdrawal. On 25 November 2018, the EU ratified the UK's withdrawal agreement.[1]

However, the invoking of the so-called 'Article 50 procedure' did not arise without controversy. A challenge in the courts caused the UK's highest court in the *Miller*[2] case to declare that the UK government needed parliamentary approval to trigger Article 50. Subsequently, the UK's Parliament overwhelmingly voted, on 1 February 2017, for a government bill authorising the British prime minister to invoke Article 50. Thereafter, the European Union (Notification of Withdrawal) Bill 2017[3] proceeded through the UK's parliamentary process. In any event, pursuant to Article 50(3), the EU Treaties will cease to apply

1 <https://ec.europa.eu/commission/sites/beta-political/files/draft_withdrawal_agreement_0.pdf>.

2 *R (On the application of Miller) v. Secretary of State for Exiting the EU* [2017] UKSC 5.

3 An Act since 26 June 2018.

'from the date of entry into force of the withdrawal agreement or, failing that, two years after'. Therefore, from 31 January 2020, the UK returns to its own sovereignty and its own legal order.

Brexit: the changing legal order

The EU's 'new legal order' was born in 1962 following the *Van Gend en Loos*[4] landmark ruling of the Court of Justice of the EU (CJEU). This case not only illustrated the power of the jurisprudence of the CJEU, as it created the concept of direct effect, but it settled that the EU Treaty is directly effective in their application against the State. Therefore, this landmark ruling enabled a procedure of enforcement of European law at the national level. Accordingly, it reinforced the supremacy of EU law. Therefore, the most important piece of UK legislation that will be repealed upon the withdrawal of the UK from the EU (i.e. Brexit) will be the European Communities Act 1972, which provides for the supremacy of EU law. Repealing this UK statute will ultimately bring an end to the constitutional relationship that exists between EU and UK law. Moreover, the vast amounts of secondary legislation that have been passed with the objective and justification of implementing EU law will have to be reconsidered by the government.

Whilst the UK government intends to repeal the European Communities Act 1972 with the European Union (Withdrawal) Act 2018. Such seeks to convert all existing EU-derived law into domestic law, allowing the UK government to decide over time what laws it wishes to retain. This approach is intended to avoid the significant gaps and consequent uncertainty if all EU-derived law was repealed without replacement.

Within a commercial context, even if the UK decided not to retain any EU law, companies looking to trade in the EU would nevertheless still be required to comply with EU laws such as EU competition rules, regulations and standards. However, the UK will need to address EU provisions which regulate the relationship between EU Member States themselves or are based on reciprocity. More specifically, Brexit focuses all legal minds on the following:

1. legislation which relies on an EU regulator or grants jurisdiction to the CJEU;
2. numerous treaties which have been signed by the EU and are currently directly applicable in the UK by virtue of s. 2(1) of the European Communities Act 1972; and,
3. the fact that references in EU laws to actions being taken within the EU will not cover actions taken within the UK after 31 January 2020.

Consequently, due to these concerns, the EU (Withdrawal) Act 2018[5] contains wide-ranging powers to amend EU-derived law by secondary legislation. In

4 C26/62, Van Gend.
5 <https://services.parliament.uk/bills/2017-19/europeanunionwithdrawal.html>.

the UK government's view, these powers will give sufficient scope to correct or remove laws that would otherwise not function properly post-Brexit. Whatever the UK Parliament legislates, since EU directives require implementation into UK law in order to have effect, this conversely creates the task for any UK government overseeing Brexit of deciding whether to embark on a process of reviewing Acts of Parliament and statutory instruments with a view to ascertaining whether or not to maintain, replace or repeal each piece of legislation. However, does this mean that the UK is in search of a new legal order?

EU regulations rely on the principle of direct applicability, which means that unlike EU directives, they are directly implemented into UK law without the need for legislation from the UK Parliament. In this light, regulations are more powerful legislative tools for the EU because of their immediate applicability. Therefore, in many instances, amending regulations will likely be needed in order to take into account the UK's new relationship with the EU. More significantly, the CJEU is currently the final arbiter on questions of the interpretation of EU law. That jurisdiction will cease on Brexit. Consequently, the EU (Withdrawal) Act 2018 sets out the future relationship between courts in the United Kingdom and EU law, including EU court decisions. UK courts, other than the UK's Supreme Court, will continue to be bound by EU laws and court decisions made before Brexit. This is an attempt to preserve continuity given that previous CJEU decisions have influenced many areas of English case law, and similarly, the English courts have looked at the wording of EU directives for the purposes of construing UK legislation which was passed to give them effect. It is highly likely that the UK courts will move away from such jurisprudence once the UK is no longer bound by EU law and/or such decisions may be superseded post-Brexit.

Typically, in readiness for a change in legal order post-Brexit, the UK's Department for Exiting the European Union has produced reports on the economic impact on 58 UK industries on leaving the EU.[6] Notably, post-Brexit the decline in EEA immigration is likely to have an adverse impact on the British health sector. Further, there is overwhelming agreement among economists that leaving the EU will adversely affect the British economy in the medium and long-term. However, there is substantial uncertainty over how large the effect will be, with plausible estimates of the cost ranging between 1% and 10% of the UK's income per capita. These estimates differ depending on whether the UK stays in the European Single Market (for instance, by joining the EEA – so-called soft Brexit), making a free trade agreement with the EU, or reverts to the trade rules that govern relations between all World Trade Organization members (so-called hard Brexit). Notably, in January 2018, the UK government's own Brexit analysis showed that UK economic growth would be stunted by 2% to 8% for at least 15 years following secession from the EU, depending on the leave scenario.

6 <www.ft.com/content/f0c20820-7835-34d4-b736-a95d7ca972a2>.

Further, on 14 November 2018, the UK government published its draft withdrawal agreement from the EU.[7] This caused two UK government ministers to resign.[8] This document, consisting of 585 pages, covered the key areas involved in the UK's withdrawal, including arbitration clauses, trade and the single marker 'borders' issue. An EU summit to discuss this draft text was convened on 25 November 2018. Subsequently, the EU accepted the UK's withdrawal agreement. Yet, at the time of writing, this agreement is still to be assented to by the UK's Parliament. Such parliamentary deadlock and rancour caused British Prime Minister Theresa May to resign in May 2019. Her successor as British Prime Minister, Boris Johnson, reaffirmed the UK's commitment to Brexit after 31 January 2020.

UK post-Brexit: 'in search of a new legal order'

A human rights deficit will be created by the UK government's EU withdrawal. Namely, the UK's Equality Human Rights Commission (EHRC) warns that 'BREXIT will not protect people's rights in the UK because it removes the EU charter of fundamental rights from UK law'.[9] Whilst the UK government maintains that the charter will cease to be part of UK law when the UK leaves the EU, it also insists that UK rights will not be weakened following Brexit. Yet, the EHRC persistently asserts that rights will be lost where such rights do not have direct equivalents in other UK human rights law; for example, a freestanding right to non-discrimination, protection of a child's best interests and the right to human dignity. Such legal implications of Brexit could potentially endanger the independence of the British judiciary, namely the UK government's plans to grant British judges a wide discretion in deciding what weight to attach to decisions of the CJEU after the UK had left the EU jurisdiction.

Typically, whilst there are uncertainties around the form Brexit will take, there are a number of existing legal models for relationships between the EU and non-EU countries, which may form the basis for the UK's continuing relationship with the EU post-Brexit:

- **EFTA/EEA model:** the UK could apply to join the European Free Trade Association (EFTA) and then the European Economic Area (EEA). As a member of the EEA, the UK would participate in the Single Market (apart from in the Common Agricultural Policy and the Common Fisheries Policy). It would continue to participate in the four freedoms, including the free

7 <https://ec.europa.eu/commission/files/draft-agreement-withdrawal-united-kingdom-great-britain-and-northern-ireland-european-union-and-european-atomic-energy-community-agreed-negotiators-level-14-november-2018_en>.

8 Dominic Raab MP – the then Brexit Minister; and, Ester McVeigh MP – the Work and Pensions Minister.

9 <www.equalityhumanrights.com/en/our-work/news/joint-statement-uks-human-rights-and-equality-bodies-brexit>.

movement of people. However, it would not be subject to the jurisdiction of the CJEU, although the EFTA court would have jurisdiction;

- **Swiss model:** Switzerland is a member of EFTA but voted not to apply to join the EEA, after which it negotiated a number of bilateral agreements with the EU in order to gain some access to the Single Market. Switzerland is subject to the freedom of goods and people but not to services and capital. It is not bound by the CJEU but follows the EFTA court, and it makes a lower contribution to the EU than those made by the non-EU EEA States and has no say in EU law;
- **Turkish model:** Turkey belongs to a customs union with the EU. This gives Turkey tariff-free access to the Single Market for goods (but not services) without quotas. It is not subject to the four freedoms, has no say in EU legislation and is not bound by the CJEU. It is, however, required to harmonise its own laws with those of the EU in certain areas including consumer protection, competition and intellectual property. It is also restricted in its ability to enter into third-country trade agreements without EU approval and has to adopt a common tariff in line with that of the EU for third-country goods;
- **Canadian model:** Free Trade Agreement (FTA): Canada has negotiated an FTA with the European Union. The negotiations have taken a decade, and Romania is currently threatening to veto the agreement. FTAs tend to be restricted to goods;

  and,

- **Rest of the World model:** the UK is a member of the World Trade Organisation (WTO). If it were to trade with the EU on this basis, it would not be subject to EU law, nor to the four freedoms and would not have to make contributions to the EU budget. It would, however, be subject to trade tariffs and to EU standards; for example, product standards in order to trade with the EU. For example, the CARICOM has such an agreement with the EU. Notably, the EUCARINET is a four-year Coordination Action, the main goal of which is to strengthen bi-regional sustainable policy dialogue on science and between EU Member States, Associated States and in the Caribbean region, the Caribbean ACP States, the overseas Departments and Collectives, the Overseas Countries and Territories (OCTs). The Project works at policy, programme and institutional (research entities) levels and contributes to the creation of the conditions of the sustainable multiple stakeholders' policy dialogue on technology between EU, its Member States and the Caribbean region. Also, it seeks to foster inter-regional (EU-Caribbean) and intra-regional cooperation in leading to the identification and prioritisation of common research areas of mutual interest and benefit, as well as stimulate and support the participation of Caribbean Research stakeholders on 'People Programme'.

Presently it remains unclear and uncertain as to which of these models, if any, the UK will adopt post-Brexit. This particularly is the position, given that the decision will not be made by the UK alone but in negotiation with and will have to be agreed by the EU (i.e. all EU Member States if taking place after Brexit or by qualified majority and with European parliamentary approval if included in the UK's negotiated exit agreement). The degree to which the UK will remain tied to the EU will undoubtedly impact on the extent to which we have to continue to comply with EU law, but it is not the only consideration.

In any event, post-Brexit the UK's search for a new legal order will begin in haste. The existing legal models within the EU, under the umbrella of the EU's legal order, will remain (Anglo-)Irish; Romano-Germanic; Nordic systems and the Central and the Eastern European. However, a complex body of case law dictates principles of supremacy of EU law and whether or not certain laws have a direct effect (can be relied on in Member State courts) or indirect effect (Member State courts are required to interpret Member State law consistently with the relevant EU law). It is hard to quantify exactly how much UK law has been adopted as a result of EU requirements; estimates of how much UK law was influenced by EU law between 1973–2016 vary from around 13% to 62%. What is certain is that the UK has voluminous EU-derived law already on the British statute books, and there are major questions as to how this will be dealt with and how the UK will deal with new EU law, which it might be required to follow in order to continue trading with the EU in certain areas; for example, in consumer sales of goods, services and digital content, post-Brexit.

Evidently, since there is no precedent for leaving the European Union under the current treaty provisions.[10] As a result, uncertainty prevails. The situation is all the more uncertain because under Article 50(4) of the Treaty on the European Union, 'the member of the European Council or of the Council representing the withdrawing Member State shall not participate in the discussions of the European Council or Council or in decisions concerning it'. In other words, much of the negotiation for the terms of the UK's withdrawal between the continuing EU Member States will take place without the UK's participation, given that the Article 50 provisions are untested and raise a considerable degree of uncertainty. There is also a distinction to be made between an exit agreement which is supposed to set out withdrawal arrangements 'taking account of the framework of its future relationship with the Union' and post-Brexit trade agreements which will have to be approved by every single Member State. Moreover, a post-Brexit agreement covering services is even more of an unknown quantity unless the UK were to join the EEA. However, what will the legal effect be on UK law? To that end, the UK in search of a legal order post-Brexit will be determined by the respective UK legal positions on the following:

- ***Current law***: legally, on conclusion of the exit agreement or expiration of the two-year period (unless extended) if earlier, the UK will no longer be subject to the EU treaties unless the terms of any exit or post-Brexit

10 Greenland left the EEC in 1985 after three years' negotiation under previous legislative arrangements.

agreement (such as EEA membership) dictates otherwise. Therefore, the EU treaties, as well as EU regulations, which are not otherwise preserved by UK national law, will no longer have effect. As there is no requirement to introduce implementing legislation for EU regulations, in theory, they will simply cease to apply; but many have related local legislation dealing with the effects of regulations, and it will be a complex process of disentanglement to work out which pieces of legislation are left standing. In relation to legislation implementing directives, the situation about what is still in effect is likely to be less complex as they are implemented into UK law by UK legislation, which will remain valid until repealed or superseded. CJEU decisions interpret EU law. To the extent that CJEU rulings have been reflected in subsequent UK law (including court decisions), they will also continue to apply;

and,

- ***Post-Brexit law***: legally, the UK will NOT be required to adopt any new EU legislation and will not be subject to the jurisdiction of the CJEU after exit (unless it agrees to either under the exit agreement or any future agreement).

Consequently, the practical impact of Brexit on UK law is a very different evaluation:

- ***Existing jurisprudence*** – it is highly unlikely and it will be impracticable for the UK for the government or even Parliament to expunge all EU-derived law upon exit from the EU. Moreover, it is also highly unlikely that the UK government will replace the majority of it, although it may have the option to do so. Plainly, the fact is that, in many areas, if the UK does not comply with EU law, the UK will simply not be able to trade with the EU. Areas of law which are particularly unlikely to change include data protection, consumer protection, financial services and product liability. The key problem which remains is how to manage the incompatibility between former EU-derived laws and new post-Brexit laws, moving forward. Such a situation, it is anticipated, will provide a plentiful supply of cases for the courts, requiring them to interpret and declare incompatibility where necessary and provide much needed clarity;

  and,

- ***Future (post-Brexit) legal reasoning*** – in certain areas (although not all), if the UK does not comply with EU legislation and must take into account any CJEU rulings on relevant legislation, the UK will significantly restrict its ability to trade with the EU. Notably, should the UK determine to retain a piece of EU-derived legislation or adopt a new piece, arguably the UK will need, from a practical perspective, to apply any CJEU decisions in respect of those laws; for example, in the area of data protection, where CJEU rulings can significantly affect non-EU members.

Given these analyses, whilst many UK pro-Brexiteers contend that exiting the EU will dramatically reduce bureaucracy and return sovereignty to the UK, in reality and in the short to medium terms, Brexit in legal terms is more likely to cause greater complexity through the legal ramifications and contingent uncertainty.

Conclusions

The possibility of 'law without boundaries' post-Brexit, as this chapter has highlighted, presents both challenges and uncertainty, as well as potential opportunities for a new legal order for the UK. However, ever since the end of the Second World War, with the creation of the United Nations, the rules and structure of the traditional inter-state community have been changing. In more recent decades, international law has been increasingly shifting its focus from the State to the individual. Furthermore, State sovereignty has been redefined by developments in the field of the safeguard of human rights, peoples' law, the 'human' environment, the common heritage of mankind, cultural heritage, sustainable development and international trade. New norms protect the universal community's interests. New actors, other than States, have emerged on the international scene, as well as new international norms which permit individuals, groups of individuals, corporations, and non-governmental organisations to bring claims before international jurisdictions.

More significantly, structurally, including Brexit, in the international sphere in legal terms we are witnessing an ongoing and gradual 'verticalisation' of power. Notably, judicial organs and institutionalised procedures to monitor States' activities have been established. In recent years, there has been a proliferation of international courts and tribunals and, in general, of mechanisms and compliance control procedures which, from their position of authority, ensure respect of norms. Consequently, international organisations – in particular those of a universal character – partake in the management of international power by carrying out 'some' general functions in several areas of law. The erosion of States' sovereignty is giving way to a global community and a new international power structure based on multilateral decision processes aimed at protecting fundamental interests and global values. However, all of these changes raise the question of whether the birth of a global community gave rise to a new set of international norms and whether such norms amount to a system coherent enough to be called 'Global Law'.

The advent of the global economy and the ever-pervasive globalisation is changing not only modern socio-economic and politico-cultural systems but also the law, decision-making processes, enforcement strategies, and the interrelations between multiple normative systems and sub-systems. The emerging international legal order is no longer that of the EU era but also as a result of the deep transformation of the traditional model of the international community and its constitutive structure. At its core, the development of a multiplicity of supra-national normative regimes and of sub-systems, distinct sets of secondary norms, or relating to a branch of "special" international law. Such an expansive new landscape of global regulatory regimes, especially in economic and social areas, from a multiplicity of actors takes part in global governance and makes the current legal framework more complex.

In conclusion, the complexity of legal sources is, therefore, the result of the new global order, characterised by growth in interconnection, by changes in social, economic and political dynamics and by a multi-polar power structure, with continual horizontal and vertical shifts in power. Yet it remains the duty of the courts, in fulfilling their role of applying the norms of international law, to contribute to its harmonious development, eliminating the points of conflict which may arise from the interplay between international rules or between these rules and domestic laws, as well as from the co-existence of different international courts and tribunals. Global law is therefore flexible so as to empower and integrate the heterogeneous elements of the various and different legal orders into a unitary framework. This bodes well for the UK, post-Brexit, as it searches for a new legal order, reclaims its former pre-EU order or, alternatively, retains its EU-influenced jurisprudence. Whatever legal orders prevail post-Brexit, like the recent UK Supreme Court ruling[11] guided, 'an unhappy marriage does not necessarily substantiate grounds for divorce'. So, whilst the UK's divorce to the EU is being made out, the future of UK law remains uncertain, and to some extent the search for a new legal order continues in vain.

11 *Owens v. Owens* [2018] UKSC 41.

3 The impact of the UK's Brexit on anti-suit injunctions

Margaret Liu

It was widely held that the lengthy debate on the use of anti-suit injunctions had been ended by the Court of Justice of European Union (hereinafter CJEU) in the *Turner* and *West Tankers* cases; the *Gazprom* case reignited the new wave of debate in the context of arbitration. The *Gazprom* case sheds light on whether a court of Member States is obliged to recognize and enforce or refuse the recognition and enforcement of an arbitral award, or so-called anti-suit award.

The anti-suit injunction is a procedural mechanism utilised by most common law courts to give effect to the choice of court or arbitration agreements, aiming to prohibit vexatious and abusive manipulations of forum by malicious parties.[1] Arbitral anti-suit orders have the same purpose as the anti-suit injunctions – they are an injunctive relief device granted by arbitrators to prevent a party from commencing and/or pursuing proceedings before a forum, other than the chosen arbitral tribunal.[2] Anti-suit injunctions and anti-suit orders are devices granted in order to lock proceedings in a specific forum, thereby preventing a risk of parallel proceedings and conflicting judgments.[3]

It is noted that the issuance of anti-suit injunctions has been banned by the CJEU in the *West Tankers* and *Turner* cases. However, it has been suggested that the granting of anti-suit injunctions may be permissible in the context of arbitration under the Brussels I Recast Regulation. One of the contentious issues during the recasting of the Brussels I Regulation was the scope of the arbitration exclusion contained in Article 1(2)(d). Although arbitration is excluded from the scope of the Brussels I Regulation, the interface between it and the international commercial arbitration fall within the material scope of the Brussels I Regulation.[4] Recital 12 clarifies the scope of the arbitration exclusion by addressing: i) Recital 12 does not only exclude arbitration in line with the arbitration

1 W Hueske, 'Rules, Britannia! A Proposed Revival of the British Antisuit Injunction in the EU Legal Framework' (2009) George Washington International Law Review 433–34.

2 R Moloo, 'Arbitrators Granting Anti-suit Orders: When Should They and What Authority?' (2009) Journal of International Arbitration 675–700, 676; P Clifford and O Browne, 'Lost at Sea or a Storm in a Teacup? Anti-suit Injunctions after West Tankers' (2009) International Arbitration Law Review 19–22, 21.

3 C P Ojiegbe, 'From West Tankers to Gazprom: Anti-suit Injunctions, Arbitral Anti-suit Orders and the Brussels I Recast' (2015) 11(2) Journal of Private International Law, 267–97, 268.

4 ibid. 270.

exclusion in the main provision of Article 1(2)(d) of Brussels I Recast Regulation, but it also allows the courts of Member States the liberty to rule on the existence and validity of arbitration agreements without the judgment being subject to the rules of recognition and enforcement laid down in Brussels I Recast Regulation, regardless of whether the Member State's court decided the scope of the arbitration agreement as a principal issue or as an incidental question.

This chapter first examines the relationship of anti-suit injunctions and the Brussels Conventions before considering the rationale for the prohibition of anti-suit injunctions within the EU judicial areas. It then critically assesses the prohibition of anti-suit injunctions in the *Turner* and *West Tankers* cases. Consideration will then shift to whether anti-suit injunctions are permissible under the Brussels I Recast Regulation through the *Gazprom* case. Finally, this chapter will explore the Brexit effect on anti-suit injunctions.

Anti-suit injunctions and the Brussel Regulation

Anti-suit injunctions, in Anglo-Saxon law, rather than continental law, are orders directing a party not to initiate or pursue legal action in a different jurisdiction, or if they had already initiated it, that they withdraw it. Failure to do so would place them in contempt of court and may carry pecuniary penalties.[5]

In England and Wales, the Court of Appeal, the High Court of Justice and the Crown Court (hereinafter, senior courts) have a 'general power' to issue an anti-suit injunction under s 37(1) of the Senior Court Act 1981 in cases in which it appears for the courts to be 'convenient' to do so. The Supreme Court in *Ust-Kamenogorsk Hydroppower Plant*[6] made it clear that the source of the power of the English senior courts to grant anti-suit injunctions in support of arbitration agreements is enshrined in Section 37 of the Senior Court Act 1981. However, these courts exercise this general power cautiously and 'sensitively' in the arbitration context 'with due regard for the scheme and terms' of the Arbitration Act 1996.[7] Under section 44(2) of the Arbitration Act 1996, senior courts are empowered with a supervisory role to grant interim injunctions in support of arbitration proceedings. The English courts will usually grant anti-suit injunctions where there is a breach of an arbitration agreement or a choice of court agreement.[8] In *Angelic Crace*,[9] the Court of Appeal held that an anti-suit injunction

5 M J Elvira Benayas, 'Is There Any Possibility, However, Small, of Saving Our Own? The Anti-suit Injunction and the Brussels Convention on the Subject of the STJCE of 27 April 2004m C-159/02' Electronic Journal of International Studies.

6 *Ust-Kamenogorsk Hydroppower Plant LLP v Ust-Kamenogorsk Hydropower Plant JSC* [2013] UKSC 35; [2013] 1 WLR 1889; [2013] Bus LR 1357 at [48].

7 *Ust-Kamenogorsk Hydroppower Plant* [2013] 1 WLR 1889; [2013] Bus LR 1357 at [60].

8 C Chatterjee, 'The Legal Effect of the Exclusive Jurisdiction Clause in the Brussels Convention in Relation to Banking Matters' (1995) Journal of International Banking and Financial Law 334–40; *Continental Bank NA v Aeakos Compania Naviera SA and Others* [1994] 1 WLR 588.

9 *Aggeliki Charis Compania Maritima ApA v Pagnan SpA* (*The Angelic Grace*) [1995] 1 Lloyd's Rep. 87, Court of Appeal, Neil, Leggatt and Millett LJJ.

will be granted where there is a breach of an arbitration agreement provided the application is sought expeditiously and before the foreign proceedings have advanced.[10] The indication shows the English courts' willingness to grant anti-suit injunctions in order to safeguard an arbitration agreement.[11] The reason for granting anti-suit injunctions is because the defendant had earlier promised not to commence them by consenting to the jurisdiction agreement.[12] The purpose of granting an anti-suit injunction, in breach of a jurisdiction agreement, is to prevent the claimant in the foreign proceedings from putting the other party through the cost and inconvenience of a wrongly initiate set of proceedings.[13] This means that a defendant who violates the order of an anti-suit injunction may be held liable for contempt of court,[14] imprisoned, fined or his property seized,[15] and any judgment obtained by the defendant from a foreign court in breach of the order of an anti-suit injunction granted against him may not be enforced.[16] In other words, where there are two parallel actions, one of the actions commenced in England and the other brought in a foreign country with the intention of vexing the defendant, the English senior courts have the power to restrain the party pursuing foreign proceedings.[17]

Within the EU, the jurisdictional concerns are exacerbated by the existence of the Brussels regimes of allocating jurisdiction. In 1968 the European legislators began to set out a series of guidelines to determine jurisdiction in cases that affect citizens resident in the European Union. It also established channels to facilitate the recognition and enforcement in Member States of judgments issued in another Member State. This path began with the Brussels Convention 1968 and had crystallised in Regulation 44/2001 of 22 December 2000 on Jurisdiction and Recognition and Enforcement of Judgments in Civil and Commercial Matters (hereinafter Brussels I Regulation), which serves to clarify some points and takes a step towards procedural harmonisation, with its ultimate milestone to date being the enactment of Regulation 1215/2012, known as Brussels I Recast.

Manifestly, this has been maintained in subsequent amendments that the Convention in its common Article 1[18] established that the arbitration was excluded

10 *Aggeliki Chairs Compania Maritima SA v Pagnan "The Angelic Grace"* [1995] 1 Lloyd's Rep. 87. 96 (Millet, L.J).

11 R Reece, 'Anti-suit Injunctions and Arbitration Proceedings' (2006) Arbitration 207–16, 211.

12 *Cheshire, North & Fawcett: Private International Law* (14th edn, OUP 2008) 475.

13 *West Tankers Inc v Ras Riunione Adriatica Di Sicurta 'The Front Comor'* [2005] 2 Llyod's Rep. 257, 268[50].

14 *West Tankers Inc v Allianze SpA* [2009] ECR 1–00663, [14] (Advocate General Kokott).

15 T Hartley, 'The Brussels I Regulation and Arbitration' (2014) International and Comparative Law Quarterly 843–66, 861; A Briggs, *Private International Law in English Courts* (OUP 2014) para 4.33.

16 M Black and R Reece, 'Anti-suit Injunctions and Arbitration Proceedings' (2006) Arbitration 207–16, 211.

17 C Chatterjee, 'The Legal Effect of the Exclusive Jurisdiction Clause in Brussels Convention in Relation to Banking Matters' (1995) Journal of International Banking and Financial Law 334–40.

18 See Art. 1(2)(d) of both Brussels I Regulation and Brussels I Recast.

from its scope. Along the way, the Supreme Court[19] echoed this doctrine, declaring that Brussel I Regulation was not applicable to the incidental control of an arbitration agreement since arbitration was a matter excluded thereof. *Turner v Grovit*[20] is a case in point in which the House of Lords ruled that an anti-suit injunction does not infringe upon the Brussels I Regulation. In particular, Lord Hobhouse explained that the *ratio decidendi* for the judgment was that anti-suit injunctions

> come into the picture at an earlier stage and involve not a decision upon the jurisdiction of the foreign court but an assessment of the conduct of the relevant party in invoking that jurisdiction. English law makes these distinctions. Indeed, the typical situation in which a restraining order is made is one where the foreign court has or is willing to assume jurisdiction; if these were not so, no restraining order would be necessary and none should be granted.[21]

Evidently, *Turner v Grovit*[22] was understood not to apply to arbitration clauses. Further, such anti-suit injunctions are not issued against the court of another EU Member State but rather against the party in breach of an arbitration clause. It is an in personam order[23] preventing a party from commencing and/or continuing proceedings in a foreign jurisdiction other than in accordance with the choice of court or arbitration agreements.[24] But this reassurance went awry when the court extended the incompatibility with the Brussels Regulation of the anti-suit injunction in the *West Tankers*[25] ruling, affirmed in *Gazprom*,[26] which reiterated that anti-suit injunctions are incompatible with the Brussels Regulation.

West Tankers decisions

The *West Tankers*[27] is a landmark case with significant impact on the fate of anti-suit injunctions. In the case, the UK House of Lords and the European Court of Justice both directly ruled on the arbitration exception in the Brussels I Regulation.[28]

19 Judgment of the Supreme Court of 17 May 2007.
20 *Turner v Grovit* [2001] UKHL 65; [2002] WLR 107.
21 ibid. at [119].
22 ibid.
23 *Turner v Grovit and Others* [2002] 1 WLR 107, 117 at [23].
24 T Raphael, *The Anti-suit Injunction* (OUP 2008) 1.05; T C Hartley, 'Comity and the Use of Antisuit Injunctions in International Litigation' (1987) American Journal of Comparative Law 487–511, 487.
25 Judgment of the European Court of Justice of 10 February 2009.
26 *Aggeliki Charis Compania Maritima ApA v Pagnan SpA* (*The Angelic Grace*) [1995] 1 Lloyd's Rep. 87, Court of Appeal, Neil, Leggatt and Millett LJJ.
27 *West Tankers Inc v RAS Riunione Adriatica Di Sicurta ApA* (*The Front Comor*) [2005] EWHC 454 (Comm); [2005] 2 Lloyds's Rep. 257; and [2007] UKHL 4; [2007] 1All E. R. (Comm) 794.
28 The Regulation has since then amended, with consequential renumbering of its articles, by Regulation (EU) No 1215/2012 on jurisdiction and recognition and enforcement of

Since 2001, the Brussels I Regulation has been the starting point when considering the jurisdiction of a court in a Brussels Regulation Member State to hear a dispute. The Brussels I Regulation in Article 27 provides that

> where proceedings involving the same cause of action and between the same parties are brought in the courts of different Member States, any court other than the court first seized shall of its own motion stay its proceedings until such time as the jurisdiction of the court first seized is established.

The strict application of this article (even, for example, where the first proceedings were commenced in bad faith) has been repeatedly emphasised by the CJEU.[29] The CJEU explained its approach as being predicted on the principles of uniformity of approach and 'mutual trust' which buttress the Brussels Regulation. It requires that each EU Member State court rules only in its own jurisdiction and not to assume exclusive jurisdiction of another Member State court.[30] The *Erich Gasser* [31] case best confirmed where the ECJ held that under the Brussels Regulation

> the court second seized is never in a better position than the court first seized to determine whether the latter has jurisdiction. That jurisdiction is determined directly by the rules of Brussels Regulation, which are common to both courts.[32]

The case arose from an incident where the *West Tankers,* owned by an English company, collided with a jetty owned by an Italian company, Erg Petroli SpA. Erg claimed compensation and received money from its insurers, Allianz SpA, for damages relating to the collision but commenced an arbitration in London against *West Tankers* seeking payment of the excess. Sometime later, Allianz SpA started proceedings against *West Tankers* in an Italian court (under the same charter party agreement by the right of subrogation) seeking to recover the amount it paid to Erg. *West Tankers* challenged the jurisdiction of the Italian court and applied to the English courts to issue an injunction restraining Allianz SpA from continuing the Italian proceedings, claiming that the dispute arose out of the charter party and that it was governed by English law with any disputes to be resolved by arbitration in London. Allianz SpA was bound by the agreement.

---

judgments in civil and commercial matters (recast) ('The Judgments Regulation') which applies to legal proceedings instituted on or after 10 January 2015.

29 See, for example, *Erich Gasser GmbH v MISAT SRL* (C-116/02; [2004] 1 Lloyds Rep. 222); *Turner v Grovit* (C-159/02; [2004] 2 Lloyds Rep. 169.

30 *Turner v Grovit* (C-159/02) EU:C:2004:228; [2005] 1 AC 101; [2004] 3 WLR 1193 at [20].

31 *Erich Gasser GmbH v MISAT SRL* (C-116/02)EU:C:2003:657; [2005] QB 1; [2004] ILPr 7 at 164.

32 *Erich Gasser* (C-116/02)[2005] QB 1; [2004] ILPr 7 at 164.

In the Queen's Bench Division[33] Colman J – following the approach taken by the Court of Appeal in *The Hari Buram*[34] – made an order for an anti-suit injunction restricting the insurers' further steps in the Italian proceedings. During the proceedings, Allianz SpA questioned whether it would be consistent with the Brussels Regulation for an English court to grant an injunction restricting proceedings in another Member State. Leave was granted to appeal on this issue directly to the then House of Lords.

Lord Hoffman upheld Justice Coleman's decision and added that there is no 'doctrinal necessity or practical advantage for the European Community to handicap itself by denying its courts the right to grant anti-suit injunctions[35] on the ground that such proceedings were in breach of an arbitration agreement. Despite giving the impression that the House of Lords was convinced by this approach, his Lordship also held that there were varying views on the issue and that it was a matter of considerable importance. In this regard, Lord Hoffman referred the case to the CJEU for a preliminary ruling on whether it was consistent with the Brussels Regulation, a Member State commencing proceedings in another Member State on the grounds that it was in breach of an arbitration agreement.[36]

In fact, the CJEU did not follow the House of Lords decision but instead issued its judgment on 10 February 2009, preferring the opinion of Advocate General Kokott whose approach[37] was that 'an anti-suit injunction should not be brought to restrain court proceedings in another EU Member State even where it is brought apparently in breach of an arbitration agreement'.[38] Accordingly, the ECJ held that the prohibition on anti-suit injunctions set out in the ECJ decision in *Turner v Grovit*[39] extends even where there is an arbitration agreement and that 'it is incompatible with Council Regulation (EC) No 44/2001 . . . for a court of a Member State to make an order to restrain a person from commencing or continuing proceedings before the court of another Member State'.[40] The rationale for the CJEU's decision was as follows, inter alia:

1 In order to determine whether a dispute falls within the scope of Brussels I Regulation, reference must be made solely to the subject matter of the proceedings – that is the subject matter of the Italian proceedings (a damages

33 *West Tankers* [2005] 2 Lloyd's Rep. 257; [2005] 1 CLC 347.
34 [2005] 1 Lloyd's Rep. 67 (CA); affirming [2004] 1 Lloyd's Rep. 206.
35 *West Tankers* [2005] 2 Lloyd's Rep. 257; [2005] 1 CLC 347 at [52].
36 *West Tankers* [2007] UKHL 4; [2007] 1 All E. R. (Comm) 794; [2007] ILPr 20 at 307 and 312.
37 Advocate General Opinion Kokott *Allianz SpA (formly Riunione Adriatica di Sicurta SpA) v West Tankers Inc* (C-185/07)ECLI:EU:C:2008:466 at [15].
38 Case C-185/07, Judgment of the Court (Grand Chamber) of 10 February 2009).
39 *Turner v Grovit* [2001] UKHL 65; [2002] WLR 107.
40 'ECJ Hand Down Judgment in *West Tankers* Confirming that Anti-suit Injunctions in Support of Arbitration Agreements are Incompatible with the Brussels Regulation', *Lexology* <www.lexology.com/library/detail.aspx?g=3c36c54-59c5-4f>.

claim in tort), and the preliminary questions as to whether the arbitration agreement was applicable fell within the scope of the Brussels Regulation.

2 However, even proceedings which do not fall within the scope of the Regulation may have consequences which undermine its effectiveness. This is because the unification of the rules of conflict of jurisdiction will be impeded where the use of an anti-suit injunction prevents a court in a Member State from ruling on the very applicability of the Brussels Regulation and strips that court's power to rule in its own jurisdiction[41] as conferred by the Brussels Regulation.

3 There is no need for issuance of anti-suit injunction because the chances for a party to circumnavigate arbitration are minimal given that article II (3) of the New York Convention (NYC) requires Member State courts to refer parties' arbitration where there is a valid arbitration agreement.[42]

4 The mere fact there is an arbitration clause does not confer an exclusive right to the arbitral body to examine the clause.[43] This is because such an approach would deny a claimant judicial protection because they would not have an opportunity to make a claim to the court that the arbitration agreement is invalid.[44]

Impact of the CJEU's ruling

This ruling has its pros and cons. On the one hand, the CJEU's decision maintains the principle of mutual trust among EU Member State courts because it ensures that no Member State courts can interfere with the judicial sovereignty of other Member State courts by determining jurisdiction or reviewing a decision of another Member State court owing to its inconsistency with the aim of the Brussels Regulation.[45] In this way, it can thus be argued that the CJEU puts EU law and, more importantly, judicial sovereignty above commercial interest.[46]

But, on the other hand, arbitration in England or any other Brussels Regulation jurisdiction will now have to wait until any proceedings brought in a foreign court in apparent breach of an arbitration agreement have been stayed or jurisdiction has been declined by another court. Potentially, this could protract a process, involving a full review and possible appeals depending on the procedural rules of the court in question.

Undoubtedly, this undermines the concept of party autonomy as regards choice of arbitration seat, denying some of the benefit of 'arbitration-friendly'

41 *Allianz SpA* (C-185/07) EU: C:2009:69; [2008] 2 Lloyd's Rep. 661 at [28].

42 ibid. at [33].

43 D M Ndolo and M Liu, 'Does the Will of the Parties Supersede the Sovereignty of the State? Anti-suit Injunctions in the UK' (2017) 10(2/2017) Global Competition Litigation Review 53–61.

44 Advocate General Opinion Kokott *Allianz SpA (formly Riunione Adriatica di Sicurta SpA) v West Tankers Inc* (C-185/07) ECLI:EU:C:2008:466 at [58].

45 Ojiegbe (n 3) 277.

46 Ndolo and Liu (n 43).

jurisdiction where courts limit any pre-award review to a minimum. It is also incompatible with the concept of competence-competence – allowing arbitrators to primarily determine their jurisdiction. The CJEU decision is problematic as it is easy to envisage a situation where an opportunistic potential defendant could exploit the position created by the CJEU's decision by commencing tactical proceedings in a Member State court which have the effect of delaying the resolution of the substantive dispute.[47] Furthermore, the CJEU's decision is also inconsistent with Article 1(2)(d) of the Brussels Regulation, which contained an arbitration exception by virtue of which *Turner v Grovit*[48] was understood not to apply to arbitration clauses. The English Court has replied by concluding that there is nothing to prevent it from granting an injunction to restrain proceedings which are (or would be) in breach of an arbitration clause.[49]

At the heart of the concerns is the effect of this decision on arbitration in London, and this concern was highlighted by Lord Hoffman in the then House of Lords when he claimed that the ability to issue anti-suit injunctions is one of the advantages that London is able to offer as it is an 'important valuable weapon' in the hands of the English courts to exercise their supervisory role over arbitration.[50] Such an effective tactical weapon in management of international commercial arbitration was deprived by the CJEU's decision in the *West Tankers case.* In this regard, Lord Mance stated that it is commercial practice of no or little comfort or use for the only remedy for the parties is to be engaged in foreign proceedings pursued in disregard of the arbitration clause, because this is exactly what the party aimed and bargained to avoid.[51]

However, these comments were dismissed by the Advocate General as being of a 'purely economic nature' and therefore could not justify infringement of Community law.[52] The Advocate General also added that from the point of view of procedural economy, an anti-suit injunction may lead to an unsatisfactory result that 'runs counter' to the principle of mutual trust between courts of Member States.[53] Therefore, the CJEU prohibits use of anti-suit injunctions in support of arbitration agreements in the EU that the principle endorsed by a case such as *Turner v Grovit*[54] in the context of proceedings being brought in apparent breach of exclusive jurisdiction clauses, given the specific exclusion of arbitration from the scope of the Brussels I Regulation.

47 N Archer, 'The Practical Implications of the West Tankers Decision' (2009) April *Slaughter and May.*

48 [2002] 1 WLR 107; [2002] CLC 463 at [23]–[25].

49 See, for example, the Court Appeal's judgment in *Through Mutual Insurance Association (Eursia) Ltd v New India Assurance Co Ltd (The Hari Bhum)* (No 1) [2005] 1 Lloyd's Rep. 67).

50 *West Tankers* [2007] UKLH 4 at [19].

51 C Ambrose, 'Can Anti-suit Injunctions Survive in European Community Law?' (2003) 52 ICLQ 401–42, 413.

52 Advocate General Opinion Kokott *Allianz SpA* (C-185/07) ECLI: EU: C:2008:466 at [66].

53 *Allianz SpA* (C-185/07) EU: C: 2009:69; [2008] 2 Lloyd's Rep. 661 at [30].

54 *Turner v Grovit* [2001] UKHL 65; [2002] WLR 107.

The decision was criticised by the international arbitration community for extending the scope of the Brussels I Regulation to arbitration in a way that undermined the effectiveness of the arbitration agreements. Critics argued that the decisions gave parties free rein to ignore arbitration agreements and commence proceedings in their preferred court concerning the existence and validity of an arbitration in order to delay or frustrate an arbitration: so-called torpedo actions.

Does the Brussels I Recast Regulation reverse the *West Tankers* decision?

The Brussels Recast was adopted in 2012 and came into force on 10 January 2015, which clarified the scope of the arbitration exception by adding Recital 12 and Article 73(2), along with retaining Article 1(2)(d), and seems to have swept away the *West Tankers* decision, thus allowing anti-suit injunctions to be issued.

Following the prohibition of anti-suit injunctions by the CJEU in the *West Tankers* case, the question arises as to whether this prohibition extends to the arbitral tribunals. This is because, as it was affirmed in *Nordsee*,[55] for the purposes of the EU law, arbitral tribunals do not fall within the meaning of "court or tribunal" to the effect that they cannot even make a direct reference to the CJEU through Article 267 of the Treaty of the Functioning of the European Union 2009 (hereinafter TFEU). In *Gazprom*,[56] the Lithuanian Supreme Court made a reference to the CJEU on this issue. The CJEU held that the Brussels Regulation only governs conflicts of jurisdiction between Member States' court and tribunals; as arbitral tribunals are neither, the principle of mutual trust under the Brussels Regulation is not infringed by an arbitral tribunal anti-suit injunction/order.[57]

Importantly, *Gazprom*[58] raised the questions on the compatibility of the anti-suit injunctions in Brussels I Recast Regulation, which came into force on 10 January 2015 with the aim of revising the Brussels Regulation. Simply, in the Brussels I Recast arbitration exclusion, Article 1(2)(d) of Brussels I Regulation survives. Indeed, the exclusion is amplified and reinforced by a new Article 73(2) and Recital 12 which expressly state that the Regulation should not apply to arbitration. Of particular interest in the Brussels Recast is the fourth paragraph of Recital 12 which clarifies that the Regulation should not apply to

> any action or ancillary proceedings relating to, in particular, the establishment of the tribunal, the powers of arbitrator, the conduct of the arbitration procedure or any other aspects of such a procedure, nor to any action or

55 *Nordsee Deustche Hochseefischerei GmbH v Reederei Mond Hochseeficherei Nordstern AG & Co KG* (102/8) EU:C:1982:107; [1982] Com LR 154.

56 *Gazprom* OAO (C-536/13) EU: C:2015:316; [2015] 1 WLR 4937; [2015] ILPr 31.

57 *Nordsee Deustche Hochseefischerei GmbH v Reederei Mond Hochseeficherei Nordstern AG & Co KG* (102/8)EU:C:1982:107; [1982] Com LR 154; also see Gazprom OAO (C-536/13) EU:C:2015:316; [2015] 1 WLR 4937; [2015] ILPr 31.

58 *Gazprom* OAO (C-536/13) EU:C: 2015:316; [2015] 1 WLR 4937; [2015] ILPr 31.

> judgment concerning the annulment, review, appeal, recognition or enforcement of an arbitral award.

It is noted that in *Nori Holding b Bank Ottritie*,[59] Justice Males in the High Court issued an anti-suit injunction to restrain court proceedings commenced in Russia in breach of an arbitration clause but refused to issue an anti-suit injunction to restrain similar court proceedings commenced in Cyprus on the ground that he was bound by the CJEU's decision in *West Tankers*, reaffirmed in *Gazprom*, which prevented the grant of such anti-suit injunctions.

The *Gazprom* case arose out of a shareholder dispute between Russian energy giant, Gazprom, and Lithuania's energy ministry over the management of gas provider, Lietuvos Dujos.

In 2012, Gazprom obtained an arbitration award against Lithuania's energy ministry from a Stockholm Chamber of Commerce (hereinafter SCC) tribunal ordering the ministry to 'withdraw or limit' some of the claims pending before local courts. However, the Lithuanian courts refused to enforce this anti-suit award, leading to the Lithuanian Supreme Courts' referral of the matter to the CJEU in 2013. Simply, the *Gazprom* case brought out parallel claims in the Lithuanian Courts and in an arbitration conducted under SCC rules in Sweden.

Interestingly, while delivering his opinion in *Gazprom*, Advocate General Wathelet relied heavily on the Brussels I Recast[60] and explained that if *West Tankers* was decided under the Brussels I Recast, in those circumstances of the case with anti-suit injunction forming the subject matter of the judgment, it would not have been held to be incompatible with the Brussels I Regulation.[61] His argument was affirmed by the fourth paragraph of Recital 12 of the Brussels I Recast (as discussed earlier) on the ground that

> not only does that paragraph exclude the recognition and enforcement of arbitral awards from the scope of that (Brussels I Recast) regulation . . . but it also excludes ancillary proceedings, which in my view covers anti-suit injunctions issued by national courts in their capacity as court supporting the arbitration.[62]

Clearly, the Advocate General's opinion triggers the debate of the compatibility of anti-suit injunctions in the arbitration context of Brussels I Recast and also raises the possibility that CJEU would overturn the decision in *West Tankers* in the future.[63] However, although the CJEU judgment did not address the impact

59 [2018] EWHC 1343 (Comm).
60 Opinion of the Advocate General Wathelet in Gazprom (C-536/13)EU:C:2014:2414.
61 ibid. at [133].
62 ibid. at [138].
63 See V Clark, 'Gazprom, Anti-suit Injunctions and Arbitration: The Debate Goes On' (*Berwin Leighton Paisner*, 21 May 2015) <www.blplaw.com/expert-legal-insights/articles/gazprom-anti-suit-injunctions-arbitration-debate-goes>.

of the Brussels I Recast on the anti-suit injunctions, the CJEU made references to the *West Tankers* decision and buttressed the principle of mutual trust among EU Member State courts. The CJEU, however, did not engage with AG Wathelet's opinion in the Brussels Recast Regulation. Instead, the CJEU decided the case on the Brussels I Regulation and left the position of anti-suit injunctions under the Brussels I Recast entirely open. Justice Males held that the CJEU in *Gazprom* was 'crystal clear' that anti-suit injunction was incompatible with the Brussels Regulation. He considered Recital 12 of the Brussels I Recast and observed that nothing in it undermines the principles affirmed in *West Tankers* and *Gazprom.* He thus held that that 'the opinion of the Advocate General on this issue was fundamentally flawed' and that if the EU legislation had wanted to reserve *West Tankers* through the Brussels Recast, it 'chose an odd way in which to do so'. He reiterated 'there is nothing in (the Recast) to cast doubt on the continuing validity of the (CJEU) decision in West Tankers case'. [64]

Justice Males therefore did not grant an anti-suit injunction to stop Cyprus court proceedings commenced in breach of the arbitration agreement, and left it either to Cyprus to stay the proceedings or to the claimants to apply to the arbitrators to issue such an anti-suit injunction (as *Gazprom* allows).

This decision reaffirms the CJEU's decision on *West Tankers* as good law and in doing so clears up most of the confusion that had been brought up by the AG opinion in the *Gazprom* case in relation to the arbitration exception in the Brussels Recast Regulation. It must be emphasised that the Brussels I Recast does not reserve *West Tankers* that anti-suit injunctions cannot be issued by courts to restrain court proceedings in other EU Member States.

The Brexit effect

Having assessed the prohibition of anti-suit injunctions by the CJEU in the *Turner v Grovit*, the *West Tankers* and *Gazprom* cases, this paper now focuses on the unique position of the UK. This is because the UK will be leaving the EU (Brexit) two years after Article 50 of the Treaty on the Functioning of the European Union (TFEU) to echo a result of the EU referendum vote in 23 June 2016. In doing so, it is necessary to examine the potential effect of post-Brexit on arbitration – the granting of anti-suit injunctions as an 'independent' State.

One of the main issues that led to the Brexit vote was to take back control of the UK law and bring an end to the jurisdiction of the CJEU when Britain leaves the EU on 29 March 2019.[65] At present, as a Member of the EU, the UK courts have to adopt the CJEU decisions in *West Tankers*, *Turner v Grovit* and *Gazprom*, although the highest Court in the UK, the then House of Lords (now the UK's Supreme Court) as discussed earlier, did not share the same views. However, if after Brexit, EU law and CJEU decisions no longer apply in the UK, the UK

64 *West Tankers Inc v Allianz SpA* (Case C-185/07) [2009] AC.

65 Department for Exiting the European Union, Policy Paper 'Ongoing Union Judicial and Administrative Proceedings – Position Paper', 13 July 2017.

courts may regain their power to issue anti-suit injunctions. As British Prime Minister Theresa May put in in her Lancaster House Speech in January 2017, 'juridical independence is a totemic issue for Brexiteers' and "leaving the European Union will mean that our laws will be made in Westminster, Edinburgh, Cardiff and Belfast. And those laws will be interpreted by judges not in Luxembourg but in courts across this country'.[66]

However, despite then Prime Minister May's declaration, it must be emphasised that the impact of Brexit on anti-suit injunctions will depend on the terms of the Brexit negotiations.[67] If the UK negotiates to opt out of all EU law, including the Brussels Regulations, the UK courts will revert back to the full power of granting anti-suit injunctions, which might increase London's competitiveness as an arbitral seat and spark a rise in London-seated arbitrations.[68] English companies would also be given a competitive edge as they can go to the English courts, which would not be bound by the Brussels Regulations, to seek anti-suit injunctions. If this would be the case, all the restrictions associated with the ECJ decisions in *West Tankers* will be evaded, and all the positives of anti-suit injunctions including preventing parallel proceedings would apply *mutatis mutandis*.

It must be admitted that even if the UK adopts such an approach, the power to grant an anti-suit injunction would not be completely unfettered on the grounds: i) the UK anti-suit injunction can only be issued by the senior courts; ii) anti-suit injunctions under the English law are used as a fault remedy which requires the defendant to prove his actions are *inter alia* unconscionable, an abuse of justice, vexatious or oppressive, in the eyes of English law. In principal, English courts would not issue an anti-suit injunction where it is not appropriate to do so even if the seat of arbitration is London. The *U & M Mining*[69] case further strengthens the assertion made earlier. In this case, undoubtedly, the agreed seat of arbitration was London, and thus the claimant sought an anti-suit injunction in the English court to stop Zambian proceedings started against it by the defendant. However, upon careful consideration of the facts, Blair J refused to grant an anti-suit injunction because this dispute concerned the operation of a copper mine in Zambia between two Zambian companies. Blair upheld that:

> The matter is of national as well as local importance since, as I have been told, the mine contributes a substantial proportion of Zambia's total GDP. So far as judicial assistance by way of interim measures pending the appointment of

66 J Grierson, H Stewart and R Mason, 'UK Will Keep "Half an Eye" on ECJ Rulings after Brexit, says Justice Minster', Wednesday 23 August 2017 <www.theguardian.com/law/2017/aug/23/uk-will-keep-half-an-eye-on-ecj-rulings-after-brexit-says-just>.

67 See K Davies and V Kirsey, 'Anti-suit Injunctions in Support of London Seated Arbitrations Post-Brexit: Are all things New Just Well-Forgotten Past?' (2016) 4(1) International Journal of Arbitration 501, 502.

68 J Rogers, S Goodall and C Golsong, 'How Will Brexit Impact Arbitration in England and Wales?' (2016) 7 International Arbitration Report 15, 17–18.

69 *U & M Mining* [2013] 2 Llood's Rep. 218; [2013] 1. CLC 456 at [72].

> the arbitrators is required, in my view the natural forum for such proceedings is in Zambia, not in England.[70]

Although Blair J's decision in *U & M Mining*[71] may be seen as anti-arbitration and/or interference with the parties' choice to select the seat of arbitration, there is a rationale behind this decision of the English court which is clearly justifiable as it is commercially sound and pragmatic. It is because in certain circumstances, practical factors may make it more convenient and effective to proceed in another jurisdiction, although the seat of arbitration is the natural forum for seeking an anti-suit injunction in ordinary circumstances.[72]

Conclusions

However, from the analysis provided in this chapter, the rest of the EU Member State courts would be equally free to grant anti-suit injunctions to restrain a party from pursuing a claim before the English courts. Furthermore, there is also a risk that where an anti-suit injunction is granted to stop proceedings in another Member State's court, those courts might later refuse to recognise and enforce the arbitral award owing to it being contrary to the country's public policy by virtue of Article V2(b) of the New York Convention, which allows national courts to refuse an arbitral award where the 'recognition or enforcement of the award would be contrary to the public policy of that country'.

If it is not what is negotiated for, as the UK could negotiate to sign up to the Lugano Convention 2007 on the jurisdiction and the recognition and enforcement of judgments, which extends the effect of the Brussels Regulation to Iceland, Switzerland and Norway. If such an approach is taken, although it is still unclear what the terms of the agreement would be, it is unlikely that the UK would still be bound by the Brussels Regulation and not the CJEU decisions on the Brussels Regulation. Therefore, the advantage of such an approach is that UK judicial sovereignty would be protected through *West Tankers* and the mutual trust principle from anti-suit injunctions in EU Member State courts.

In conclusion, the UK might alternatively negotiate for a Denmark-like approach. As per Article 21 of the Brussels I Regulation, Denmark opted out of the Brussels Regulation; however, the EU concluded an agreement on jurisdiction and the recognition and enforcement of judgments in civil and commercial matters which ensures the application of the provisions of the Brussels Regulation in Denmark from 1 July 2007.[73] In this way, therefore, the UK and the rest of

70 ibid.

71 ibid.

72 A Singh, 'Supervisory Jurisdiction of the Courts of the Seat: Primary, Not Exclusive – A Comment on *U & M Mining Zambia Ltd v Konkola Copper Mines Plc* (2013) 16(3) Int ALR N23, N24.

73 Commission of the European Communities, 'Report from the Commission to the European Parliament, The Council of The European Economic and Social Committee on the

the EU Member States will negotiate an agreement either to duplicate or 'keep but amend' or one that will completely replace the Brussels Regulation. As the UK will be negotiating while leaving the EU and thus from a different position to that of Denmark, it is more likely that it would prefer a 'keep but amend' agreement. This is also a possibility because the CJEU decisions in *West Tankers* and *Turner v Grovit* clearly expose the weaknesses of the current UK regulatory framework relating to anti-suit injunctions.

As international commercial arbitration is increasingly becoming a preferred method for disputes resolution internationally, and so are national courts increasingly issuing anti-suit injunctions. In a judgment delivered on 13 February 2018, the Grant Court of the Cayman Islands granted an anti-suit injunction to restrain the joint official liquidators of Argyle Funds SPC (Argyle) from continuing litigation commenced in the Supreme Court of the State of New York against Argyle's former statutory auditor (BDO Cayman) and three related parties.[74] The court enforced 'sole recourse' provisions in the engagement letters between Argyle and BDO that disputes were 'to be resolved via arbitration in the Cayman Islands'.[75] Although anti-suit injunctions have undeniable extra-territorial effects, they are granted on the basis of the court's in personam jurisdiction over the party enjoined. Their grant has no direct effect on the foreign proceedings, but the defendant will be personally liable for contempt of court if they breach the terms of the order. The impacts of issuing an anti-suit injunction in favour of arbitration is accelerating in Caribbean countries upholding the primacy of the arbitration agreement.

---

application of Council Regulation (EC) No 44/2001 on the jurisdiction and the recognition and enforcement of judgements in civil and commercial matters' (COM/2009/0174 final). S. 1. 1.

74 Campbells Advisory, 'Anti-suit Injunction Granted by Grant Court to Restrain Cayman Liquidators from Continuing New York Litigation', 15 February 2018 <www.mondaq.com/caymanislands/x/674028/offshore+financial+centres/AntiSuit+Injunction+Granted+By+Grand+Court+To+Restrain+Cayman+Liquidators+From+Continuing+New+York+Litigation>.

75 For details of the case, see *Petroleum Company of Trinidad and Tobago Limited and Samsung Engineering Trinidad Co. Limited*, Case No. HT-2017-000235, Neutral Citation Number: [2017] EWHC 3055 (TCC).

Part II

Trade and security in EU-CARICOM

4 EU-CARICOM trade law as a tool for development?

Achim Rogmann

Trade relations between the EU and the CARIFORUM nations are governed by multilateral and bilateral trade agreements. The bilateral provisions should be in compliance with the multilateral framework that is governed by WTO law. Hence, I will first address the issue of which trade rules have to be obeyed as a consequence of membership of the WTO. In addition, trade agreements between CARIFORUM and the EU have to be in conformity with the instruments adopted under the auspices of the World Customs Organization (WCO).

WTO agreements

Pursuant to Article II(2) of the WTO Agreement, the WTO multilateral agreements are 'binding on all Members'.[1] Under article XVI(4) of the WTO Agreement, members must ensure the conformity of their laws, regulations, and administrative procedures with the substantive obligations of the WTO Agreement.

One of the core elements of the trading system governed by the WTO rules is the elimination of discriminatory treatment in international trade relations.[2] The principle of non-discrimination comprises two main elements: the obligation of most favoured nation (MFN) treatment under article I GATT 1994 and the national treatment (NT) obligation pursuant to article III GATT 1994. While the MFN obligation restricts the right of members to discriminate 'between and among like products of different origins', the NT obligation prohibits the discriminatory treatment of lawfully 'imported products vis-à-vis like domestic products'.[3] As the intention of EU-CARICOM trade relations is to enhance bilateral trade relations, I will restrict my survey to the MFN principle. Pursuant to the MFN obligation, WTO members must extend any advantage immediately and unconditionally to all WTO members. This obligation covers all relevant

1 Mituso Matsushita and others, *The World Trade Organization: Law, Practice and Policy* (3rd edn, OUP 2015) 32.
2 See Marrakesh Agreement establishing the World Trade Organization [1994] UNTS. 154, 33 ILM. 1144 para 3 Preamble.
3 Matsushita and others (n 1) 155–56.

measures governing market access. If a WTO member intends to grant preferred market access to any other nation, it has to take the MFN obligation into consideration.

The preferential treatment of individual trade partners is in contradiction to the MFN obligation, which ensures that WTO members have an equal opportunity to compete for market share in other Member States.[4] As of 17 January 2020, 303 preferential trade agreements were already in force, and 483 had been notified by WTO members.[5] These arrangements function as exceptions to the MFN treatment,[6] but the exceptions can only be used under certain conditions, which I will address in the context of the CARIFORUM – EC agreement.

The TFA[7] was agreed in order to make the import and export across all WTO member countries more efficient and less costly by increasing transparency and improving customs procedures,[8] and it was one of the main outcomes of the WTO ministerial conference in Bali. In general, there is a broad understanding of the term 'trade facilitation', which covers the reduction of red tape in international trade, especially with regards to customs and other trade and border procedures.[9] The core task of the TFA was to clarify GATT 1994 provisions that already existed (articles V, VIII and X), hence leaving big policy issues untouched and refraining from expanding the scope of GATT.[10]

The TFA entered into force on 22 February 2017 by virtue of its ratification by two-thirds of the WTO members. By May 2020, 150 of the 164 WTO members, including the EU[11] and most of the CARIFORUM countries,[12] had ratified the TFA.[13] Hence, trade relations between the EU and the CARIFORUM nations have to be in compliance with the provisions of the TFA. Since uniform trade provisions have to be applied by all parties to the CARIFORUM-EU trade

4 ibid. 157.

5 Counting goods, services and accessions separately, see <www.wto.org/english/tratop_e/region_e/region_e.htm>.

6 Matsushita and others (n 1) 157.

7 Protocol of 28 November 2014 amending the Marrakesh Agreement establishing the WTO [2014] WT/L/940.

8 Hans-Michael Wolffgang and Edward Kafeero, 'Old Wine in New Skins: Analysis of the Trade Facilitation Agreement vis-à-vis the Revised Kyoto Convention' (2014) 8(2) World Customs Journal 27.

9 Andrew Grainger, 'The WTO Trade Facilitation Agreement: Consulting the Private Sector' (2014) 48(6) Journal of World Trade Law 1167, 1168.

10 Tom Cachet, 'The World Trade Organization Trade Facilitation Agreement: Legal Consequences and Impact on the Union Customs Code' (2017) 12(2) Global Trade and Customs Journal 74, 81.

11 See the Council Decision (EU) 2015/1947 on the conclusion, on behalf of the European Union, of the Protocol amending the Marrakesh Agreement establishing the World Trade Organisation [2015] OJ 2015 L 284/1.

12 The TFA has not yet been ratified by The Bahamas, Haiti or Suriname. The Commonwealth of The Bahamas is the only CARIFORUM nation that is not yet a WTO member. WTO membership is expected by 2021.

13 See <www.tfafacility.org/ratifications>.

agreements, it is not possible to exclude individual partners to the agreement from specific provisions by not implementing the TFA provisions.

WCO agreements

Not as well-known as the WTO legal system are the agreements negotiated and agreed under the auspices of the World Customs Organization (WCO). The WCO is the only intergovernmental organisation to be exclusively focused on customs matters. It was established in order to enhance the efficiency and effectiveness of customs administrations, with a view to securing the highest possible degree of harmony and uniformity of customs systems across the world. In order to remove obstacles to trade, it administers a wide range of international agreements and instruments, and pursues the development of further global standards[14] to address the challenges of an ever-changing trade environment. Today the WCO counts 183 members, which include 12 CARIFORUM countries[15] and the EU, whose status is 'akin to' membership.[16]

One of the WCO's flagship conventions is the Revised Kyoto Convention on the Simplification and Harmonisation of Customs Procedures (RKC). This provides a set of comprehensive customs procedures to facilitate legitimate international trade while effecting customs controls, including the protection of customs revenue and society. The RKC delivers the principles of simplified and harmonised customs procedures like predictability, transparency, due process, maximum use of information technology, and modern customs techniques,[17] and these are also fundamental to CARICOM – EU trade relations. Unlike the WTO, the WCO does not follow the single undertaking approach,[18] which has the effect that WCO members do not have the obligation to accede to the RKC. The WCO is restricted to persuading its members to accede to the RKC by highlighting the benefits.[19] The consequence of sharing common definitions and customs procedures in accordance with the RKC is that the RKC contracting parties are supported in facilitating burdensome negotiations on customs-related provisions when they negotiate trade agreements. Moreover, certain provisions that go beyond the RKC level of commitment can be agreed upon between the negotiating parties on the basis of the RKC principles.[20]

14 See Tokio Yamaoka, 'The De Facto Accession of the European Communities to the World Customs Organization: Process and Significance' (2013) 8(4) Global Trade and Customs Journal 92, 93.

15 By August 2019 Dominica, Grenada, St. Kitts and Nevis as well as St. Vincent and the Grenadines are not members of the WCO.

16 See Yamaoka (n 14) 96–99 for the reasons for and the consequences of the EU's special status.

17 Tadashi Yasui, 'Benefits of the Revised Kyoto Convention' (2010) WCO Research Paper No. 6, 1 <www.wcoomd.org/~/media/wco/public/global/pdf/topics/research/research-paper-series/rkc_benefits.pdf?la=en>.

18 Yamaoka (n 14) 96.

19 Yasui (n 17) 1.

20 ibid. 2–3.

Despite the fact that to date a total of 116 countries and territories have acceded to the RKC, none of the CARICOM nations has yet signed or ratified the Convention, which opened for signatures in June 1999.[21] From the bigger group of CARIFORUM States, only Cuba and the Dominican Republic are RKC contracting parties. In March 2018, WCO's Secretary-General pointed out the importance of implementing WCO standards and called on CARICOM members who were also members of the WCO to ratify the RKC. Countries that are not a party to the RKC can apply elements of the Convention on a voluntary basis. It is reported that the CARICOM states are following the major guidelines of the RKC and are to implement the RKC as part of the trade facilitation initiative.[22]

The EU and all of its Member States are signatories to the RKC, which illustrates that the European partners in the CARIFORUM-EU trade relationship have accepted the obligation to implement the core elements of the RKC. This can have the effect that CARIFORUM States have to follow the RKC standards under the bilateral trade agreement, since the EU and its Member States may not fall short of their WCO obligations. Article 31 of the CARIFORUM-EU Economic Partnership Agreement (EPA)[23] reflects this need to follow international rules, by stipulating that signatories must base their external trade regime on substantive elements of the RKC.

Furthermore, it is remarkable that most CARIFORUM States have signed the WTO TFA but have abstained from accepting the RKC. This decision might be based largely on political reasons, as almost all of the content of the TFA is a reflection of the provisions of the RKC. Other instruments and tools developed by the WCO that are not part of the RKC have also been integrated into the TFA.[24] Given that a large proportion of the standards and practices set out in the RKC are optional, and that there is a need to apply at least the binding parts via the EPA, it cannot easily be explained why the CARIFORUM States have not yet officially acceded to the RKC.

EU – ACP trade relations

The current legal basis for trade relations was preceded by a sequence of agreements between the then European Economic Community (EEC) and the group of African, Caribbean and Pacific states. These agreements precluded individual trade arrangements between EEC and Caribbean states.

21 WCO General Secretariat, Document on Position as Regards Ratifications and Accessions at 7 November 2018 (2018) PG0287E1a.

22 Karen Adair, 'The Scope of a Multilateral Agreement on Trade Facilitation in the Interest of Caribbean Countries: Enhancement of Trade Competitiveness through Capacity Building' (2006) Diagnostic & Negotiating Position Report <https://caricom.org/documents/10171-multilateral_agreement_on_trade_facilitation.pdf>.

23 See Part III for details on this agreement.

24 Wolffgang and Kafeero (n 8) 28–34.

Lomé Convention for the post-colonial era

Specific trade relations between the EEC/EU and the Caribbean nations have a long tradition. The first Lomé Convention between the EEC and 46 developing counties belonging to the newly created African, Caribbean and Pacific Group of States (ACP) was signed on 28 April 1975.[25] The main objective of the ACP was the joint negotiation and implementation of cooperation agreements with the EEC.[26] Signing the Lomé Convention can be seen as a consequence of the accession of the United Kingdom to the EEC's Common Market in 1973, when responsibility for trade relations with the post-colonial developing countries of the Commonwealth was handed over to the EEC.[27]

Under the Lomé Convention, the EEC granted unilateral trade preferences in favour of the ACP states, while EEC products did not enjoy any preferential access to the ACP markets. Furthermore, the Convention included a non-discrimination clause stipulating that the EEC had to abstain from discriminating between ACP states in terms of trade provisions.[28] Since article XXIV GATT 1994 only permits breaches of the MFN clause if a free trade area or customs union is formed that bilaterally eliminates trade barriers, the EEC had to ensure compliance with GATT 1994 for the special trade relations with the ACP nations. Even if the EEC treated the market access provisions under the Lomé Convention as compliant with the GATT 1994 provisions, it was necessary to apply for a waiver from the obligations under the MFN clause in article I(1) under article XXV(5) GATT 1994. A corresponding waiver was granted in 1994 until the expiry of the Lomé Convention.[29] However, basing trade relations with Caribbean nations on a waiver was not a comfortable situation for the EEC, as a waiver, under article IX(3) WTO Agreement, has to be granted by consensus of all WTO members.

From Lomé to Cotonou

The Lomé Convention was renegotiated and extended three times until the last version (Lomé IV) expired in 2000. The exception from the MFN obligation allowing trade preferences to be granted to the ACP states was based on the 'Decision on Differential and More Favourable Treatment, Reciprocity and Fuller Participation of Developing Countries' (the 'Enabling Clause'[30]), adopted

25 Matthew Louis Bishop, Tony Heron and Anthony Payne, 'Caribbean Development Alternatives and the CARIFORUM – European Union Economic Partnership Agreement' (2013) 16(1) Journal of International Relations and Development 82, 90.

26 See <www.acp.int/node/7>.

27 Bishop, Heron and Payne (n 25) 90.

28 Jürgen Huber, 'The Past, Present and Future ACP-EC Trade Regime and the WTO' (2000) 11(2) European Journal of International Law 427, 429.

29 ibid. 429–30.

30 GATT Decision on differential and more favourable treatment, reciprocity and fuller participation of developing countries [1979] L/4903.

under the former GATT 1947 in 1979.[31] In 2000 the Lomé Convention was replaced by the Cotonou Agreement, which granted preferential market access to 78 ACP states. The core reasons for signing a new agreement were the alleged inability of the trade provisions of the Lomé Convention to increase the market share of the ACP countries in the EU,[32] and the need to achieve conformity with WTO obligations.[33] Under the Enabling Clause, tariff preferences granted by developed countries must not discriminate between developing countries, except that it is possible to provide more generous treatment to all the least-developed countries (LDC). Different treatment for different developing countries may not be granted just on geographical criteria.[34] The preferences granted by the EU to the ACP countries under the Lomé Convention were not covered by the Enabling Clause. In order to achieve compatibility with the WTO rules, the new trade agreement had to differentiate between trading partners only on the basis of their levels of development.[35]

The Trade, Aid and Political Agreement signed in Cotonou in June 2000 between the ACP states and the EC set ambitious goals for a period of 20 years. The Agreement foresees Economic Partnership Agreements (EPAs) that will set up an entirely new framework for trade and investment flows between the EU and contracting ACP states. The Agreement entered into force in April 2003 and was revised in 2005 and 2010.

With regard to trade relations, the Cotonou Agreement functions more as a bridge towards new trade relations rather than the implementation of such relations: the trade chapter of the agreement governs the new trade relationship and the expiry of preferences at the end of 2007. Furthermore, the parties agreed to conclude new, WTO-compatible, trading arrangements, progressively removing barriers to trade between them and enhancing cooperation in all relevant areas of trade.[36]

In order to facilitate the transition to the new trading arrangements, the non-reciprocal trade preferences applied under the Lomé IV Convention were maintained during the preparatory period for all ACP countries, under the conditions defined in Annex V to the Agreement.[37] Because of the unilateral liberalisation of market access, the continued incompatibility with the MFN obligation could only be solved by another WTO waiver being issued. However, it was not in the interests of the EC/EU to be dependent on a WTO waiver for a substantial part

31 Huber (n 28) 436.
32 Lars Nilsson, 'Trading Relations: Is the Roadmap from Lomé to Cotonou Correct?' (2010) 34(4) Applied Economics 439, 451.
33 ibid. 439.
34 Huber (n 28) 436.
35 Stephen R Hurt, 'Co-operation and Coercion? The Cotonou Agreement between the European Union and ACP States and the End of the Lomé Convention' (2003) 24(1) Third World Quarterly 161, 164–65.
36 European Parliament Resolution of 5 February 2009 on the development impact of Economic Partnership Agreements (EPAs) (2008/2170(INI)), OJ 2010 C 67E/120, 122.
37 Art 36.3 Lomé IV Convention.

of its external trade regime.[38] As the waiver was to expire in 2007, negotiations with seven ACP regions were conducted in order to achieve agreements in accordance with article XXIV GATT 1994.[39] The CARIFORUM-EC EPA is the core legal basis for trade relations between CARIFORUM and the EU states.

Autonomous EU trade provisions for CARIFORUM States

When establishing specific trade regulations with a third country or region, the EU has the choice between adopting autonomous trade provisions and signing bilateral or regional trade agreements.[40] Since 1971, the (former) European Community has granted autonomous trade measures to developing countries under its scheme for generalised tariff preferences governed by the Lomé framework. Today, the EU's autonomous trade regime is reflected in the provisions of Regulation No 978/2012,[41] applying the General System of Preferences (GSP) without an additional framework agreement. As unilateral trade preferences are not in compliance with article I(1) GATT 1994, the GSP has to be based on an exception from the MFN clause. For this purpose, the EU has based the GSP Regulation on the Enabling Clause.

The GSP Regulation was adopted using the power given to the EU under the Common Commercial Policy (CCP) as stipulated in article 207 TFEU. The CCP has to be consistent with and to consolidate the objectives of the EU's policy in the field of development cooperation, as laid down in article 208 TFEU, which relate in particular to the eradication of poverty and the promotion of sustainable development and good governance in developing countries.[42]

In the *EC – Tariff Preferences* dispute settlement case, the WTO's Appellate Body (AB) held[43] that the WTO Enabling Clause entitles developed countries to grant better tariff treatment to some developing countries than it does to others, subject to certain conditions. The AB held that these conditions were not met by the EU's previous GSP Regulation, and this led to modified conditions under the follow-up regulations adopted by the EU.[44]

38 Huber (n 28) 433–34.

39 Tony Heron and Peg Murray-Evans, 'Limits to Market Power: Strategic Discourse and Institutional Path Dependence in the European Union – African, Caribbean and Pacific Economic Partnership Agreements' (2017) 23(2) European Journal of International Relations 341, 347.

40 Under specific circumstances autonomous trade measures can even be applied to countries that have already signed a trade agreement with the EU, see e.g. European Parliament and Council Regulation (EU) 2017/1566 on the introduction of temporary autonomous trade measures for Ukraine supplementing the trade concessions available under the Association Agreement [2017] OJ 2017 L 254/1.

41 European Parliament and Council Regulation (EU) No 978/2012 on applying a scheme of generalised tariff preferences [2012] OJ 2012 L 313/1.

42 European Parliament and Council Regulation (EU) No 978/2012 on applying a scheme of generalised tariff preferences [2012] OJ L301/1, consideration (4).

43 WTO Appellate Body Report, *EC – Tariff Preferences* (2004) WT/DS246/AB/R.

44 Lorand Bartels, 'The WTO Legality of the EU's GSP+ Arrangement' (2007) 10(4) Journal of International Economic Law 869.

As a result of the massive changes within the global economy and the different levels of economic progress in the group of 'developing countries', the EU implemented a reform of the GSP to make sure that the preferences benefited those countries most in need.[45] The EU considered that the growing diversity of developing countries calls for more differentiation in the design and implementation of EU policies, because a number of developing countries had been successfully integrated into global markets and were putting pressure on the exports of much poorer countries that genuinely needed help.[46] The corresponding reform led to a reduction in the number of GSP beneficiaries from 178 to 92 countries by 2014. Among those countries that were excluded from the GSP benefits is a group of 14 CARIFORUM States.[47]

Under the current GSP Regulation, LDC countries continue to benefit from duty-free and quota-free access to the EU market for all 'legal' products (the so-called Everything But Arms (EBA) initiative). In the absence of a contractual commitment to maintain preferential market access, the special status can be withdrawn by the EU unilaterally.[48] Under the GSP Regulation, only countries with LDC status can be beneficiaries of the EBA initiative, with the effect that the only Caribbean state benefiting from the EBA programme is Haiti.[49] In consequence, no other CARIFORUM state can be found on the list of beneficiaries under the schemes for tariff preferences according to the GSP Regulation.

The market access regulation

In addition to the already quite complex trade relations governed by the GSP Regulation and the EPA, the EU enacted the so-called Market Access Regulation (MAR)[50] in 2007. This regulation takes into account that agreements establishing – or leading to the establishment of – EPAs for which negotiations have been concluded encourage the parties to take steps to apply the agreement

45 Commission, 'Proposal for a Regulation of the European Parliament and of the Council Applying a Scheme of Generalised Tariff Preferences' COM (2011) 241 final; Commission, 'Communication on Trade, Growth and Development' COM (2012) 22 final.

46 Commission, 'Proposal for a Regulation of the European Parliament and of the Council Applying a Scheme of Generalised Tariff Preferences' COM (2011) 241 final, 2.

47 Commission (2015) information document on the EU's Generalised Scheme of Preferences (GSP), Annex II <http://trade.ec.europa.eu/doclib/docs/2015/august/tradoc_153732.pdf>; see also Gabriel Siles-Brügge, 'EU Trade and Development Policy beyond the ACP: Subordinating Developmental to Commercial Imperatives in the Reform of GSP' (2014) 20(1) Contemporary Politics 49, arguing that the EU's developmental trade agenda is increasingly subordinated to commercial interests.

48 Huber (n 28) 436.

49 Art 1(2)(c) and Annex IV of the GSP Regulation.

50 Council Regulation (EC) No 1528/2007 on applying the arrangements for products originating in certain states which are part of the African, Caribbean and Pacific (ACP) Group of States provided for in agreements establishing, or leading to the establishment of, economic partnership agreements (2007) OJ 2007 No L 348/1, recast by Regulation (EU) 2016/1076, OJ 2016 L 185/1.

before a provisional application, on a mutual basis.[51] The MAR was enacted in order to apply the agreements on the basis of those provisions.

The background is a provision in the Cotonou Agreement[52] for an assessment of the situation of non-LDC ACP states that have decided after consultation with the EU that they are not in a position to negotiate and sign an EPA. In such cases the EU has to offer an alternative in order to grant market access equivalent to the previous situation under Lomé IV and in conformity with WTO rules.[53]

Today all the CARIFORUM States, with the exception of Cuba, are signatories to the CARIFORUM-EC EPA, which has applied provisionally since 2008. Cuba did not participate in the EPA negotiations despite its status as a CARIFORUM Member State. For political reasons the EU did not enact any other preferential provisions for trade relations with Cuba. Here the MFN treatment under article I(1) GATT 1994 governs the bilateral trade relations. Since the Republic of Haiti signed the EPA but has not taken the necessary steps towards ratification of the EPA, Annex I to the MAR has been amended to remove Haiti from that Annex with effect from 1 October 2014.[54] In consequence, the MAR is not applicable to any of the CARIFORUM countries.

Despite the fact that there is no room for the application of the MAR to the 14 CARIFORUM States that have ratified the EPA, those countries are still listed in Annex I to the MAR. This leads to a conflict in that, from the EU's perspective, two different preferential arrangements are applicable to the cross-border movement of goods that originate from the CARIFORUM States in question. However, under article 216(2) TFEU the EPA prevails over the MAR. Even if this article did not contain an express provision on the position of international agreements within the EU legal order, it can be concluded from the legal effect of those agreements that they rank in the hierarchy of EU legal sources below the primary sources but above secondary sources of EU law like the MAR. As a consequence, secondary law cannot be contrary to such international agreements.[55] Therefore, any shortfalls in terms of market access under the MAR have to be resolved by only applying the EPA as far as it has direct effect, which is the case for provisions that are unconditional and sufficiently precise.[56] For preferential agreements in particular, the ECJ found that these conditions are fulfilled in terms of creating a system of free trade that includes provisions on abolishing customs duties.[57] The former EC followed this hierarchical approach and

51 Consideration (4) MAR 2007.

52 Art 37(6).

53 Huber (n 28) 432.

54 European Parliament and Council Regulation (EU) 527/2013 amending Council Regulation (EC) 1528/2007 as regards the exclusion of a number of countries from the list of regions or states which have concluded negotiations, OJ 2013 L 165/59.

55 Agoston Mohay, 'The Status of International Agreements concluded by the European Union in the EU Legal Order' (2017) 33 Pravni Vjesnik BR 151, 157–58.

56 Case C-344/04 *IATA and ELFAA v Department for Transport* [2006] ECR I-00403, para 39.

57 Case 140/81 *Kupferberg* [1982] ECR 3641, para 24.

gave information about international trade in a notice concerning the provisional application of the CARIFORUM-EC EPA that some provisions of that Agreement would supersede the provisions contained in the MAR.[58]

The CARIFORUM-EU economic partnership agreement

The CARIFORUM-EU EPA is one of the seven regional EPAs between the EU and ACP states that were planned to supersede the Lomé Convention. The EPA was negotiated[59] in order to achieve an agreement compatible with article XXIV GATT 1994 and without applying a WTO waiver. The (former) EC and the CARIFORUM States had to agree upon a comprehensive free trade agreement. This is reflected in the EPA, as the parties agree that nothing in the agreement requires them to act in a manner inconsistent with their WTO obligations.[60]

The EPA was signed in October 2008 and has been provisionally applied since 29 December 2008.[61] Moreover, the EPA partners agreed to apply the agreement even before the provisional application, as stipulated in article 243(4) TFEU. This pre-provisional application was governed on the side of the EU by the MAR.

The provisional application of the EPA is provided for in article 243 EPA and was to be effective as soon as possible, but no later than 31 October 2008. The instrument of provisional application before entry into force is based on article 218(5) TFEU and is quite common in the sphere of international agreements concluded by the EU. The reason is that many of those agreements contain provisions which fall within the joint competence of EU and its Member States and are concluded by them, acting jointly, rather than the EU simply acting on its own.[62] In consequence, mixed agreements have to be ratified by the EU and its Member States, sometimes even by regional parliaments. However, in the case of mixed agreements the Council may only decide to provisionally apply those parts of the agreement that fall within the competence of the EU,[63] even though in this case article 243(3) EPA entitled the parties to provisionally apply the agreement in full.

Even though the approval by the European Parliament followed in March 2009, the EPA is still only provisionally applicable and has not yet come into

58 OJ 2008 No L 352/62.

59 For details of the complex negotiations, see Richard L Bernal, *Globalization, Trade and Economic Development: The CARIFORUM-EU Economic Partnership Agreement* (Palgrave Macmillan US 2013) 27–90.

60 Art 242 EPA.

61 Council Decision 2008/805/EC on the signature and provisional application of the Economic Partnership Agreement between the CARIFORUM States, of the one part, and the European Community and its Member States, of the other part (2008) OJ 2008 No L 289/1.

62 Piet Eeckhout, *EU External Relations Law* (2nd edn, OUP 2011) 212.

63 Frank Hoffmeister, 'Curse or Blessing? Mixed Agreements in the Recent Practice of the European Union and Its Member States' in Christophe Hillion and Panos Koutrakos (eds), *Mixed Agreements Revisited: The EU and Its Member States in the World* (Hart 2010) 258.

force. Full application can only be achieved after ratification of the EPA by all signatories. At the moment, ratifications from five Caribbean and five European signatories (including the EU itself) are still pending.[64]

EPA's market access provisions

The EU aims to define and pursue common policies and actions in order to foster the sustainable economic, social and environmental development of developing countries, with the primary aim of eradicating poverty.[65] The Common Commercial Policy must be seen here as one of the pillars to support developing countries.

One core instrument to foster development in weaker and more vulnerable economies is to provide preferential access to the high-income EU market in order to enhance the trade and investment flows between the EC/EU and CARIFORUM and to create a new trading dynamic between the parties by means of the progressive, asymmetrical liberalisation of trade.[66] The overarching objective of the EPA is the promotion of sustainable economic development[67] by establishing a 'Trade Partnership for Sustainable Development'.[68] Trade preferences assist developing countries in their efforts to reduce poverty and promote good governance and sustainable development, by helping them to generate additional revenue through international trade, which can then be reinvested for the benefit of their own development and, in addition, to diversify their economies.[69]

In this context a line must be drawn to the United Nations Sustainable Development Goals (SDGs), particularly the goals of no poverty (SDG 1), zero hunger (SDG 2), decent work and economic growth (SDG 8), industry, innovation and infrastructure (SDG 9) and global partnership (SDG 17).[70] An essential component of SDG 17 is trade facilitation,[71] and the integration of this into the EPA will be described in the following subsection (b).

The instruments by which increased trade can support the development goals are manifold. They can range from increased export earnings, gains from specialisation according to comparative advantage, economies of scale, impact on

64 <www.consilium.europa.eu/en/documents-publications/treaties-agreements/agreement/?id=2008034&DocLanguage=en>.
65 Arts 3(5) and 21(2)(d) TFEU.
66 Art 1(f) EPA; Bernal (n 59) 109.
67 Bernal (n 59) 127.
68 Headline to Part 1 and art 3 EPA.
69 See e.g. European Commission, Report on the application of Regulation (EU) No 978/2012 applying a scheme of generalised tariff preferences and repealing Council Regulation (EC) No 732/2008, COM (2018) 665 final, 1.
70 For a critical analysis of trade and the SDGs see Sam Adelman, 'The Sustainable Development Goals, Anthropocentrism and Neoliberalism' in Duncan French and Louis J Kotze (eds), *Sustainable Development Goals: Law, Theory and Implementation* (Edward Elgar Publishing 2018) 2.
71 Trade facilitation is being described as 'a powerful tool to foster global competitiveness under SDG targets 17.10, 17.11 and 17.12', see World Bank Group, *Atlas of Sustainable Development Goals 2017*, 104, <https://openknowledge.worldbank.org/handle/10986/26306>.

productivity, impact on investment and capital accumulation, technology transfer and greater incentives to improve domestic physical and institutional infrastructures to improved access to higher-quality intermediates.[72] In order to benefit most, it is essential to have a bilateral opening of markets.

Trade liberalisation

The CARIFORUM States have defined increasing economic growth and expansion, as well as diversification of exports to foster growth, as important goals of the EPA.[73] As the EC and CARIFORUM agreed to establish a free trade area in order to improve trade relations, the EPA had to follow the reciprocal approach, which means that all signatories have to remove import duties on substantially all trade. The parties agreed on an asymmetric market opening: the EU has opened all tariff lines immediately, leading to duty- and quota-free market access from day one with short transition periods for sugar and rice,[74] whereas the CARIFORUM States will open about 92% of their trade over a 25-year period (beginning from 2008, hence lasting until 2033).[75] The agreed asymmetric opening commitments of the CARICOM partners can be seen as interim agreements under article XXIV(5)(c) GATT 1994, which accepts arrangements needed for the formation of a free trade area within a reasonable length of time. However, this extra time should exceed ten years only in exceptional and justified cases.[76]

The provisions on abolishing or reducing import duties must apply to *all goods* originating from an EC party or any CARIFORUM state,[77] demonstrating the comprehensive scope of the EPA. In order to eliminate customs duties on (originating) exports, duties of this kind had to be banned for exports from all EPA parties with immediate effect.[78] The EPA also abolishes any import or export prohibitions or restrictions on originating imports or exports, whether made effective through quotas, import or export licenses or other measures.[79]

Trade liberalisation is restricted to goods *originating* in the CARIFORUM parties. 'Originating' means qualifying under the rules of origin set out in Protocol I to the EPA,[80] where the relevant Rules of Origin (RoO) are laid down; these are the criteria that determine whether a product can be deemed to come from an EPA signatory, giving preferential market access, in order to avoid trade deflection. One of the key challenges when designing RoO is to offer the proper

72 Xavier Cirera, Francesca Foliano and Michael Gasiorek, 'The Impact of Preferences on Developing Countries Exports to the European Union: Bilateral Gravity Modelling at the Product Level' (2016) 50(1) Empirical Economics 59, 61.

73 Bernal (n 59) 127.

74 Art 15 EPA with reference to Annex II.

75 Art 16 EPA with reference to Annex III; Bernal (n 59) 142–43.

76 WTO, 'Understanding on the Interpretation of Article XXIV of GATT 1994'.

77 Art 9 EPA.

78 Art 14 EPA.

79 Art 26 EPA.

80 Art 10 EPA.

balance between producer flexibility (related to the sourcing of materials and processing obligations) and sufficient incentive for producers to add value locally.[81] RoO can be restrictive or more flexible. Hence, the effectiveness of trade liberalising measures depends on the concepts and methods used to determine the origin of goods. These rules can also be an important factor in determining the investment decisions of multinational companies. At the start of the negotiations, the EC sought far-reaching changes to the RoO compared to the provisions under the Cotonou Agreement.[82] In comparison to the Lomé Convention, the EPA provides for less restrictive RoO, especially in the textile and clothing sector and for fish and fish products.[83] In particular, when compared to the only alternative to the EPA – the GSP – the agreement's RoO are more liberal for trade.

Trade facilitation

In general, the reduction and elimination of import duties is only one core aspect in fostering trade relations. The easing of non-tariff barriers also plays a fundamental role in creating increased export opportunities.[84] For this reason, the operational aspects that increase the cost of transporting and trading goods across borders have to be taken into consideration. Dissatisfaction experienced by businesses when moving goods across borders, with regard to inefficient border management practices as well as trade and customs procedures, has led to the conclusion of the WTO TFA,[85] which is younger than the EPA but is already governing trade relations between the EPA parties.

In addition to the international framework, the EPA provides for trade facilitation between parties. It includes a wide range of provisions governing the facilitation of trade between partners to the agreement. Chapter 4 of the EPA addresses the issue of 'customs and trade facilitation' and recognises its importance for the development of CARIFORUM-EU and also intra-CARIFORUM trade.

Measures in this area comprise, inter alia:

- customs and administrative cooperation;[86]
- all trade and customs legislation, provisions and procedures being based upon the relevant international instruments and standards;[87]
- relations with the business community being based on best practice, and as few trade restrictions as possible being maintained.[88]

81 Eckart Naumann, 'Rules of Origin in EU – ACP Economic Partnership Agreements' (2010) International Centre for Trade and Sustainable Development, 2.
82 Bernal (n 59) 132–33.
83 Naumann (n 81) 23.
84 Bernal (n 59) 130.
85 Grainger (n 9) 1167.
86 Arts 30 and 35 EPA.
87 Art 31(1) EPA.
88 Art 32 EPA.

Insofar as the EPA requires the implementation of international instruments and standards into the relevant legislation, most of these standards already form part of the national or EU legal framework. In particular, Article 34 of the EPA can only have a declaratory character as it requires the WTO customs valuation rules to be applied to the trade between the parties. These provisions form part of the WTO's single package and are anyway mandatory for all WTO members. A specific challenge is the need to base all trade and customs procedures on global standards. Here the benchmark is not just the implementation of these standards but their proper application.

EPA and CARICOM integration process

The EPA is designed not just to benefit the relationship between the CARIFORUM States and the EU but also to improve the relationships among the Caribbean states. The CARIFORUM States have committed to offering each other the same preferential treatment as the treatment they give to the EU. In consequence, all the CARIFORUM States will form a free trade area at the end of the phasing in period for market access commitments by the parties on the Caribbean side of the EPA.

Here, the membership of CARICOM becomes crucial. Even if the EPA does not require the acceleration of the implementation of the CARICOM single market,[89] the CARICOM Member States have already internally achieved a deeper form of integration. Under the Revised Treaty of Chaguaramas establishing the Caribbean Community and Common Market (RTC, article 83), the Member States must establish and maintain a common external tariff. This feature is the deciding instrument when establishing a customs union under article XXIV(8)(a)(ii) GATT 1994. Accordingly, the RTC was notified to the WTO as a Customs Union & Economic Integration Agreement. However, the free movement of goods internally is restricted to goods originating in one of the CARICOM states (community origin),[90] which implies the application of RoO.[91] Restricting free trade between the constituent members of an integration area to goods originating in territories of the members is in turn a core element of a free trade area under article XXIV(8)(b) GATT 1994. However, article XXIV(8)(a)(i) GATT 1994 provides for a specific type of a customs union where trade liberalisation is only conducted for all trade in products originating in the constituent territories. Obviously, the CARICOM members decided to establish the 'weaker' form of a customs union. To gain the full benefit of the CARICOM customs union, it would be advisable to transform it into a customs union based on the principle of free circulation, hence obviating the need to apply costly and trade-restricting RoO.

The EPA's regional preference provision does not prevent the CARIFORUM nations from granting each other more favourable treatment without conferring

89 Bernal (n 59) 140.
90 Art 78(3)(b) and Art 79(3) RTC.
91 Art 84 RTC.

such treatment on the EU.[92] Hence, the CARICOM integration process is already ahead of the commitments flowing from the EPA. The impact of the integration clause is restricted to the trade relations with the Dominican Republic, where a free trade agreement had already been signed in 1998.

The different aspects of the EPA that are the subject of this contribution demonstrate that the EPA offers the CARIFORUM States a significant enhancement of their access to the EU market, which can also encourage companies to begin exports in new goods and hence to diversify exports and to attract foreign investors. In general, preferential regimes implementing lower tariffs and larger preference margins are effective in increasing trade, especially if they are introduced by means of a free trade agreement.[93] However, this kind of agreement can only be successful if traders make use of the trade preferences that are on offer. They may refrain from making use of these preferences if the complexity of the offered regimes (such as the RoO) means that the compliance costs are too high for them to bear. In the case of the CARIFORUM-EC EPA, the use of preferences on imports into the EU has increased from 79% in 2013 to at least 92% in 2016,[94] showing a high degree of acceptance.

Despite the wide-ranging opening of the EU market and the high usage of the EPA, trade with the CARIFORUM States fluctuated during the first decade after the EPA was implemented. Exports from Caribbean EPA countries to the EU even decreased in 2016 by 23% compared to 2015.[95] Looking at the evolution of agri-food imports from EPA CARIFORUM States in 2017, a decrease of 11% has been reported compared to the year before.[96] Just recently, the European Parliament stated that there were 'only modest new trade flows' from CARIFORUM countries to the EU.[97]

The attractiveness of an exporting nation for investors and exporters obviously does not just depend on the existence of a trade agreement. A number of other factors have to be taken into consideration, like the overall economic conditions (which comprise fiscal incentives, taxation, the cost of labour and commodity prices), infrastructure, transparency of rules, political stability, integrity, good governance and an overall respect for the rule of law.

Room for improvement can be seen in the fact that only ten out of the 15 CARIFORUM States have applied the tariff reductions which had been agreed

92 Bernal (n 59) 141.

93 Cirera, Foliano and Gasiorek (n 72) 62.

94 European Commission, 'Country Reports and Info Sheets on Implementation of EU FTA' SW (2017) 364 final, 39–40.

95 ibid. 113–14.

96 European Commission, 'Agri-Food Trade Statistical Factsheet' (2018) 8 <https://ec.europa.eu/agriculture/sites/agriculture/files/trade-analysis/statistics/outside-eu/countries/agrifood-usa_en.pdf>.

97 European Parliamentary Research Service, 'EU trade with Latin America and the Caribbean' PE 625.186 (September 2018) 16 <www.europarl.europa.eu/RegData/etudes/IDAN/2018/625186/EPRS_IDA(2018)625186_EN.pdf>.

for 2013, and export duties have so far only been partially eliminated.[98] Also the Doing Business Report 2019, published by the World Bank Group, gives information about options for improving the business environment. Under the category 'trading across borders' in the ease of doing business ranking, the CARIFORUM States are ranked between 63 (Dominican Republic, which was ranked 59th in 2018) and 161 (The Bahamas, ranked 157th in 2018) in a total of 190 economies. It is worth mentioning that it is not only high-income countries that achieved higher rankings in the total ease of doing business ranking – for example, Georgia was ranked sixth and Mauritius 20th. In the category 'trading across borders', countries like Bhutan and Eswatini are ranked in the higher echelons.

Consequences of Brexit

The UK's invocation of Article 50 TEU in order to withdraw from the EU raises the question of the consequences of Brexit on the EPA with regard to trade between the UK and the CARIFORUM countries. The UK signed and also ratified the EPA separately from the EU only because of the division of power between the EU and its Member States. This consent cannot be interpreted to mean that any Member State has entered into a trade agreement with any CARIFORUM state individually. The perpetuation of the membership of the CARIFORUM-EC EPA depends on membership of the EU. This principle has been fundamental for the EPA, as it is concluded on the European side only by the 'European Community or its Member States or the European Community and its Member States, within their respective areas of competence'.[99] Furthermore, as regards the territorial application, the EPA applies only to the territories in which the Treaty establishing the European Community (now the TFEU) is applied,[100] and the UK's intention is to terminate the application of the TFEU to its territory. Finally, under the EPA any new Member State of the EU shall accede to the agreement from the date of its accession to the EU. In consequence, any Member State leaving the EU must leave the EPA as well.

One of the most important purposes of Brexit is to allow the UK to conduct a commercial policy that is different from that pursued by the EU. An independent UK would be free to agree on any WTO-compatible agreement with the CARIFORUM group or individual Caribbean states. The consequence of a 'hard' Brexit would be that the UK regained full autonomy immediately. However, in November 2018 the EU and UK agreed on a draft withdrawal agreement providing for a transition period that would end on 31 December 2020.[101] Union law – including international agreements – would be applicable to and in the UK would have the same effect as in the Member States.[102] During the

98 ibid.
99 Art 223(1) EPA.
100 Art 245 EPA.
101 Art 126 Draft Agreement.
102 Art 129(1) Draft Agreement.

transition period, the UK would be able to negotiate, sign and ratify international agreements in its own capacity in the areas of exclusive competence of the EU, as long as those agreements did not enter into force or apply during the transition period, unless so authorised by the EU.[103]

In order to ensure the continuation of trade agreements after Brexit, the UK government intends to 'provide a technical replication of the conditions' stipulated in the agreements. This could be done by means of a transitional adoption of free trade agreements for which the third countries concerned have already signalled their support.[104] This preliminary continuation of the EPA could be ended by a new trade agreement signed between the UK and the CARIFORUM nations. However, it is questionable whether the UK would have an equivalent position in negotiations compared to the joint forces of the EU in trade negotiations.

Conclusions

This contribution has examined the complex trade regime between the CARICOM and the EU nations, which can be described as asymmetric as it is partly governed by international and bilateral trade agreements and partly by autonomous trade provisions that depend on the country in question, leading to different levels of market access on the two sides of the Atlantic Ocean. Despite the far-reaching trade liberalisation for exports to the high-income EU market, the trade increases resulting from the EPA have not yet arrived. The reasons can be seen to lie in the lack of the full implementation and application of the EPA. Moreover, the effect on trade creation of the EPA can only be sparked if the full potential of trade facilitation measures and a better economic environment for foreign investors have been achieved. Further negative effects from Brexit can be prevented if the EPA provisions can continue to constitute a basis for CARIFORUM-UK trade relations until a new trade agreement can enter into force.

103 Art 129(4) Draft Agreement.

104 House of Commons, 'Continuing Application of EU Trade Agreements after Brexit' (2018) HC 520, 10–15.

5 Building a digital anchor

A legal perspective on a prospective improvement of electronic data interchange in maritime trade

Hannes Prochno

Nowadays, far beyond 80% of the world's trade volume is carried by sea, with the Caribbean Community (CARICOM) and European Union (EU) Member States bearing a disproportional share. Still, the net amount of cargo transported by ship will prospectively grow over the upcoming decades according to the United Nations Conference on Trade and Development (UNCTAD).[1] Due to recent trends of digitalisation, policymakers are and will be confronted with legal issues to ensure and further promote sustainable development with regard to the interchange of electronic data in shipping, in particular between private parties involved in the business and public authorities.

Two chances, but also challenges, in this context have been pointed out in the latest *UNCTAD Review of Maritime Transport 2018*, which might improve the processing of data transfer for both sides: First, there is the implementation of a so-called Single Window (SW) concept, which in general promotes the interchange of trade-relevant electronic data between private companies and public figures via a single electronic hub; second, there is the recent approach of introducing blockchain technology into the digital infrastructure of shipping in order to improve the level of security and promote smart business by simplifying the processing of data.[2] Both innovations may therefore be considered as essential tools for trade facilitation. On the basis of international law, organisations such as the World Trade Organization (WTO), the International Maritime Organization (IMO) or the World Customs Organization (WCO) have partially built the legal framework for the establishment of this presumable digital evolution. However, the process of implementation appears to be a continuing challenge for states concerned. Especially supranational institutions like the EU, already taking the initiative, seem to be struggling with an encompassing realisation of the appropriate structure.

The economic impact as well as potential threats, arising from the implementation of a SW environment as well as blockchain technology in maritime trade

1 United Nation Conference on Trade and Development, *Review of Maritime Transport 2018* (UNCTAD/RMT/2018) 23 <https://unctad.org/en/PublicationsLibrary/rmt2018_en.pdf>.
2 ibid. 87.

and beyond need to be evaluated with regard to trade facilitation. The chosen benchmark for this evaluation is the UN Sustainable Development Goals (SDGs) since they constitute, according to none other than UN Secretary-General H.E. Antonio Guterres, an all-encompassing set of progressive targets for the future of humankind.[3]

Data interchange in maritime trade between private and public figures

Digitalisation in all kinds of business is pervasive. Maritime trade is no exception here but rather an exceeding digitalised sector. This is due to the exceptional requirements for safety and security as well as economic efficiency, which are needed with regard to the transportation of cargo. The following should provide an adequate overview on the figures involved and the kind of data exchanged.

The seaborne trade of goods involves multiple private companies and public figures. They have to be divided into different groups who send or receive data from each other. The Facilitation Committee (FAL Committee) of the IMO provides a detailed overview here.[4] With regard to private companies whose task is to actively submit data in this context, a distinction between different process groups is essential: there are parties involved in transport services like inter alia consignor, forwarder, carrier, ship's agent and consignee on the one side and parties involved in ship operation like owner, charterer and manager on the other side.[5] The parties receiving those data can be in general identified as public authorities like inter alia clearance authorities (or port authorities), customs authorities, health authorities, immigration authorities, port state inspection authorities, statistics authorities, veterinary authorities and waste authorities.[6]

The FAL Committee also provides a detailed overview on the data elements occurring in maritime trade with a primary reference to the requirements from the FAL Convention as well as the requirements with regard to the International Ship and Port Facility Security Code (ISPS-Code) of the International Convention for the Safety of Life at Sea (SOLAS).[7] These maps also contain cross

3 Antonio Guterres, 'Preface' in *Global Goals Yearbook 2018: Partnership for the Goals* (Macondo Foundation 2018) 3.

4 Facilitation Committee of the International Maritime Organization, *Guidelines for Setting Up a Single Window System in Maritime Transport* (FAL. 5- Circ. 36 2011).

5 ibid. para 4.1.

6 ibid. para 5.9.

7 The ISPS-Code established under SOLAS chapter XI-2 in 2004 is designed to improve the assessment of security threats in shipping for everyone involved, which includes inter alia the establishment of a common international framework, the allocation of responsibilities, cooperation and exchange of security-related information; For more information, see International Maritime Organization, *Guide to Maritime Security and the ISPS Code* (IMO 2012) paras 2–4.

references to the WCO data model.[8] It would go beyond the intended scope of this contribution to list all the individual data elements. In general, these elements contain mainly ship-related (concerning e.g. ship crew, arrival and departure of vessel, voyage and ship waste and so on) or rather cargo-related (concerning e.g. description of loaded goods and net tonnage) information. Anyway, this information is required in terms of security, ship safety, the environment, port operations or the payment of import and export duties.[9]

Single window concept for maritime trade

As described by the UN/CEFACT,[10] several slightly varying definitions of SW concepts occur on an international level. Bringing those together, it is understood as a 'facility that allows parties involved in trade and transport to lodge standardised information and documents, (mainly electronic) with a single-entry point to fulfil all import, export and transit-related regulatory requirements'.[11] SWs are identified as an essential tool for trade facilitation for everyone involved in the submission of data.[12] The economic advantages for transport service parties as well as ship operations parties on the one side seem obvious: SWs, in consequence, promote the acceleration of the process of ships entering and leaving ports as well as loading, discharging and handling cargo where somehow electronic data submission is required. For governments and their acting authorities on the other side, SWs promise an improvement of risk management as well as security within their jurisdiction or administrative area since all data is faster and more easily accessible.[13]

SWs must be traditionally categorised into two different types. First, there is the so-called customs-centric SW usually based on a single authority system. This model focuses on customs specific activities in a national or customs union environment. Second, there is the so-called port-centric SW, which is based on an automated information transaction system or single automated system since several authorities are involved in the formal process of cargo-loaded vessels sailing to or from ports.[14] Both types have been implemented with varying degrees of

8 Facilitation Committee of the International Maritime Organization (n 4) para 5.8; See also the Data Model Data Harmonization itself <www.wcoomd.org/-/media/wco/public/global/pdf/topics/facilitation/instruments-and-tools/tools/single-window/single-window-data-harmonisation.pdf>.

9 ibid. para 5.9.

10 United Nations Centre for Trade Facilitation and Electronic Business, *Recommendation and Guidelines on establishing a Single Window to enhance the efficient exchange of information between trade and government* (2005) ECE/TRADE/352.

11 ibid. 3.

12 Dennis Ndonga, *Single Windows and Trade Facilitation: A Tool for Development* (Wolters Kluwer 2015) 25.

13 Achim Rogmann and Kateryna Zelenska, 'The EU and Its Member States on the Way towards a Customs Single Window' (2017) 7 Customs Scientific Journal 20, 21.

14 Ndonga (n 12) 25–26.

comprehensiveness across the globe, also of course in an airport and road border environment.[15] This evaluation will be focusing on a third model, the so-called Maritime SW, which can be understood as a merger of or the establishment of a close link between the two original models. Because requirements for specific electronic information for customs, port and other authorities are combined, an automated information transaction system or single automated system is required as well.[16] Reviewing the beneficiary aspects of SWs described previously, it seems quite obvious that the level of impact on trade facilitation is dependent on the quantity of data a SW encompasses. A Maritime SW therefore constitutes the desirable model in this regard. However, it seems also quite obvious that the more authorities are involved in the merging process, the more complex and complicated an establishment becomes.[17]

Understanding blockchain technology in maritime trade

While SWs constitute a concept to facilitate data interchange in maritime trade, blockchain technology constitutes a technical tool to potentially implement such a concept. This evaluation will focus on the potential role of the technology within the maritime supply chain. Its original use in relation to crypto currency, creating an immense hype around it, shall retreat into the background. However, several general characteristics need to be pointed out: its wording already implies a number of transactional records (block), which are transferred in a closed structure (chain). The specialty of this structure is that it is decentralised without any authority that is able to monitor, check or validate all the transactions taking place (so-called distributed leger).[18]

The advantages that are promised by blockchain technology are to foster greater trust and therefore security between everybody involved in the supply chain while reducing the complexity of data interchange in trade to boost economic growth.[19] In the context of maritime trade and the interchange of data between parties involved in transport service and shipping operations with public authorities, these advantages are essential. A trust-build secure environment will provide public authorities the access to the data required through the blockchain. This shall essentially improve the verification, as well as tracking and tracing of data for everyone involved in the process.[20] There seems to be no good reasons

15 Christian Volpe Martincus, *Out of the Border Labyrinth: An Assessment of Trade Facilitation Initiatives in Latin America and the Caribbean* (Inter-American Development Bank 2016) 174.
16 Ndonga (n 12) 25–26.
17 Martincus (n 15) 174.
18 Yotaro Okazaki, 'Unveiling the Potential of Blockchain for Customs' (2018) WCO Research Paper No. 45, 6 <www.wcoomd.org/-/media/wco/public/global/pdf/topics/research/research-paper-series/45_yotaro_okazaki_unveiling_the_potential_of_blockchain_for_customs.pdf?la=fi>.
19 Jorien Kerstens and James Canham, 'Blockchain: Mapping New Trade Routes to Trust' (2018) 87 WCO News 52, 53.
20 United Nation Conference on Trade and Development (n 1) 9; Okazaki (n 18) 10.

why the example provided by Kerstens and Canham of accessing the data for an Entry Summary Declaration, which is the requirement of transport service parties (here carrier) to submit detailed cargo descriptions 24 hours prior to loading,[21] via a blockchain, should not be transferrable to other data required by public authorities as well.[22] Furthermore, the relatable data interchange between the public authorities itself, on a national level or in a common cross-border environment like the EU, may be also executed through a blockchain.[23]

As presumed earlier, building a bridge from blockchain to SWs in this context is inevitable. In general, it has been pointed out that SWs must be accompanied by a suitable technology in order to appropriately generate the trade facilitating effect.[24] It is assumed that the power of blockchain technology in particular could leverage a SW system for the purpose of cross-border management.[25] A potential example of usage is also provided by Kerstens and Canham, referring to agricultural licenses which are granted by a ministry of agriculture, controlled by health authorities or veterinarians at point of entry and are supervised (within an import declaration) by customs authorities.[26] Accordingly, an encompassing Maritime SW in this regard will again be most beneficial, as already described previously.

However, one should not forget in this regard that there is still a high degree of uncertainty when it comes to the application of blockchain technology in maritime trade and electronic data interchange. At least the implementation on a private level and public-private partnership level (inter alia the ports of Antwerp and Rotterdam) with regard to container distribution, tracking and tracing[27] will shed more light on the functioning and risks of the technology beyond crypto currency.

Legal perspective and prospective development

The economic-advantageous characteristics of the SW concept as well as blockchain technology must be legally connected to trade facilitation, which is described by Ndonga as 'the efficient application of trade rules and regulations'.[28] While SWs have been an integral part of national and international regulatory developments over the last decade, blockchain regulation is obviously quite new on the agenda. When it comes to maritime trade, the three international organisations

21 See Parliament and Council Regulation (EU) 952/2013 laying down the Union Customs Code [2013] OJ L269/1 Art. 127.

22 Kerstens and Canham (n 19) 54.

23 ibid. 54–55.

24 Illustrated by the Trade SW of Costa Rica, see Martincus (n 15) 209 ff.

25 Okazaki (n 18) 17.

26 Kerstens and Canham (n 19) 55.

27 United Nation Conference on Trade and Development (n 1) 89, a detailed description of the port of Rotterdam as well as Antwerp (not mentioned in the port) can be found at <www.portofrotterdam.com/en/news-and-press-releases/port-authority-and-municipality-of-rotterdam-launch-blockchain-technology>; and <www.portofantwerp.com/en/news/smart-port-blockchain>.

28 Ndonga (n 12) 10.

mentioned earlier, which are the WTO, the IMO and WCO, share the primary entitlement to address data interchange in maritime trade legally.

The UN/CEFACT Recommendation No. 33 must be understood as the origin of the SW concept on which the regulatory assessment of IMO, WTO and WCO was founded. The legal status of SWs within those three international organisations shall be briefly reviewed at first.

The IMO's Convention on Facilitation of International Maritime Traffic (FAL Convention) after its latest amendments in 2016[29] obligates its signatories to establish systems of electronic information exchange until 8 April 2019 pursuant to Art. 1.3. of the Annex. The provision further provides a clear definition of SWs and highly encourages its Member States to establish one in the context of arrival, stay and departure of ships, persons and cargo. There is a similar approach within the WTOs Trade Facilitation Agreement (TFA), entering into force in 2017, with the encouragement to establish a SW for traders according to Art. 10 para 4.1. The different addresses of these articles derive of course from the different originating backgrounds of these organisations and their legal instruments. However, with regard to the characteristics of a Maritime SW, the approach of the IMO appears more suitable and approachable, bearing in mind the rather 'motivating' than 'dictating' nature of the FAL provision. The WCO on the other side remains regulatory inactive but is addressing the topic with encompassing guidelines and other reference papers based on the TFA from a customs perspective.[30] It is also noticeable at this point that a certain degree of trans-organisational reference between IMO, WTO and WCO is apparent, which might further lead to extended cooperation when it comes to SWs.

Blockchain technology on the other hand has not yet been legally introduced in particular in this context yet. The UN/CEFACT has initiated a first step in this regard by issuing a first version of a white paper overview on blockchain for trade, highlighting its potential for trade facilitation.[31] There are, however, certain regulations that might cover it within their scope of application indirectly. The TFA inter alia promotes the use of information technology to its members to support a SW according to Art. 10 para 4.4 TFA. Reconsidering the impact of blockchain technology on a SW, a regulatory link appears well-grounded. A similar approach is taken in the FAL Convention in Annex Section 1.3 as well. Such a direct link cannot be found within the WCO legal instruments; however, the issue has been on the agenda of their legal research.[32]

29 Facilitation Committee of the International Maritime Organization Resolution on the Amendments to the Annex of the Convention on Facilitation of International Maritime Traffic, 1965 FAL. 12(40) 2016.

30 The full selection can be found at <www.wcoomd.org/en/topics/facilitation/instrument-and-tools/tools/single-window-guidelines.aspx>.

31 See UN/CEFACT White Paper, Overview of Blockchain for Trade, Version 1, ECE/TRADE/C/CEFACT/2019/9, 5 <www.unece.org/fileadmin/DAM/cefact/GuidanceMater ials/WhitePaperBlockchain.pdf>.

32 See inter alia Okazaki (n 18) 17; The use of blockchain by customs authorities has also been the topic of the 17th WCO IT Conference & Exhibition on 8 June 2018.

European legal framework for single windows and status of blockchain technology

Within the described international legal framework, the EU has developed its own version of a SW environment for maritime trade. While the Union shares competence with its Member States when it comes to transport pursuant to Art. 4(2g) Treaty of the Functioning of the European Union (TFEU), it has an exclusive competence with regard to the customs union pursuant to Art. 3(1a) TFEU. Maritime SWs, also including customs-related information, are legally allocated to the former. Therefore, the concept is manifested in the area of transport policy through the Reporting Formalities Directive (RFD)[33] from 2010 based on Art. 100(2) TFEU. Including a reference to the FAL Convention, Art 5.1. RFD obligates every EU Member State to establish a national SW linking the SafeSeaNet,[34] e-customs and other electronic systems not later than 1 June 2015. Beyond the scope of national implementation, Art. 3.2. RFD further obligates the EU Commission and EU Member States to develop mechanisms for the harmonisation of reporting formalities.

A Regulatory Fitness and Performance programme (REFIT) evaluation, launched by the EU Commission in October 2016, came to the conclusion that only a few EU Member States had achieved the aim of establishing a well-functioning national SW.[35] Furthermore, with regard to Art. 3.2. RFD the evaluation claims that the intention to cooperate and share data is not sufficiently existent among the port authorities of several EU Member States. A lack of harmonisation was therefore identified.[36] That statement was supported by shipping companies which participated in a survey for the evaluation. It is claimed that those deficits lie within the regulatory limitation of the RFD.[37]

Just as on an international level, blockchain technology in relation to maritime trade is regulatory unaddressed by the European legislators. However, it is not unnoticed. In particular, the blockchain Partnership Declaration signed in April 2018, originally and belatedly joined by 25 EU Member States plus Norway, promises an enhanced cooperation in order to integrate blockchain technology

33 See Parliament and Council Directive 2010/65/EU on reporting formalities for ships arriving in and/or departing from ports of the Member States [2010] OJ L/283/1.

34 The SafeSeaNet is a vessel traffic monitoring and information system used by the Member States of the EU, Norway and Iceland. It has been originally introduced via Parliament and Council Directive 2002/59/EC on establishing a Community vessel traffic monitoring and information system [2002] OJ L 208. It was established to enhance 'maritime safety, port and maritime security, marine environment protection and efficiency of maritime traffic and maritime transport' (See Preface No. 4).

35 EU Commission, 'Synopsis report on the public consultation on the REFIT evaluation of Directives 2010/65/EU on Reporting Formalities for ships arriving in and/or departing from ports of the Member States (RFD) and 2002/59/EC on the Vessel Traffic Monitoring and Information System (VTMIS)' para 3.2.4 <https://ec.europa.eu/transport/sites/transport/files/2017-rfd-vtmis-synopsis-report.pdf>.

36 ibid. para 3.3.

37 ibid. para 3.5.

into the digital infrastructure.[38] Based on this declaration, as well as with regard to the UN/CEFACT White Paper and the TFA, the European Parliament adopted a resolution[39] pointing out the potential of blockchain technology for trade in general and calls on the European Commission to develop guiding principles for application and the need to integrate the topic into the regulatory environment.[40]

Prospective development

On an international level, the already collaborating organisations will prospectively further expand their cooperation and mutual reference. With regard to the ongoing and upcoming implementation and research, this most likely includes blockchain technology in general as well as its function as a potential technology to implement a SW appropriately.

The prospective path for the EU in this context seems nebulous. Referring to the results from the REFIT evaluation, the Council of the EU, in the "Valletta Declaration" from March 2017, urged the Commission to initiate a follow-up for the RFD directive to establish a harmonised European Maritime SW environment.[41] This follow-up is needed to further harmonise the IT standards in the EU; otherwise, an establishment seems rather unlikely.[42] More than one year later, the stand of this appeal is unclear. There seems to be no current necessity to establish a maritime SW, also because the EU as a supranational organisation is not part of the IMO. In contrast to its Member States, the Union is not required to fulfil the deadline for the establishment of a system of electronic data exchange set in the FAL Convention.[43] Due to this seemingly legal standstill situation, a further regulatory integration of blockchain technology into a SW environment appears unlikely in the close future. Nevertheless, even though there is no legal obligation, the EU should still have a particular economic interest in progressing this issue.

Impact of SW and blockchain technology in maritime trade according to the Sustainable Development Goals

The approach to connect the legal implementation of the SW concept and blockchain technology in maritime trade to the SDGs might appear rather unusual on first

38 The declaration can be found here: <https://ec.europa.eu/digital-single-market/en/news/european-countries-join-blockchain-partnership>.

39 See European Parliament resolution of 13 December 2018 on blockchain: a forward-looking trade policy, Procedure 2018/2085(INI), Doc A8-0407/2018.

40 ibid. para 35.

41 Council of the European Union Report, 'Ministerial Declaration on Priorities for the EU's Maritime Transport Policy until 2020: Competitiveness, Decarbonisation, Digitalisation to Ensure Global Connectivity, an Efficient Internal Market and a World-Class Maritime Cluster (Valetta Declaration)' 9150/17 para 16 <http://data.consilium.europa.eu/doc/document/ST-9150-2017-INIT/en/pdfm>.

42 Rogmann and Zelenska (n 13) 31.

43 This was probably most famously underlined by the CJEU in Case C-366/10 Air Transport Association of America and Others v Secretary of State for Energy and Climate Change [2011] ECR I-13755, para 71 ff.

sight. This unusualness is antagonised by the above-mentioned perspective from UN Secretary-General Guterres, which also includes the status of SDGs as a 'collective response to building a fair globalization' within the 'extraordinary expansion of the global economy over the last decades'.[44] Furthermore, the UN/CEFACT has indicated only on the surface the potential of blockchain contributing to SDGs.[45] It has been pointed out that the SDGs, above everything else, constitute policy objectives and that law might play the pivotal role in achieving the Goals on the one side or might be a hindrance to achieving them on the other side.[46] Keeping this in mind, the bridge build is rather inevitable of everything beyond the improvement of technical delicacies to improve electronic data interchange in maritime trade. Therefore, the most relevant SDGs shall be evaluated in this context.

Enhancing SDG 17: Global Partnership for the Goals

The most obvious line between instruments of trade facilitation and SDGs must be drawn in the context of Global Partnership. Trade facilitation needs to be funded to improve global competitiveness and economic growth. These considerations in the context of SDG 17 are therefore especially relevant for the economies of developing countries,[47] like several of the CARICOM Member States.[48] A particular example provided are the required average days by national customs authorities for clearance of exported goods, where especially Latin American and African countries are identified as inefficient in a timely manner.[49] The beneficial aspects of SWs and blockchain technology on the clearance of goods speak for themselves in this context.

However, the implementation of this approach has been heavily criticised by some: Global Partnership on behalf of the WTO multilateral trading system in particular cannot comply with sustainable production as well as consumption and can be considered as an engine for global inequality.[50] Despite these developments, SDG 17 even suggests for an enhancement of competences for the WTO to promote trade liberalisation.[51] A clear lack of enhancing 'macroeconomic stability through policy coordination' is denounced with regard to the implementation of Global Partnership.[52]

44 Guterres (n 3) 3.
45 See UN/CEFACT White paper (n 31) 3.
46 Duncan French and Louis J Kotze (also eds), 'Introduction' in *Sustainable Development Goals: Law, Theory and Implementation* (Edward Elgar Publishing 2018) 3–4.
47 World Bank Group, 'Atlas of Sustainable Development Goals 2017', 98, 104, https://openknowledge.worldbank.org/handle/10986/26306.
48 United Nations, 'World Economic Situation and Prospects 2018', 142, https://www.un.org/development/desa/dpad/wp-content/uploads/sites/45/publication/WESP2018_Full_Web-1.pdf.
49 ibid.
50 Sam Adelman, 'The Sustainable Development Goals, Anthropocentrism and Neoliberalism' in Duncan French and Louis J Kotze (eds), (n 46) 15, 36.
51 SDG 17.10; ibid. 115.
52 Adelman (n 50) 36.

Promoting SDG 8: Balancing Economic Growth

The term balancing growth in this context implies sustained, inclusive and sustainable growth.[53] In consequence, SDG 8 is especially relevant for the least developed countries, which are in an urgent need for economic growth with a benefit for the common population and not at the expense of natural resources.[54] Trade facilitation has been identified as an essential tool to achieve such economic growth for developing countries (and therefore the least developed countries as well). It has the potential to add about 0.9% annually to the GDP of developing countries, compared to only 0.25% to the GDP of developed countries according to the WTO in its World Trade Report from 2015, focusing on the impact of the TFA.[55] SWs and blockchain technology in particular, not underlined by percent disclosure, have been identified, as already mentioned, as relevant tools for trade facilitation, especially for developing countries.[56] The combination of both innovations might thus be considered as even more beneficial for the fulfilment of SDG 8. Therefore, even though the EU has initiated the process of building up this digital infrastructure, it might be even more beneficial for the CARICOM Member States in terms of economic development. Beyond balancing economic growth, the transition is obviously apparent to other SDGs such as End Poverty (SDG 1) and Zero Hunger (SDG 2) with the special recognition of developing and least developed countries as well as Innovation & Infrastructure (SDG 9) in terms of building a more resilient digital infrastructure in maritime shipping.

Although these assessments and prospects appear promising, it must be questioned whether the mentioned beneficiaries are reached in this regard. Especially the involved WTO has again been criticised for not improving the trade position of the least developed countries over the years.[57] In the context of trade facilitation through SWs and blockchain technology, only bigger shipping companies might benefit as well as States, which will not allocate appropriately their revenue to the poorer population.

Compatibility with SDG 13: Climate Action

Another major challenge, pointed out in the latest UNCTAD review of maritime transport, is the one of the amounts of greenhouse gas emissions caused by the shipping industry.[58] Those maritime emissions will prospectively increase essentially (between 50% and 250% until 2050) over the upcoming decades since legal

53 World Bank Group (n 47) 44.

54 ibid.

55 World Trade Organization, 'World Trade Report 2015', 134, <https://www.wto.org/english/res_e/booksp_e/world_trade_report15_e.pdf>.

56 See Ndonga (n 12) 36; World Trade Organization, 'World Trade Report 2018', 9, <https://www.wto.org/english/res_e/publications_e/world_trade_report18_e.pdf>.

57 Heloise Weber, 'Politics of "Leaving No One Behind": Contesting the 2030 Sustainable Development Goals Agenda' (2017) 14 Globalizations 399, 409.

58 United Nation Conference on Trade and Development (n 1) 89 ff.

and economic measures addressing efficiency and mitigation cannot comply with the worldwide trade expansion.[59] This makes shipping on the one side by far the most influencing mode of transportation with regard to global warming. On the other side is shipping (together with rail transport) by far the most climate friendly mode of transportation when it comes to the amount of goods and tones that are transported (tone of CO2 emitted per freight tonne),[60] keeping those at about 80% of trade volume in mind already mentioned at the beginning of the evaluation.[61]

Therefore, it must be concluded that trade facilitation instruments for maritime shipping, such as SWs and blockchain technology, are beneficial for economic development. However, it will also further boost the prospective trade expansion, potentially aggravating other concerning issues such as climate change and further environmental damages with regard to inter alia waste removal or ship breaking,[62] which are considered adverse to Life below Water (SDG 14) and Life on Land (SDG 15).[63] This discrepancy between the objectives of SDG 14 and SDG 8 is not one in terms of trade facilitation alone but is identified as a problematic issue in general. The issue is the required extent of improved resource efficiency, which cannot be sufficiently achieved at all according to some in a constantly growing economy.[64] Therefore, the appropriate balance in terms of sustainable development seems to be crucial at this point.

Conclusions

Due to recent trends of digitalisation, data interchange in maritime trade bears potential for improvement in terms of trade facilitation. The establishment of a SW is the most discussed improvement in this regard. Several types and models are on the table because of the different international organisations involved and their regulatory competences. It has been pointed out that the most beneficial for trade facilitation will be an all-encompassing Maritime SW including data for inter alia port, clearance, customs and immigration authorities and many more. In practice, there seem to be difficulties in adopting such a SW on a national as

59 International Maritime Organization, Third IMO GHG Study 2014, ix <www.imo.org/en/Our Work/Environment/PollutionPrevention/AirPollution/Documents/Third%20Greenhouse%20Gas%20Study/GHG3%20Executive%20Summary%20and%20Report.pdf>.

60 Ralph Sims and Roberto Schaeffer, Chapter 8 on 'Transport' of the 'Fifth Assessment Report of the International Panel on Climate Change' (2014) 610 <www.ipcc.ch/pdf/assessment-report/ar5/wg3/ipcc_wg3_ar5_chapter8.pdf>; A legal evaluation is also provided by Judith Van Leeuwen and Kristine Kern, 'The External Dimension of European Union Marine Governance: Institutional Interplay between the EU and the International Maritime Organization (2013) 13 Global Environmental Politics 69.

61 United Nation Conference on Trade and Development (n 1) 23.

62 The environmental consequences of ship breaking, fostered through the expansion of maritime trade, are described by Tony George Puthutcherill, *From Shipbreaking to Sustainable Ship Recycling: Evolution of a Legal Regime* (Brill Nijhoff Publishers 2010) 36.

63 World Bank Group (n 47) 80, 86 ff.

64 Adelman (n 50) 36.

well as supranational level. Further cooperation and mutual reference among the three concerned organisations IMO, WTO and WCO is required, which also falls under the scope and is pursued but also is probably worthy of improvement with regard to policy coordination by Global Partnership. From a European perspective, the difficulties arise from regulatory deficits on a supranational level, exemplified most essential through the EU RFD, which is not up to date anymore. Even though there is only little research on this behalf, it must be assumed that blockchain technology could further boost a SW in a trade facilitating matter. Even though applied research needs to be further conducted, a regulatory link should be pursued already.

Since trade facilitation provides a path to economic growth, especially for developing countries, regions and communities like the CARICOM, these technical innovations can be interpreted in general in favour of sustainable development. The critics in relation to the global partnership system who contend that it does not appropriately facilitate the distribution of wealth must be taken seriously though. Furthermore, to find the appropriate balance, the negative impacts like increasing greenhouse gas emissions and other environmental damages from trade expansion need to be considered as well. Therefore, the compatibility with the SDGs needs to be further evaluated and be part of the regulatory process.

6 European Union and CARICOM

Current challenges and potential solutions in the energy and investment sector

Claudia Kurkin

The CARIFORUM-EU Economic Partnership Agreement (EPA) signed in June 2008 is the latest development in trade relations between the Caribbean and Europe, and it is a WTO-compatible trade agreement.[1] The EPA between CARIFORUM States and EU is a trade and development arrangement that provides CARIFORUM economies' goods and services exports favourable, reciprocal and asymmetric access into EU markets.[2] The overarching objective of the EPA is the promotion of sustainable economic development.[3] This is more than an agreement with a development dimension. The components of meaningful sustainable economic development are given clear expression in an overarching chapter on development in the EPA, which provides a holistic framework for the subject-specific measures in subsequent chapters.[4] Just before, in April 2008, the Caribbean Community CARICOM Secretariat commenced the Energy Programme as one of the programmes within the Directorate of Trade and Economic Integration (TEI).[5] The Energy Programme was assigned

1 Richard L Bernal, *Globalization, Trade, and Economic Development: The CARIFORUM-EU Economic Partnership Agreement* (New York 2013) XIII and XVII.

2 Sheldon McLean and Jeetendra Khadan, *An Assessment of the Performance of CARICOM Extra-Regional Trade Agreements: An Initial Scoping Exercise* (Santiago 2014) 18.

3 Bernal (n 1) XVII, The government of CARIFORUM organised themselves to negotiate as a single group with one common position, no easy task given the diversity of interests, languages and cooperation experience. The agreement was based on the principle of special and differential treatment (SDT) for small developing economies. Through collective action a group of small CARIFORUM States managed to conclude the EPA negotiations against the vastly more powerful EU, Most Honorable PJ Patterson, 'Preface' in Bernal (n 1) X and XI. During the negotiations considerable time was spent explaining the goals of the CARIFORUM i.e. by consulting the private sector and civil society, Bernal (n 1) XIV.

4 Bernal (n 1) XVIII. A detailed analysis of the status quo of the EPA-Agreement (Art 138 EPA) for the energy and investment sector, in particular taking into account the strengths and weaknesses of the EPA-Agreement must be reserved for a separate study. With regard to trade under the CARIFORUM-EU EPA, the leading export products from the Caribbean to the EU are fuels and mining products, particularly gas and petroleum, McLean and Khadan (n 2) 18.

5 <www.caricom.org/our-work/energy>.

the responsibility of implementing a programmatic approach to energy sector developments in the region. This establishes a departure from the mere projectised approach and aims to facilitate greater responsiveness in carrying out the energy-related Community's mandates as well as fostering a more harmonised approach to energy issues. The Energy Programme is executed by the Energy Unit within the Trade and Economic Integration. The energy sector is by far the largest economic sector in Trinidad and Tobago.[6] By its nature, size and reach, the sector has an unprecedented opportunity to develop the people, businesses, technology and capital markets of Trinidad and Tobago.[7] Energy is generally one of the essential drivers for economic and social development.[8] And the oil and gas sector is the leading sector in developing social investments worldwide.[9] But the current international investment law system is insufficiently compatible with sustainable development.[10]

Energy security is increasingly becoming a vital issue worldwide.[11] This is even more so the case for the European Union (EU). Indeed, coupled with the fact that the EU is the biggest energy customer in the world,[12] the Union's large dependency on energy supplies from the outside world renders its future on the energy front all the more uncertain.[13] The EU's unsteady stand is perilous to a

6 Anthony E Paul, 'Maximizing National Value: Ownership, National Participation, Local Content and Sustainable Development' in Trevor M Boopsingh and Gregory McGuire (eds), *From Oil to Gas and Beyond: A Review of the Trinidad and Tobago Model and Analysis of Future Challenges* (Plymouth 2014) 140.

7 ibid. 141.

8 The absence of reliable and sustainable energy restricts the provision of basic services for human activities, Tae Yong Jung, Minkyung Huh and Jongwoo Moon, 'Goal 7: Affordable and Clean Energy' in Tae Yong Jung (ed), *Sustainable Development Goals in the Republic of Korea* (Abingdon Oxon 2018) 65.

9 Rafaela Costa Camoes Rabello, Vivienne Anderson and Karen Nairn, 'An Exploration of Social Investment Discourses in the Oil and Gas Sector' in David Crowther, Shahla Seifi and Abdul Moyeen (eds), *The Goals of Sustainable Development, Responsibility and Governance* (Singapore 2018) 139.

10 Manjiao Chi, *Integrating Sustainable Development in International Investment Law, Normative Incompatibility, System Integration and Governance Implications* (Abingdon 2018) I.

11 Rafael Leal-Arcas and Juan Alemany Rios, 'The Creation of a European Energy Union' (2015) 5(3) European Energy Journal 24.

12 The EU spends up to 400 billion on energy per year; China is the largest energy consumer in the world, Leal Arcas and Rios (n 11) 24, see further <http://ec.europa.eu/eurostat/statistics-explained/index.php/Consumption_of_energy> because UK is a major export market for important sectors of the EU economy, including for energy, this is an important issue for both parties, and the UK government has said it is considering all options for the future of the energy market with the EU. But that the critical issue is that certain models of energy relationships are dependent on decision-making power remaining with the EU, which is contrary to some core goals of the UK government as stated in its Brexit mandate, Kim Jensen and Markus Gehring, 'Renewable Energy in the Member States of the EU, Chapter 27 – United Kingdom' in Dörte Fouquet (ed), *EU Energy Law, Volume III, Renewable Energy in the Member States of the EU* (2nd edn, Claeys & Casteels Law Publishers 2018) 1210.

13 The empirical findings do not support the idea that energy security in a liberalised market structure means a depoliticisation of energy dependence and energy affairs, Andrea Prontera,

greater extent in that it currently relies on a very sparse number of energy suppliers[14] which, in addition, tend to brandish energy as a political weapon.

In March 2015, the European Council adopted the Framework Strategy for a Resilient Energy Union with a Forward-Looking Climate Strategy in a 2030 perspective, launching the process of establishing the European Energy Union.[15] In December of that year, the United Nations General Assembly agreed on the Sustainable Development Goals, also in a 2030 perspective.[16] Of the 17 Sustainable Development Goals formulated in the agenda, which replaced the UN Millennium Development Goals, Goal 7 Affordable and Clean Energy and Goal 13 Climate Action are relevant to energy policy. Both envisage the managed transition from a carbon-dependent to a low-carbon energy system, one of the most complex regulatory tasks ever undertaken and one with far-reaching consequences.[17] Energy has become a laboratory of international and European governance and law-making with which the State level is aligning itself. Aiming to formulate a theory of energy law is increasing.[18] For the investment sector Goal 8 Decent Work and Economic Growth is relevant. Goal 17 Partnership for the Goals deals with the implementation of the goals. They are each specified by sub-goals. Ideally, a successful energy policy will translate the Goals into a right to universal access to sustainable and modern energy, a right to action against climate change and for the investment sector into a right to sustainable economic growth. Following on from the EU competence sphere, the problem areas of sustainability, international investment protection and energy will be presented in order to identify current significant challenges or developments, of which a key issue or challenge is the legal transformation of the named Sustainable Development Goals into the energy and investment sector, to highlight selected problem constellations in the EU-CARICOM area with a focus on the EU and to discuss potential solutions.[19]

The New Politics of Energy Security in the European Union and Beyond, States, Markets, Institutions (Abingdon 2017) 232.

14 Russia is the EU's biggest energy supplier, and this was the first time in the EU's history when energy supplies from Russia were affected not by purely technical but deliberate political and economic factors, Umut Turksen, *EU Energy Relations with Russia: Solidarity and the Rule of Law* (New York 2018) 1.

15 Communication from the Commission to the European Parliament, the Council, the European Economic and Social Committee, the Committee of the Regions and the European Investment Bank, 'A Framework Strategy for a Resilient Energy Union with a Forward-Looking Climate Change Policy' <https://eur-lex.europa.eu/legal-content/EN/TXT/?uri=CELEX:52015DC0080>.

16 Resolution of the UN General Assembly, 'Transforming Our World: The 2030 Agenda for Sustainable Development, adopted on 25.9.2015' (A/RES/70/1) <www.un.org/Depts/german/gv-70/band1/ar70001.pdf>.

17 Volker Roeben, *Towards a European Energy Union, European Energy Strategy in International Law* (Cambridge 2018) 1.

18 Raphael J Heffron, 'Preface' in Vicente López-Ibor Mayor (ed), *Clean Energy, Law and Regulation, Climate Change, Energy Union and International Governance* (London 2017) XVII.

19 For example, the following questions require further consideration: given that industrialised nations are primarily responsible for many of the global environmental problems we face today, such as climate change, should these countries be held responsible for remedying these

Sphere of EU competence: sustainability, investment protection and energy

Since the Treaty of Lisbon (2009) was enacted, the EU's dual responsibilities for investment protection (Art 206 and 207 Treaty on the Functioning of the European Union) and sustainability as well as for energy policy (Art 194 TFEU) have been united in the European sphere of competence. In devising its foreign policy, the European Union must give due consideration to the rule of law and principles of international law. These issues can be viewed as core elements of sustainable development and good governance.[20] In addition, Union law provides for the identification of material sustainability contents in primary law, sustainability regulations in secondary law and organisational or procedural sustainability regulations for legislative procedures.[21] And the EU has committed to implement the SDGs both in its internal and external policies.[22]

Content and legal significance of the sustainability concept

The concept of sustainable development roots in the political philosophy of the ancient and was for a long time pursued by the United Nations as a political strategy of development.[23] The concept of sustainability reflects a conceptual synthesis of 30 years of development policy with different strategies, approaches and experiences.[24] And still its content is controversial not only among the discipline of jurisprudence. In the Brundtland Report is 'Sustainable development' understood as 'development that meets the needs of the present without compromising the ability of future generations to meet their own needs'.[25]

---

problems (i.e. the *polluter pays* principle is invoked? What actions could be taken? How might these actions impact the development opportunities of emerging economies?) See further Henrik Gudmundsson, Ralph P Hall, Greg Marsden and Josias Zietsman, *Sustainable Transportation, Indicators, Frameworks, and Performance Management* (Heidelberg 2016) 32.

20 Katja Gehne, 'Das Nachhaltigkeitskonzept als rechtliche Kategorie im Spannungsfeld zwischen staatlichen Regulierungsinteressen und Investorschutz' in Marc Bungenberg, Jörn Griebel and Steffen Hindelang (eds), *Internationaler Investitionsschutz und Europarecht* (Baden-Baden 2010) 271.

21 Klaus Meßerschmidt, 'Nachhaltigkeit im EU-Gesetzgebungsverfahren' in Wolfgang Kahl (ed), *Nachhaltigkeit durch Organisation und Verfahren* (Tübingen 2016) 195.

22 <https://ec.europa.eu/europeaid/policies/sustainable-development-goals_en>.

23 "Ideas underlying sustainable development have governed the practices of many cultures for thousands of years", Markus Gehring and Andrew Newcombe, 'An Introduction to Sustainable Development in World Investment Law' in Marie-Claire Cordonier Segger, Markus Gehring, and Andrew Newcombe (eds), *Sustainable Development in World Investment Law* (Alphen aan den Rijn 2011) 3 with further proof.

24 Gehne (n 20) 273, see further Claudia Kurkin, 'Risiko und Nachhaltigkeit im internationalen Wirtschaftsrecht' in A Michalke, M Rambke and S Zeranski (eds), *Vernetztes Risiko- und Nachhaltigkeitsmanagement, erfolgreiche Navigation durch die Komplexität und Dynamik des Risikos* (Springer Gabler 2018) 97.

25 Report of the World Commission on Environment and Development: Our Common Future, 1987, Chapter 2, IV, Ziff. 1, 41 <www.un-documents.net/our-common-future.

Against the background of the Brundtland Report and various development theories that have spawned the concept of sustainability, *Katja Gehne* highlights that the concept is essentially demanding interdependencies between environmental issues, especially resource protection, social objectives, such as good governance and principles of justice, and also economic objectives, inter alia principles of modern liberal economics.[26] These issues must be brought together as efficiently as possible with a view to supporting the long-term prosperity of a society.[27] This perspective requires thereafter identifying relationships and exploiting them systematically for the benefit of social, environmental and economic objectives, for which it is one of investment in environmental technology. This includes to identify trade-offs such as the use of wood energy at the expense of forest and compensate as much as possible or to minimise and to obtain and promote social capacities and natural resources in terms of the living conditions of future generations.

Following the Brundtland Commission, it is addressed to all countries and levels of government, regardless of their level of development.[28] The Sustainability Responsibility reach is where social processes are politically controlled and governed by law (government function) or affected (companies). The UN General Assembly resolution on the Global Agenda is a recommendation under Article 10 UN Charter and therefore not legally binding. Recently, however, it has become increasingly evident that the contents of the resolution are being integrated by states into international treaties and into national legal systems, so that they become hard law as well as being taken up by private organisations such as the Global Compact as soft law.[29]

Current developments in international investment law

The concept of sustainable development and international investment law is still segmented both in jurisprudence and in the case law. So those lines of development largely proceeded independently. This may be due to chance. However, a probable cause is likely to be in the international investment law for a long

pdf>. It contains two key concepts: the concept of "needs", in particular the essential needs of the world's poor, to which overriding priority should be given and the idea of limitations imposed by the state of technology and social organisation on the environment's ability to meet present and future needs, Chi (n 10) 10.

26 Gehne (n 20) 274.

27 Report of the World Commission on Environment and Development: Our Common Future, Transmitted to the General Assembly as an Annex to document A/42/427-Development and International Co-operation: Environment.

28 Agenda 21, Kapitel 30; die Arbeit des UN Secretary-General's Special Representative on business and human rights. John Ruggie, 'Information and Reports' <http://www2.ohchr.org/english/issues/trans_corporations/index.htm>.

29 Winfried Huck and Claudia Kurkin, 'Die UN-Sustainable Development Goals (SDGs) im transnationalen Mehrebensystem' (2018) 2 Zeitschrift für ausländisches öffentliches Recht und Völkerrecht (ZaöRV)/Heidelberg Journal of International Law (HJIL) 375 <https://papers.ssrn.com/sol3/results.cfm>.

time dominant economic paradigm, giving priority to growth and reaffirming that the concept of sustainability has been neglected,[30] so hereafter both areas appeared not quite compatible. However, it is characterised more recently, not least because of the risk posed by climate change's threat of natural resources, a paradigm shift.[31] Increasingly, the need to incorporate the concept of sustainability into international investment law is being recognised. So consider Marie-Claire Cordonier Segger and Andrew Newcombe as 'significant challenge facing the world community today . . . the pressing need to increase investment flows to foster sustainable development in developing countries'.[32] Because the past few years have recorded an increasing number of investment agreements, international investment law has become more important as well as the concept of sustainability, which the UN Member States have recently confirmed in the SDGs. In its communication titled 'Towards a Comprehensive European International Investment Policy', the European Commission has stated that International Investment Agreements (Articles 206 & 207, TFEU) on the protection of foreign direct investment should be consistent with the other policies of the Union and its Member States, including policies on the protection of the environment, consumer protection, and development policy.[33] On a global level, International Investment Agreements are not negotiated primarily for the purpose of sustainable development promotion. The provisions are connected with sustainable development to varying extents.[34] Nevertheless, so far no standard practice that considers sustainability within international investment law has been established. Increasingly, companies consider environmental challenges and development issues as 'business case'.[35] But sustainability aspects are not only considered as

30 Katja Gehne, *Nachhaltige Entwicklung als Rechtsprinzip, Normativer Aussagegehalt, rechtstheoretische Einordnung, Funktionen im Recht* (Tübingen 2011), 34.

31 For the exemplary question 'What should be the basic paradigm determining how responsibilities, burdens, benefits and risks should be divided between countries and peoples?', four paradigms are differentiated: the liability paradigm, the leadership paradigm, the mainstreaming paradigm, and the human rights paradigm, Joyeeta Gupta, 'Climate Change and Shifting Paradigms' in Duncan French (ed), *Global Justice and Sustainable Development* (Leiden 2010) 167.

32 Marie-Claire Cordonier Segger and Andrew Newcombe, 'An Integrated Agenda for Sustainable Development in International Investment Law' in Marie-Claire Cordonier Segger, Andrew Newcombe and Markus Gehring (eds), *Sustainable Development in World Investment Law* (Alphen aan den Rijn 2011) 101.

33 European Commission, Towards a Comprehensive European International Investment Policy, Communication of 7 July 2010 <http://trade.ec.europa.eu/doclib/docs/2010/july/tradoc_146307.pdf>. Markus Krajewski correctly points out that objectives and goals of energy policy and regulation have not been analysed much. As with most investment law research, the focus has been on the protection of the rights and interests of the investor, Markus Krajewski, 'The Impact of International Investment Agreements on Energy Regulation' in Christoph Herrmann, Markus Krajewski and Jörg Philipp Terhechte (eds), *European Yearbook of International Economic Law* (Springer 2013) 2.

34 Chi (n 10) 1.

35 Andreas Georg Scherer and Guido Palazzo, 'Globalization and Corporate Social Responsibility' in Andrew Crane, Abagail McWilliams, Dirk Matten, Jeffrey Moon and Donald Siegel (eds), *The Oxford Handbook of Corporate Social Responsibility* (OUP 2008) 413.

an economic potential (investment funds, environmental goods). Against this background, the legal prior understanding with which investment law issues are approached can hardly be reduced to the protection and promotion of investments. If the aspect of overall societal efficiency is to be taken into account, and since investment impacts upon a society and its environment over a period of time, the focus must be broadened, and it is particularly urgent to develop a legal mechanism that integrates sustainability and makes investor interests and public policies more clearly assessable and legally predictable.

Concept, legal grounds and status quo of the European Energy Union

The European Energy Union is a transformative political-legal project.[36] Fulfilling the mandate of the Lisbon Treaty, the European Council in March 2015 adopted the strategy for establishing a European Energy Union. In answering what this project is for, it is arguable that the new European Energy Union embodies the claim of the political system to determine the future structure of the energy system rather than the market.[37] The objectives of the Energy Union range from the development of energy infrastructure to the structuring of raw material imports and, for reasons of security of supply, cover almost the entire area of energy law.[38] The EU places a significant emphasis on coordinating and harmonising its energy transition towards a secure, sustainable, competitive and affordable future energy system in addition to market reforms through the various energy packages.[39] It will facilitate the free flow of energy across borders and a secure supply in every EU country for every European citizen. Through the European Energy Union, the EU assumes responsibility for the social-State function of providing EU citizens with equal access to secure, sustainable and affordable energy as a public good.[40] This responsibility legitimises the EU in establishing rules-based network governance over energy, in Europe and worldwide, as it will be accountable not just to the citizens of the European Union but also to the international community of States and, ultimately, humanity.

The absence of global energy governance and a distinct agreement governing energy in a comprehensive manner contributes to widening the existing legal

36 Roeben (n 17) 3.

37 The design is a European concern, not just a national one, Roeben (n 17) 5.

38 Claas Friedrich Germelmann, 'Die Energieunion – Eine neue Perspektive für die europäische Energiepolitik?' (2016) 1 Europarecht (EuR) 3.

39 European Commission, 'Building the Energy Union' <https://ec.europa.eu/energy/en/topics/energy-strategy-and-energy-union/building-energy-union>. The principle of solidarity is recognised in the Treaty to strengthen the political and economic power of the EU, but its application is diverse and ineffective in EU energy policy, Turksen (n 14) 75.

40 Roeben (n 17) 3. Another perspective says that the notion of the EU as a regulatory state goes hand in hand with an approach to energy policy that is based on looking at energy as a private good with strong public goods characteristics, but not as a strategic good, Svein S Andersen, Andreas Goldthau, and Nick Sitter, 'Introduction: Perspectives, Aims and Contributions' in Svein S Andersen, Andreas Goldthau and Nick Sitter (eds), *Energy Union, Europe's New Liberal Mercantilism?* (London 2017) 4.

vacuum at the international level on a crucial issue. This regulation is centred on a legal regime that integrates international law, EU law and the national law of Member States. The development of this regime is shaped by the lateral co-evolution of these normative orders and their progressive vertical integration over a time span stretching to the end of the century, for which 2030 is a critical milestone. The guiding idea is to combine bottom-up with top-down decision-making. Decentralisation and plurality are to be balanced with centralisation and uniformity.[41] This Energy Union signifies deep integration of the Member States. But the fundamental role that states still play in the practice of EU energy security governance does not mean that nothing has changed in the EU's newly liberalised and de-monopolised market environment.[42] National governments have lost many of their previous means of influence, and the shift toward the market has reduced their ability to manage their energy dependency and foreign energy relations with producers. For example, the states conclude intergovernmental energy agreements with third countries, but the European Commission wants to strengthen its existing influence on Member States. As a result, governments are trying to find new strategies with which to achieve their objectives. They combine old and new policy instruments to address traditional energy security concerns, interact with state and non-state actors and pursue other policy goals in such areas as industrial and foreign policy. EU action envisaged there is complementary, serving the cross-border cooperation of the Member States and their entities, though in some areas EU action is primary, in particular, on decarbonisation and, to an extent, on the energy market. In addition to the EU's energy dependence on the outside world, other considerable difficulties arise; for example, the current regulatory framework on global energy governance is largely multi-layered and fragmented.[43]

Implementing the Sustainable Development Goals in the energy sector

Energy is one of the priorities of the European Commission for 2019–2024.[44] Among the priorities is also the implementation of the UN Sustainability Strategy and the Sustainable Development Goals. The Energy Unit of the CARICOM Secretariat has recently in June 2018 launched an initiative to formulate a region-wide communications strategy for sustainable energy.[45] The purpose of

41 Energy security in Europe is still the product of interactions between public authorities and market players, but the fragmentation of the state, along with the spread of new business models has greatly complicated the picture, Prontera (n 13) 237.

42 Prontera (n 13) 233.

43 Leal-Arcas and Rios (n 11) 24.

44 <https://ec.europa.eu/commission/priorities_en>.

45 'Communications Strategy being Formulated for Sustainable Energy in CARICOM' (Press Release, 12 June 2018), <www.caricom.org/media-center/communications/press-releases/communications-strategy-being-formulated-for-sustainable-energy-in-caricom>; Caribbean Sustainable Energy Roadmap and Strategy (C-SERMS), <https://energy.caricom.org/portfolio-items/cserms/>.

the strategy will be to create and increase awareness of challenges and opportunities in the energy sector, to facilitate behavioural change at all levels, to encourage innovation and to facilitate the transition to new energy systems.[46] Various measures are available to promote sustainable development. These include improving energy efficiency and energy infrastructures, investing in new technologies and internalising the negative environmental impact of fossil fuel-based energy production with the help of emissions trading. Due to the international nature of energy markets, external relations and international cooperation through various political dialogues are essential components of EU energy law and policy in addition to internal measures that aim to improve EU energy security. The EU and its individual Member States have entered into different bilateral and multilateral agreements with different producing countries. The implementation of the SDGs is directed not only at individual states or the international community but also at the private sector.

The SDGs formulate a universally accepted norm for energy.[47] A process of international law-making serves to legally implement the norm of universal access to sustainable energy. SDG 13 Climate Action aims at taking urgent action to combat climate change and its adverse effects.[48] The UN has undertaken further activities to concretise the resolution on the sustainability goals by adopting the new resolutions A/Res/71/223 and A/Res/72/224 'ensuring access to affordable, reliable, sustainable and modern energy for all'. The solutions for the problems of humanity, such as the ones described in the Global Agenda 2030, will not come only from philanthropy but from setting up sustainable business models, which calls for mutual trust among stakeholders and tools such as public-private partnerships.[49] In recent times the modern global economy and the international community have become a function of interdependence.[50] Jolene Lin has observed that cities are beginning to perform law-making functions in the context of transnational climate change governance.[51] Through transnational networks that form important linkages between city governments,

46 An Advisory Group facilitated by the CARICOM Secretariat will conduct research and consultations to identify ways in which challenges and opportunities related to energy access, energy security, energy efficiency, environmental protection and adaptation to climate change can best be communicated to all sectors of the Caribbean Society. The Advisory Group brings together representatives of key regional organisations such as the Caribbean Development Bank (CDB), the Caribbean Electric Utility Services Cooperation (CARILEC), and so on involved in communications in the energy sector <www.caricom.org/media-center/communications/press-releases/communications-strategy-being-formulated-for-sustainable-energy-in-caricom>.

47 Roeben (n 17) 36.

48 Tae Yong Jung, Hanbee Lee and Dohyun Park, 'Goal 13: Climate Action' in Tae Yong Jung (ed) (n 8) 138.

49 Carlos Sallé, '7=17: Universal Access with Renewable Energy as Leverage to Help Attain All SDGs' in (n 18) 274.

50 Chios Carmody, 'Interdependence and WTO Law, Chapter 8' in *Global Law and Sustainable Development* <www.glawcal.org.uk/glawcal-comments/is-interdependence-a-product-of-wto>.

51 Jolene Lin, *Governing Climate Change, Global Cities and Transnational Lawmaking* (New York 2018) 8.

states, international organisations, businesses, and civil society, cities are creating and implementing norms, practices, and voluntary standards across national boundaries. The impact of their normative output is to steer the behaviour of cities towards mitigating climate change and adapting to its unavoidable impacts. Further, the multi-level and multi-actor partnerships in which cities participate actively today transcend the public-private divide and the traditional strictures of domestic (internal) versus international (external). Hence, the transnational governance activities of cities point to the reconfiguration of the state in modern times from a monolithic, unitary entity to a mutable, variegated one in a global system densely populated by networks of components of the state; for example, networks comprising judges, antitrust enforcement agencies and central banks.

Is a new WTO agreement on trade in energy needed?

Since the EPA agreement is considered compatible with the WTO,[52] this assessment can be linked to the question of whether a new WTO agreement on trade in energy is needed.[53] The proposals submitted for this purpose are based on the general idea that such a sectoral agreement would be the solution to the archetypal problem in the area: the inadequacy of the general framework of the multilateral trading system to address the specificities of the trade in energy resources.[54] For instance, with regard to renewable energy subsidies, there is a fundamental inadequacy of existing WTO rules in this area. Paolo Davide Farah and Elena Cima aptly point out that there is inter alia insufficiency of current interpretive tools, and the non-inclusion of energy or renewable energy in any WTO agreement makes it hard for WTO rules to fully acknowledge and value the specific obstacles faced by renewable energy producers and consumers, so it is necessary to weigh the positive externalities of renewable energy use against the negative ones created by fossil fuels when evaluating national policies, and the WTO still lacks a suitable mechanism to achieve this goal.[55]

But a new WTO energy agreement may cause more problems than positive outcomes.[56] For example WTO law may sometimes and somehow appear not flexible enough to take into consideration the characteristics of this sector. If a

52 See text, footnote 1.

53 Various proposals are made to this end, for instance, J. Pauwelyn mentions a sort of General Agreement on Trade in Energy, and T. Cottier and his collaborators also opt for a similar Framework Agreement on Energy within WTO Law; see further Jenya Grigorova, 'The International Trading Regime and the Regulation of Trade in Energy Resources: Is Reform Necessary and is a New Energy Agreement within the WTO Framework the Way to Go?' in Antonio Segura Serrano (ed), *The Reform of International Economic Governance* (New York 2016) 198.

54 Grigorova (n 53) 199.

55 Paolo Davide Farah and Elena Cima, 'WTO and Renewable Energy, Lessons from the Case Law' in Antonio Segura Serrano (ed), *The Reform of International Economic Governance* (New York 2016) 231.

56 Grigorova (n 53) 194.

sectoral energy agreement is to be designed, its provisions will need to be carefully drafted in order to avoid as many interpretation predicaments as possible. However, the need of consensus on all of these issues will undoubtedly result in somewhat reduced obligations, and there is still no guarantee that all possible complications will be resolved in advance. Arguably, such a modification of the existing general framework will be insufficient. Therefore, the focus should be on the alternatives: starting from the fact that traditional energy resources are limited and exhaustible, the public attention should be focalised in the near future.

Does the EC have a new right to issue intergovernmental agreements?

If individual EU countries negotiate energy agreements with non-EU countries, they must ensure that these agreements comply with EU law. This helps to ensure the proper functioning on the EU internal energy market.[57] The European Commission wants to strengthen its existing influence on Member States in their conclusion of intergovernmental energy agreements with third countries. At the heart of its reform proposal is a compatibility assessment of the pre-conclusion agreements *ex ante* with active intervention by the Commission, based on the Member States' substantial submission on/ and implementation obligations.[58] Are such measures in conformity with EU law? Are they really limited to a legal review by the Commission?

Contrary to the wording of the proposal, the Energy Union Strategy and the explanatory memorandum of the EC proposal and recitals of the European Commission's proposal for a decision indicate that it intends to control and manage, not only legally but also politically, intergovernmental agreements between Member States in the energy sector.[59] Although the Commission's proposal for a decision is, in substance, covered by the Energy Competence Title of Article 194 TFEU. However, it is not sufficient because of its indeterminate added value and its significant intervention with regard to the Member States' obligation to present and transpose the Directive in favour of the Commission; it would be contrary to the principle of subsidiarity, namely the primary legal freedom of

57 European Commission, 'Energy, International Cooperation, Intergovernmental Agreements' <https://ec.europa.eu/energy/en/topics/international-cooperation/intergovernmental-agreements>.

58 Proposal for a decision of the European Parliament and of the Council on establishing an information exchange mechanism with regard to intergovernmental agreements and non-binding instruments between Member States and third countries in the field of energy and repealing Decision No 994/2012/EU <https://eur-lex.europa.eu/legal-content/EN/TXT/PDF/?uri=CELEX:52016PC0053&from=DE>. See further: EU Decision, Energy agreements with third countries, <www.cep.eu/fileadmin/user_upload/cep.eu/Analysen/COM_2016_53_Energieabkommen/cepAnalyse_COM_2016__53_Energieabkommen.pdf>.

59 Jens Brauneck, 'Energieunion: Neues Weisungsrecht der EU-Kommission für zwischenstaatliche Abkommen?' (2017) 1 Neue Zeitschrift für Verwaltungsrecht (NVwZ) 35.

the Member States to determine the energy supply structure. The previous decisions have not resulted in subsequent amendments of intergovernmental energy agreements by the Member States. But it must be doubted that these goals can be achieved through more stringent duties.[60] If a Member State, contrary to the Commission, considers that it is not in breach of EU law, it should also be unimpressed by the proposed new legislation and risk infringement proceedings.

Integration of the sustainability concept in international investment law

The focus is now on the question of how the sustainability concept can be effectively integrated into international investment law.[61] This perspective develops the following two theses: first, the principle of proportionality, which is especially prevalent in the German legal system but is also known as a core legal principle in many other jurisdictions worldwide, is proving to be particularly receptive to the concept of sustainability. Second, in international investment law, the principle of proportionality is also a familiar legal principle.[62] It therefore functions as an appropriate legal instrument for incorporating the concept of sustainability into investment law, using a modified proportionality test. Thereby it promotes the Sustainable Development Goals set by the Member States of the United Nations, which are targeted at all countries and stakeholders. The application of the modified proportionality test as a new legal methodology that includes the concept of sustainability leads to thoroughly balanced, reasonable and more transparent results for all parties involved, and it promotes the Sustainable Development Goals. In order to integrate the concept of sustainability in the transnational and international investment law exist several options, which are briefly explained in a moment before the sustainability concept and investment law are merged into a modified proportionality test, which is best suited for this purpose.

If the idea of sustainable development is included in the preamble or the target provisions of an agreement, it follows from Article 31 para 1 of the Vienna Convention on the law of treaties that the contract must be interpreted in the light of the sustainability concept. But this procedure is not proven to be particularly assertive for the sustainability concept because there is no mandatory requirement, to which extent can the provisions of the Treaty be interpreted in favour of the sustainability concept. Not much different is the case when in the commitments made by the European Union investitions-related trade agreements are

60 ibid. 35.

61 Title II EPA.

62 While the migration of the principle of proportionality to WTO law seems relatively settled, it is a still open issue regarding international investment law and arbitration, Valentina Vadi, 'A History of Success? Proportionality in International Economic Law' in Antonio Segura Serrano (ed), *The Reform of International Economic Governance* (New York 2016) 171. Unfortunately, the principle has so far been little associated with the sustainability concept. This is a pitiable shortcoming, and the findings could become not only relevant to the Caribbean Court of Justice (CCJ).

included or provided in a separate chapter on sustainability. Such a section is inter alia already included in the CETA-Agreement with Canada.[63] But it raises awareness of the importance of the sustainability concept, and it is foreseeable that they will in the future deal more with questions of sustainable design of investments. Although there is an ongoing trend toward the inclusion of CSR provisions into International Investment Agreements, nevertheless, having regarded the nature of both CSR instruments and International Investment Agreements, with the former being voluntary while the latter are only binding for States, the effectiveness of these clauses is still limited, constituting soft law.[64] In the literature, the proposal is also made that labour and environmental provisions in International Investment Agreements should make explicit reference to the UN Global Compact initiative.[65] Certainly, because of its universality, legitimacy, and flexible implementation, this initiative constitutes the best approach for helping host States to achieve their Sustainable Development Goals without losing their allure for foreign investors. But so far there is no empirical evidence suggesting that the inclusion of CSR measures in International Investment Agreements is what best promotes sustainable development.[66] For that reason further analysis is required.

The idea of sustainability could be anchored as an interpretation guideline within arbitration (ICSID, UNCITRAL),[67] especially more than a third of all investment disputes adjudicated under ICSID can be classified as energy-related disputes.[68] According to Katja Gehne, standard mainstreaming could be achieved on the basis of the costume of values associated with the sustainability concept, which holds a considerable potential for coherence effects. In combination with carefully elaborated, concrete exception clauses and interpretation guidelines (good faith standards), it could contribute to greater clarity and predictability in order to translate the tension between investor protection and the interests of state regulation into clearer legal criteria.

The inclusion of procedural obligations in International Investment Agreements requiring sustainability assessments to be carried out prior to investment measures could also make a contribution.[69] On the one hand, they would provide

63 Comprehensive Economic and Trade Agreement (CETA) <http://trade.ec.europa.eu/doclib/docs/2014/september/tradoc_152806.pdf>.

64 Rafael Tamayo-Àlvarez, 'How International Investment Agreements Can Better Contribute to Sustainable Development by Reflecting the UN Global Compact Principles' in Maria Alejandra Gonzalez-Perez and Liam Leonard (eds), *The UN-Global Compact: Fair Competition and Environmental and Labour Justice in International Markets* (Bingley 2015) 155.

65 None of the International Investment Agreements makes explicit reference to the UN Global Compact initiative nor reflects the universal scope of its ten principles, Tamayo-Àlvarez (n 64) 146.

66 Tamayo-Àlvarez (n 64) 155.

67 Although the UN Commission on International Trade Law (UNCITRAL) arbitration rules are of enormous importance in practice, the agenda of arbitration rules coordinated by UNCITRAL contains no sustainability considerations, Gehne (n 20) 271 and 291.

68 Krajewski (n 33) 1.

69 Andrew Newcombe, 'Sustainable Development and Investment Treaty Law' (2007) Journal of the World Investment & Trade 359.

more transparency with regard to the assessment of legitimate expectations and, on the other hand, they would allow more scope for informed political decisions in the run-up to investment measures. For example, such analyses are already mandatory for investment guarantees in the context of the International Finance Cooperation (IFC). Another aspect is Sustainability Impact Assessment (SIAs) with regard to the impact of provisions of International Investment Agreements.

Principle of proportionality, as a legal instrument for integration

The principle of proportionality is a structural instrument for dealing with conflicts between opposing interests. It formalises the process of decision-making by weighing up all relevant issues and rationally prioritising between the issues in each individual case.[70] The principle of proportionality, which refers to a bipolar structure of a collision of legal positions, is in general not suitable for an examination of the multipolar target structure of the sustainability concept.[71] However, the principle of proportionality, which is increasingly widespread in investment law,[72] is proving to be receptive to the optimisation objective pursued with the sustainability concept. Gehne correctly emphasises the common logic that makes it possible to link the sustainability concept to manageable assessment parameters.[73] Investment law is characterised by the classical bipolar structure between state intervention and the right to property, to which the principle of proportionality is tailored. Since the concept of sustainability is aimed at achieving an appropriate balance between economic (i.e. principles of modern liberal economics), social (good governance and principles of justice) and ecological (environmental and resource protection) normative concerns, it also concerns the area of tension between legitimate state regulatory interests and investment protection. They are adapted to the particularities of investment law.[74]

First and foremost, the measure must concern the scope of application of the sustainability concept (i.e. it must concern the conflict between ecological and social regulation in the public interest on the one hand and investment protection interests as an expression of macroeconomic interests on the other).[75] Moreover, a proportionality test can already take place if a tiered relationship between sovereign purpose and means is discernible in the legal system under consideration.[76] It is pointed out aptly that a weighing takes place in every legal system and that

70 Johannes Sauer, 'Die Globalisierung des Verhältnismäßigkeitsgrundsatzes' (2012) 51 Der Staat 13.

71 Katja Gehne, *Nachhaltige Entwicklung als Rechtsprinzip, Normativer Aussagegehalt, rechtstheoretische Einordnung, Funktionen im Recht* (Tübingen 2011) 229.

72 Alessandro Covi, 'Der Grundsatz der Verhältnismäßigkeit als Baustein des europäischen Investitionsschutzrechts' (Baden-Baden 2016) 125.

73 Gehne (n 20) 287, 285.

74 Covi (n 72) 116.

75 Gehne (n 20) 288.

76 Covi (n 72) 125.

the special feature of the proportionality test is its strict methodology. It is therefore not necessary to have identical terminologies or a uniform weighting of the audit steps in the individual legal systems in order to open up the scope. In view of this prior understanding, the concept of sustainability applies to normative objectives and legitimate state regulatory interests and also relates to economic interests of investors (SDG 8: Decent Work and Economic Growth).

In order to prevent the resulting normative arbitrariness in arguments in favour of the state or the investor, the state's interventions, for example using policy or legal measures or decisions, must incorporate sustainability and hold up to scrutiny with regard to the following proportionality considerations. Initially, the proposed intervention must consider any potential conflict between environmental and social regulations for the public interest on the one hand, and investment protection interests as an expression of the macroeconomic interest on the other hand.[77] The measure must take due account of the normative concerns associated with investment protection, with the provision that economic, social and environmental objectives and concerns are to be integrated in such a way that synergies are created as far as possible or trade-off situations are offset. The overall aim is to place measures in a binding and transparent legal framework consisting of proportionality considerations including the sustainability concept. Furthermore, the proposed intervention must fulfil a legitimate purpose and should be well suited to reaching its aims: namely the promotion of a specific end complemented by the concept of sustainability. There must also be a clear necessity for the policy or legal measure. Accordingly, there should be an assessment of whether a less restrictive measure is available, which would also effectively promote the regulatory and sustainability objectives, with reasonable effort and with less impact on the position of the investor. Moreover, the measure must be proportionate in both the broader and narrower sense. It must also be commensurate with the specified objectives. The intended purpose must therefore not be disproportionate to the intensity of the intervention. Therefore, measures that operate within the framework of appropriateness and serve legitimate ecological, social and economic goals in the context of sustainability can in principle be regarded as legitimate regulatory interests.

The effectiveness of the measure must be subject to re-evaluation. A sustainability offense occurs when, for economic reasons (production, profits, growth), an investment project is permitted that supports the uncontrolled, environmentally harmful extraction of raw materials without being accompanied by measures for nature conservation, health protection and benefits for the local population and development. In such a case the decision-maker has disregarded relevant environmental, social and economic concerns, as well as long- and short-term effects, and did not take synergies and trade-offs into account. This would leave future-oriented, ecological and social concerns inappropriately neglected. Such an evident non-inclusion or misweighing of the objectives in the area of sustainability

77 Gehne (n 20) 287.

is in contradiction to the requirements of the efficiency obligation of the sustainability concept. Obviously, there is no efficient solution to a conflict of objectives here. In the investment law under the heading 'legitimate expectations' common aspect of good faith, which refers to the expectations of the investor facing the state behaviour in the contract or promises and practices of the State would get in this regard a different connotation. The legitimate interests of the investor could no longer be assessed solely in terms of state actions. They would also be evaluated with respect to what an investor may expect from a state, in line with good governance including sustainability as well as the principle of proportionality. In this way, the legitimate expectations of the investor vis-à-vis the state would be subject to re-evaluation. The extent to which courts or decision-making bodies can decide on the appropriateness of a measure in the context of sustainability from a legal perspective depends decisively on the extent to which political decisions in a legal system are subject to judicial review.

Conclusions

The sustainability concept requires identifying relationships and exploiting them systematically for the benefit of social, environmental and economic objectives, for which it is one of investment in environmental technology. The UN General Assembly resolution on the Global Agenda is a recommendation under Article 10 UN Charter and therefore not legally binding. Recently, however, it has become increasingly evident that the contents of the resolution are being integrated by states into international treaties and into national legal systems, so that they become hard law as well as being taken up by private organisations such as the Global Compact as soft law.

In answering what the project European Energy Union is for, it is arguable that the new European Energy Union embodies the claim of the political system to determine the future structure of the energy system rather than the market. Thus, the European Union also assumes responsibility for bringing about rules-based energy governance worldwide, and for that it will be accountable not just to the citizens of the European Union but also to the international community of States and, ultimately, humanity. Ideally, a successful energy policy will translate the Sustainable Development Goals into a right to universal access to sustainable and modern energy, a right to action against climate change and for the investment sector into a right to sustainable economic growth. These issues must be brought together as efficiently as possible with a view to supporting the long-term prosperity of society. The guiding idea is to combine bottom-up with top-down decision-making. Decentralisation and plurality are to be balanced with centralisation and uniformity. Member State action is to be primary for most of the dimensions of the strategy. Through transnational networks that form important linkages between city governments, states, international organisations, businesses, and civil society, cities are creating and implementing norms, practices, and voluntary standards across national boundaries. In this way cities are beginning to perform law-making functions in the context of transnational climate change governance. The impact of their normative output is to steer the behaviour of cities towards mitigating climate change and adapting to its unavoidable impacts.

The principle of proportionality, which is especially prevalent in the German legal system but is also known as a core legal principle in many other jurisdictions worldwide, is proving to be particularly receptive to the concept of sustainability. In international investment law, the principle of proportionality is also a familiar legal principle. It therefore functions as an appropriate legal instrument for incorporating the concept of sustainability into investment law, using a modified proportionality test. Thereby it promotes the Sustainable Development Goals, set by the Member States of the United Nations, which are targeted at all countries and stakeholders.

Part III

Taxation and immigration in EU-CARICOM

7 Select jurisprudence of the CJEU and CCJ

A comparative perspective

Anthony Gafoor

Trade and development issues between the Caribbean and the EU can be traced to the various interactions between the two sets of countries stemming from the earliest days of colonisation which evolved into the slave trade between the Americas and Europe[1] whereby Africans and later indentured labourers from Africa and Asia respectively were brought to the Caribbean by Europeans to support the plantation economy in the 19th century.

In the 1970s this relationship entered into a new dimension with the Lomé Conventions[2] which allowed the small, developing economies of the Caribbean preferential access to the European market with the entry of one of the Caribbean's main trading partners, the UK, into the European Economic Community, later the EU.

The creation of the World Trade Organization in 1995 signalled a trend towards ending non-reciprocal trading agreements, and this development was characterised by the African, Caribbean and Pacific trading bloc entering into an agreement with the EU (the ACP-EU Agreement eventually known as the Cotonou Agreement in 2000.[3] This arrangement supported the development and negotiation of a separate treaty between the EU and CARIFORUM (which may be described as CARICOM plus in that it includes the CARICOM States as well as the Dominican Republic and Suriname inter alia from 1992 to the present date.

The history of trade and development between the EU and the Caribbean has therefore been characterised initially by informal arrangements in the light of the lack of any treaty basis for the slave trade and given that the Caribbean consisted of colonies of the European superpowers and which later evolved into trade and development relations based on treaties between sovereign states.

1 Robert Harms, 'Early Globalization and the Slave Trade' (*Yale Global Online*, 9 May 2003) <https://yaleglobal.yale.edu/content/early-globalization-and-slave-trade>.

2 The Lome Conventions granted the African, Caribbean and Pacific countries preferential access to European markets and subsisted between 1976–1999. In 1995, the USA claimed that these arrangements violated WTO rules, and this was upheld by the WTO in 1996, which brought such arrangements to an effective end.

3 *EPA Handbook for Civil Society on the CARIFORUM-EU Partnership Agreement* (CARICOM Secretariat 2013) 12.

More recently, the EU-CARIFORUM Economic Partnership Agreement (EPA), which was entered into in 2008, has sought to maintain some degree of priority access for members of CARICOM as well as Santo Domingo and Suriname on the basis that reciprocal obligations would be extended to the EU. The EPA grants quota- and tariff-free access to the EU for goods from CARIFORUM.

The success of this initiative has depended heavily on the continued financial support of the EU and, at present, the success of the EPA has been limited. However, the agreement itself was intended to be far reaching and in particular to ensure that Caribbean countries build sufficient capacity to compete within a global trade environment. The position has been helpfully described as follows:

> The overarching objectives of the EPA are to alleviate poverty in Cariforum, to promote regional integration and economic cooperation and to foster the gradual integration of the Cariforum states into the world economy by improving their trade capacity and creating an investment conducive environment. The development provisions of the EPA focus strongly on financial and technical support to cope with the challenges the EPA poses for Cariforum's public and private sectors, and on support to reform public institutions and administrations and to upgrade and diversify products and services of private actors.[4]

Given a similar approach towards regional integration in the EU and the Caribbean, it may not come as a surprise that the process of regional integration was used as a tool for furthering trade and development through the creation of a single market and economy which was intended to give rise to a seamless transition among independent sovereign states in supporting integration efforts through treaty arrangements.

Within the context of the European experience, this was characterised by a series of treaty negotiations among Member States. This evolved from the Treaty of Rome in 1958 through various stages such as the Single European Act 1986, the Treaty of Maastricht 1993,[5] and the Treaty of Lisbon 2007. Similarly, integration in the Caribbean is treaty-based and moved from CARIFTA in 1967 to the original Treaty of Chaguaramas in 1973 to the current Revised Treaty of Chaguaramas in 2001. Unlike the integration movement in Europe, which arguably had political objectives, the parallel Caribbean process was intended to be primarily economic.

4 Mareike Meyn, Christopher Stevens, Jane Kennan, Nick Highton, Sanoussi Bilal, Corinna Braun-Munzinger, Dan Lui, Jeske van Seters, Collette Campbell and John Rapley, *The Cariforum-EU Economic Partnership Agreement (EPA): The Development Component* (Directorate-General for External Policies Policy Department, European Parliament March 2009) 9.

5 Ettore Durrucci, Demosthenes Ioannou, Francesco Paolo Mongelli and Alezzio Terzi, 'A History of Europe's Economic Integration' (*World Economic Forum*) <www.weforum.org/agenda/2015/.../a-history-of-europes-economic-integration/>.

It seems virtually indisputable that global events such as the Singles European Act 1986 (which entered into force in 1987) to establish a single European market as well as the Washington Consensus 1989, which sought to foster greater trade liberalisation, encouraged the Member States of CARICOM to widen and deepen their efforts at regional integration in 1989 with the Grande Anse Declaration which led to the Revised Treaty of Chaguaramas.

Thus, while the CJEU in its original incarnation of the European Court of Justice was established with the Treaty of Rome in 1958, the CCJ was only established through a multilateral agreement among Member States in 2001 but actually commenced operations in 2005.

Role of the CJEU and the CCJ

These issues of the evolution of the two courts (though it should be noted that the ECJ itself is one of three courts under the umbrella of the CJEU) is directly relevant to matters of trade and development given that one of the key purposes for creating such judicial institutions has been to ensure that trade and development issues among Member States can be settled quickly by judges versed in the legal traditions of their respective regions. Both courts have arguably benefited from this given the thrust especially in the Caribbean towards continuing to build an indigenous jurisprudence.

There is little doubt that the establishment of the Court of Justice of the European Community (CJEU) as the legal engine which drives the EU together with the European Council, Commission and Parliament have had a seminal influence on European integration. Similarly, although the legal infrastructure in the Commonwealth Caribbean is less sophisticated in that the Caribbean Court of Justice (CCJ) is the only supranational judicial body to promote regional integration within the context of the CSME, there is a growing demand by Member States to seek greater harmonisation of legislation and, from the inter-governmentalist perspective, other Community organs such as the Heads of Government (HOGs) and the CARICOM Secretariat also drive the process of regional integration.

It should be noted at the outset that there are important differences in terms of the way both courts are established. In relation to the CJEU, its jurisdiction may be understood as constituting a final appellate court from decisions of the highest courts of Member States in most spheres save that of human rights where such appeals are heard by the European Court of Human Rights (ECHR). The CJEU primarily examines whether appellate decisions are compatible with the Treaty on the Functioning of the European Union (TFEU) which sought to consolidate the Treaty on the European Union and the Treaty on the Functioning of the European Union which emerged from the Treaty of Lisbon in 2007.

On the other hand, the CCJ acts both as a court of original jurisdiction for the purposes of interpreting the Revised Treaty of Chaguaramas as well as a final appellate court for Barbados, Guyana, Dominica and Belize, with the other Member States continuing to ventilate their appeals before the Judicial Committee of the Privy Council. Notably a common bench hears both appellate and original jurisdiction matters which potentially provide a further avenue for promoting cohesiveness within the Caribbean region in terms of the recognition and creation of legal norms. Such norms would seem to serve a dual purpose in that they articulate matters which are peculiar or characteristic of legal jurisprudence for the region but also represent some degree of consonance with international norms as established by other international tribunals.

Further, the CJEU is funded out of the budgetary contribution of Member States towards the overall EU budget whereas the CCJ is funded by an independent trust fund which further reinforces its independence and insulates it from political interference by Member States. However, the appointment of judges to the ECJ/CJEU is done through nominations by Member States, unlike the CCJ where save for the appointment of the President of the Court (which is confirmed by Member States after being nominated by a Regional Judicial and Legal Services Commission (RJLSC)), all other appointees are made by the RJLSC itself.

There are a number of areas in which both courts may exercise similar roles, and a few will be examined in terms of the jurisprudential contribution of both courts in terms of the following perspectives: accessibility; supremacy; direct effect/stare decisis; and references from domestic courts and tribunals.

Accessibility

Member States as well as private individuals are able to approach both courts for the resolution of disputes. It has been postulated that the CCJ adopts a liberal approach to the question of locus standi for private individuals under A.222 of the RTC in comparison with the CJEU which adopts a restrictive approach.[6] This treaty provision in effect seeks to weed out unmeritorious appeals by requiring private litigants to establish that they have sufficient standing to bring a substantive appeal.

In the CCJ case of *Johnson v Caricad*,[7] a case pertaining to whether an employee could pursue her termination of employment action against a Community institution, the CCJ was adamant that this was not permissible given that a Community organ was not being sued but rather an institution of the Community and thus the CCJ lacked jurisdiction to hear the matter. The CCJ in particular drew an analogy with the United Nations (UN), which consists of various organs and institutions/associate institutions which could not be considered organs of the UN themselves.[8]

Indeed, thus far, none of the 27 original jurisdiction matters emanating from Member States have involved state parties taking legal action against another CARICOM Member State. They have all involved actions by natural persons or

6 Jason Haynes, 'Revisiting the locus standi of Private Applicants in Judicial Review Proceedings under CARICOM and EU Law: A Comparative Perspective' (2015) 41(1) Commonwealth Law Bulletin 59–81.

7 [2009] CCJ 3 (OJ).

8 ibid. para 12.

corporate entities, demonstrating in many ways the extent to which non-state actors can drive the regional integration process.[9]

However, in *Douglas v Dominica*,[10] the applicant was denied special leave to pursue a legal action against Dominica on the basis that he did not have locus standi given that he had brought an action against the denial of entry into Dominica of a Jamaican artiste whose concert he had been promoting. The CCJ held that none of the treaty provisions was breached. The effect of this case was to maintain that the artiste himself may have been the more appropriate person to bring an action on the basis of the denial of free movement of Caribbean nationals for work purposes rather than the concert promoter.

The CCJ's decision at paragraph 9 is instructive in examining the scope of A.222 of the RTC:

> As a general proposition, the Article 222 conditions must be established by an Applicant in relation to that Applicant's own rights and benefits sourced from the Treaty. This is evident from the requirement that the Applicant must demonstrate that the right or benefit conferred by the RTC on a Contracting Party was intended to ensure to the benefit of the Applicant 'directly'. It is to be emphasized that the issue is not whether the Applicant suffered loss because of the breach of someone else's treaty rights but whether the Applicant suffered loss because of the breach of the Applicant's treaty rights.

In the relatively new case of *Jason Jones v Council of Legal Education*,[11] similarly the applicant was denied special leave to challenge the process whereby law students graduating from the University of the West Indies were accorded an automatic right of entry to the regional law schools in preference to graduates of other tertiary institutions who were required to take an entrance examination.

In declining to grant special leave, the CCJ found that it had no jurisdiction to review the actions of the Council of Legal Education, which in effect regulated its own affairs pursuant to a separate treaty arrangement among Member States of CARICOM. Of interest was the fact that the CCJ had rendered a similar ruling in *Doreen Johnson v CARICAD*[12] in which it had also concluded that it lacked jurisdiction over another institution of CARICOM. While this decision may be seen in effect as merely a more recent incarnation of the *Johnson* case, in declining jurisdiction the CCJ also sought to ensure that it would continue to focus on trade-related matters for which it was established rather than be tempted to stray into nebulous areas which were not envisaged by the RTC, particularly in relation to institutions which may be considered part of the regional machinery of institutions but not organs/bodies themselves of the Community.

9 See for example TCL v Guyana (2006); Myrie v Barbados (2013); Tomlinson v. Belize and Trinidad and Tobago (2016); SM Jaleel v Guyana (2017).

10 [2017] CCJ 1 (OJ).

11 [2018] CCJ 2 (OJ).

12 ibid.

Of note was the reasoning of the CCJ that:

> In *Doreen Johnson v CARICAD* this Court upheld a similar objection to jurisdiction in a claim brought against the Caribbean Centre for Development Administration (CARICAD), which the Court held was neither an Organ or Body of the Community nor an integral part of the Community. The Court stated that Institutions and Associate Institutions of the Community are autonomous inter-governmental entities, which contribute to the achievement of the objectives of the Community but are not an integral part of the Community and proceedings cannot be commenced against them in this Court. It must be even more compelling a conclusion that proceedings cannot be commenced against the Council in this Court, as the Council is further removed from the Community, being not even an institution or associated institution of the Community.[13]

In respect of the CJEU, the ability of an individual to access the Court's services is restricted to seeking annulment of an act which directly affects that person and which is in the nature of judicial review proceedings. This arises under A.263(4) of the TFEU which categorises such persons as non-preferential plaintiffs who must demonstrate some interest in having an act of an EU institution or body annulled where s/he is directly affected.[14] This may be contrasted with preferential plaintiffs which are Member States as well as the Council, Commission and Parliament. Interestingly, prior to the implementation of the TFEU, the individual test was more liberal in that one only needed to establish that the measure had to be of direct and individual concern to the legal position of the applicant.[15]

References from domestic courts

A.267 of the TFEU has been widely used by the CJEU to promote consistency and conformity with EU law. In essence, this provision mandates domestic courts to refer a matter of interpretation concerning EU law to the CJEU where such a reference is necessary to enable that court to give judgment.[16] The *El Yassini* case identified as relevant factors that such a body had to be established by law; permanent; exercise a compulsory jurisdiction; whether the proceedings were inter

13 [2017] CCJ 1 (OJ), para 12.

14 Case T-18/10 *Inuit Tapiriit Kanatami and Others v. Commission* & Judgment of 25 October 2011, Case T-262/10 *Microban v. Commission*.

15 S Peers and M Costa, 'Court of Justice of the European Union (General Chamber): Judicial Review of EU Acts after the Treaty of Lisbon' (2012) <http://openaccess.city.ac.uk/5846/>.

16 *R (Miller) v Secretary of State for Exiting the European Union*. See also the guidelines given in *H.P. Bulmer v. Bollinger S.A.* [1974] 2 All ER 1226 per Lord Denning MR where the learned Master of the Rolls stressed that such references were important in the context of being impossible to deliver a judgment otherwise.

partes; that it applied rules of law; and was independent.[17] Solanke suggests that additionally such a body would have to be required to determine a legal dispute, exercise a legal function and fall within the jurisdiction of a Member State.[18]

A similar provision exists under the RTC, A.214 which likewise permits domestic courts to refer matters involving the interpretation of Community law under the treaty to the CCJ, if necessary, to give judgment. The exercise of discretion as to whether or not to make such a reference is entirely the decision of the domestic court or tribunal and not that of the parties. In large measure, this can also be seen as correlating to A.216 of the RTC which recognises that the CCJ has a compulsory and exclusive jurisdiction to rule on matters arising under the RTC. The distinction though is that the relevant domestic court of a Member State has the ultimate say in the outcome of a matter where an issue of Community law arises before the domestic court in that, even if such a reference is made, the CCJ can only provide guidance, but the application of that guidance to the facts of the case before the domestic court remains exclusively within its jurisdiction and not that of the CCJ.

Thus far, this provision has not been used in the 15 odd years that the court has been operational. One may postulate that the absence of such referrals may be due to an unwillingness to discern that the assistance of the CCJ may be necessary to enable such a court to deliver judgment, or it may be that domestic judges are not sufficiently aware that such a provision could be a useful adjunct in clarifying issues of Community law and ensuring consistency of interpretation. Sobion takes issue with whether the CCJ does in fact interpret 'Community law' as opposed to international law citing in aid RTC A.217 which specifies that the court shall apply rules of international law in treaty interpretation and opines that this differs from the CJEU which does in fact apply Community law in the form of various pieces of legislation such as regulations and directives.[19]

Sobion further suggests that some of the reasons why national courts have not utilised A.214 are concerned with the importance of the question and whether there is reasonable doubt about the answer, which can be further classified as turning on whether the treaty provision is clear or no point of importance is raised.[20]

In the absence of case law, it is difficult to know what the reasons are for the absence of referrals. However, in so far as one can speak of Community law as opposed to pure international law, it is possible to see the RTC and the rules

17 *El Yassini* Case C416/96.

18 C 196/ 09 *Miles and Others v European Schools*. See generally Iiola Solanke, To refer or not to refer: that is the question . . . (Eutopia Law <https://eutopialaw.com/2016/12/09/to-refer-or-not-to-refer-that-is-the-ques>. Posted 9th December 2016.

19 Justin Sobion, 'The Caribbean Community, the Caribbean Single Market and Economy and the CISG: Three Ways of Promoting International Trade in the Caribbean Region' (Unpublished Master's thesis, 2014) 56.

20 ibid. 67.

pertaining to the various Community organs as constituting Community law which is distinguishable from international law per se.

Vink, Claes and Arnold opine that such provisions enable national courts to become involved in applying European law in a domestic context, though he distinguishes between instances when such a court may make such a reference (for example where this is necessary to give judgment and which is common to both the CJEU and the CCJ) as opposed to where there is doubt over the validity of a piece of legislation when national courts would lack the jurisdiction to strike down such legislation or even to declare same invalid.[21] They state further that:

> The system depends on the cooperation of the national courts and their willingness to refer. Parties do not have a right to a reference: it is ultimately for the court to decide. There are two kinds of references: questions of interpretation of European law, and questions concerning the validity of secondary European law. Any court or tribunal may refer a question to the Court on the interpretation of a rule of European law if it considers it necessary to do so in order to resolve a dispute brought before it. However, courts or tribunals against whose decisions there is no judicial remedy under national law must, as a rule, refer such a question to the Court, unless the Court has already ruled on the point (known as *acte éclairé*), or unless the correct interpretation of the rule of Community law is obvious and would be the same for any court across the EU and for each of the language versions of the relevant provision (known as *acte clair*).[22]

Supremacy of Community law

In relation to the issue of the supremacy of Community law, it has been well established within the EU that the CJEU has been instrumental in articulating the idea that Community law takes precedence over national law. There are various ways in which this proposition can be analysed.

On a fundamental level, the Vienna Convention on the Law of Treaties[23] (VCLT) A.27 specifies that national law cannot be invoked as a basis for non-compliance with treaty obligations, and this applies as much to the EU as CARICOM. Within the context of the EU, the supremacy of EU Community law over national law was not derived from the treaty but from the reasoning of the CJEU in the now renowned case of *Van Gend en Loos*[24] on the basis of the creation

21 Maarten Vink, Monica Claes and Christine Arnold, 'Explaining the Use of Preliminary References by Domestic Courts in EU Member States: A Mixed-Method Comparative Analysis' (Paper to be presented in Panel 6B 'Judicial Politics in the EU and Beyond', 11th Biennial Conference of the European Union Studies Association, Marina del Rey, Friday 24 April 2009) <http://aei.pitt.edu/33155/1/vink._maarten.pdf>.

22 ibid. 3.

23 <https://treaties.un.org/doc/publication/unts/volume%201155/volume-1155-i-18232-english.pdf>.

24 Case 26/62.

by treaty of a new legal order; this was further consolidated in *Costa v ENEL*[25]; *Simmenthal*[26] which removed any doubt that the concept of supremacy applied both to prior and future legislation; and *Factortame II*[27] which stressed that in the event of a conflict between EU law and national law, there was an obligation to ignore national law. On the one hand, protagonists of the CJEU have argued that this has the overall impact of constitutionalising the EU Treaty; on the other hand, critics have accused the CJEU of judicial activism.[28]

This 'long debate between supranationalism and intergovernmentalism' as identified by Member States unhappy with decisions of the CJEU may allow them to use the two avenues open to them of either legislative/treaty override (whereby precedence may be given to a later domestic law) or non-compliance.[29] To date neither has occurred in any meaningful way albeit that there may have been a delay in complying with some decisions. However, the concept of supranational courts may be seen as relevant to describing the actions of judicial tribunals operating at the regional level where such bodies are invested with the supreme authority to give decisions which are binding on Member States but lacking the institutional machinery to ensure compliance, unlike a judgment of a domestic court. On the other hand, intergovernmentalism is a theory which may best explain why governments may seek to cooperate with each other for the greater good, as has been used to explain the creation of the EU.[30]

It should be noted though that there has been no evidence to date of a lack of compliance with a decision of either the CJEU or the CCJ. In relation to the latter, the ability to enforce a decision domestically is supported by the requirements of A.215 of the RTC which requires member states, organs, bodies, persons or entities to whom a judgment applies to comply promptly with such a decision.

Within the Caribbean context, the approach taken by the CCJ may best be described as an application of EU-based principles with a Caribbean gloss of emphasising that the RTC and the creation of the CSME have transformed the legal system at the Community level into a new rules-based legal order which takes precedence over national law.[31] In terms of whether charges of judicial activism can be appropriately levelled at the CCJ, much turns on how one views the role of the Court. Nelson, former JCCJ, opines that: 'The economic integration

25 Case 6/64.
26 Case 106/77.
27 Case 221/89.
28 Michael Blauberger and Susanne K Schmidt, 'The European Court of Justice and Its Political Impact' (2017) 40(4) West European Politics 907–18. <http://doi.org/10.1080/01402382.2017.1281652>.
29 ibid. 908.
30 Jean-Jacques Roche, 'Intergovernmentalism' in Bertrand Badie, Dirk Berg-Schlosser and Leonardo Morlino (eds), *International Encyclopedia of Political Science*. <http://doi.org/10.4135/9781412959636.n284>. <http://sk.sagepub.com/reference/intlpoliticalscience/n284.xml>.
31 *TCL v Caribbean Community* [2009] 2 CCJ 2 (OJ). See also Rolston Nelson, 'The Applicable Law in the Caribbean Single Market' (2011) 87 Amicus Curiae 3.

treaties constitute an outline to be filled in by judge-made law. Judge-made law constitutes a useful resource for moving forward economic integration'.[32] Indeed, if the treaty is silent or unclear, then it may be surmised that the CCJ will act no differently from any other international court in seeking, as a matter of treaty interpretation, to make sense of the provisions in relation to the particular issue under consideration by reference to AA.31–33 of the VCLT.

In the subsequent case of *Shanique Myrie v Barbados*[33] the CCJ was afforded a further opportunity to emphasise the supremacy of Community law by placing reliance on a subsequent decision of the Heads of Government to endorse the free movement of CARICOM citizens to six months 'hassle free travel' within the region. Interestingly, the RTC already had this provision relating to free movement in A.45 of the RTC. However, the Conference decision could be interpreted, within the terms of the VCLT, A.31 (3) (a) as a subsequent agreement which did not modify but rather reinforced the right to free movement. In this sense, this has become the flagship decision of the CCJ to date in terms of both the purposive approach to treaty interpretation but, for present purposes, fidelity to the doctrine of supremacy of Community law over domestic law.[34]

Principle of direct effect

Given that CARICOM does not have the elaborate system of law-making as in the EU with various legal instruments such as regulations (which are binding on Member States without further domestic implementation) and directives (which are generally left to Member States to implement into domestic law), it may seem odd to include the category of direct effect in comparing the jurisprudence of the CJEU and the CCJ. In this regard, the principle of horizontal direct effect was developed by the CJEU whereby effect can be given to a treaty provision as with a regulation if certain conditions are met: the provision must be clear and precisely stated; it must be unconditional and not dependent on any other legal provision; and it must confer a specific right upon which a citizen can base a claim.[35] In the case of *Defrenne v Sabena*, the conjoint impact of the principles of direct effect and the supremacy of EU law was applied to enable a claim to be made before domestic courts to override domestic law.[36]

The CJEU has also identified the principle of vertical direct effect whereby a member state is obligated to ensure that its domestic law is compatible with EU law: *Foster v British Gas*[37]; this was also held to apply to directives, which, as

32 Nelson (n 31).

33 [2013] CCJ 3 (OJ).

34 Désirée P Bernard, 'The Revised Treaty of Chaguaramas and the Caribbean Court of Justice – Compatibility or Controversy?' (2013) 96 Amicus Curiae 9–10.

35 Case 26/62, *NV Algemene Transporten Expeditie Onderneming van Gend en Loos v Nederlandse Administratis der Belastingen* [1963] ECR 1

36 Case 43/75.

37 Case C-18-89.

previously indicated, were seen as a matter for Member States: *Van Duyn v Home Office*.[38] Further, the doctrine of indirect effect also emerged from the notion that directives were to be interpreted in conformity with EU law.

Within the CSME, it may be argued that the *Myrie* decision has much the same effect as the broad principle of direct effect in terms of treaty interpretation. There the CCJ upheld a 2007 Conference decision notwithstanding that it had not been enacted into domestic law. The CCJ made it clear that the failure of a member state to implement a Conference decision into domestic law did not affect its applicability in domestic law. Moreover, in the case of *Tomlinson v Belize and Trinidad and Tobago*,[39] the CCJ granted special leave to the applicant to challenge the domestic immigration laws of two Member States which were contended to be contrary to the right to free movement albeit that he was not actually denied entry into either jurisdiction as a member of the LGBTI community nor was he asked about his sexual orientation at the port of entry and was therefore unsuccessful in the substantive hearing.

Conclusions

It may be concluded that, in the various spheres of accessibility, references by domestic courts, supremacy of Community law and direct effect, there are significant parallels between the CJEU and the CCJ which demonstrate that both courts have been grappling with similar issues which have occurred in relation to matters pertaining to trade and development such as the free movement of persons or other related pillars of integration such as the right of establishment or to provide services. Given the fact that they have both been instrumental in promoting consistency of legal interpretation in respect of a single economic space, it is likely that they will encounter similar issues and can therefore learn from each other.

Alter and Helfer have ventured to suggest that the CJEU law has been transplanted into other jurisdictions[40] and this may raise questions as to whether this amounts to a duplication of EU principles with all of the concomitant issues that this may give rise to such as the artificial application of foreign jurisprudence without regard for different cultural and cultural norms and practices.

In the case of the CCJ, it is clear that the court is alive to this danger and has demonstrated a cautious approach towards adopting judicial precedents from other jurisdictions. However, the similarities between the EU integration scheme and the CSME are such that it is natural and legitimate for the CCJ to look towards the CJEU for guidance given the longer established vintage of the CJEU.

38 Case 41/74.
39 [2016] CCJ 1 (OJ).
40 Karen J Alter and Laurence R Helfer, *Transplanting International Courts: The Law and Politics of the Andean Tribunal of Justice* (International Courts and Tribunals Series, OUP, 2017).

As the self-proclaimed guardian of the CSME, the CCJ has demonstrated a pro-treaty approach towards interpretation which upholds the binding nature of treaties encapsulated in the familiar phrase, *pacta sunt servanda*. This is no different from the approach by the CJEU, which has itself demonstrated a fidelity and loyalty to treaty interpretation which has at its core the supremacy of EU law over domestic law.

8 From haven to blacklist

UK, EU and Caribbean cooperation on tax avoidance, after Brexit

Stuart MacLennan

The Caribbean has long played a central role in global tax avoidance. For many decades, there appeared to be little onus to do anything to curtail the practices of tax havens. Indeed, at one time, there was a considerable body of literature which took the view that tax havens were a somewhat benign phenomenon which actually mitigated the effects of large states' 'sub-optimal' levels of taxation.[1]

Concern about tax havens, however, began to grow in the late 1990s. The subsequent financial crisis of 2007–08, the resultant recession, and relatively slow rate of recovery has resulted in an unprecedented squeeze on the public finances of most developed nations. Consequently, a new onus has emerged to close the tax gap between expected revenues and actual returns. Historically, the role of coordinating national tax laws was first assumed by the League of Nations, and, following the Second World War, the Organisation for European Economic Co-operation, later the Organisation for Economic Co-operation and Development (OECD).

While the OECD has proved a formidable coordinator of tax laws, the fact that the body, in particular its Committee on Fiscal Affairs, operates on the basis of consensus means that 'creative ambiguity' has often prevailed over decisive action.[2] In this respect, the OECD could be described as a secretariat without an executive. Although the Group of 20 summit (G20) has existed at a ministerial level since 1999,[3] it was only in response to the financial crisis that the grouping took on a top-level focus as well as an enhanced role in financial management.[4] In contrast to the OECD, the G20, as a top-level summit, could be described as an executive without a secretariat. The complementariness of these bodies respective deficiencies was obvious, and, consequently, when the G20 reached conclusions as to the necessary actions to tackle harmful tax avoidance, the OECD was the

1 Joel Slemrod, 'Why Is Elvis on Burkina Faso Postage Stamps? Cross-Country Evidence on the Commercialization of State Sovereignty' (2008) 5 Journal of Empirical Legal Studies 683.

2 Hugh J Ault, 'Reflections on the Role of the OECD in Developing International Tax Norms' (2008) 34 Brook. J. Int'l L. 757, 763.

3 G7 Finance Ministers, 'Report of G7 Finance Ministers to the Köln Economic Summit' (1999) <www.g8.utoronto.ca/finance/fm061999.htm>.

4 G20, 'London Summit – Leaders' Statement' (2 April 2009) <www.g20.utoronto.ca/2009/2009communique0402.pdf>.

obvious administrative body to turn the broadly agreed principles into substantive action. The result of this impetus is the ongoing work of the OECD on base erosion and profit shifting (BEPS).

In tandem with the efforts of the OECD, many states, in particular the United Kingdom, have taken unilateral action to tackle the problem of tax avoidance. Furthermore, the European Union, which has previously only ever taken extremely limited involvement with matters of direct taxation, has sought a 'piece of the action' through re-orienting its role as the guardian of free competition in the internal market, as well as legislative intervention. However, it should not be assumed that this apparent unity of purpose is matched by either a common approach or a common objective. There remains considerable disagreement between EU Member States as to how problems of tax avoidance should be tackled. There also exists, as this paper reveals, a notable schism between those EU Member States with colonial and/or post-colonial interests in the Caribbean and those without. One of the more controversial interventions of the EU has been the decision of the council to 'blacklist' non-cooperative tax jurisdictions. This chapter is therefore split into three sections. It commences by examining the efforts that have been taken so far to tackle tax avoidance at national, regional, and international levels. This chapter proceeds to consider the different approaches and objectives of the UK, the EU, and the Caribbean states in addressing the issue of tax avoidance.

Finally, this chapter examines the role of the United Kingdom as a bridge between the Caribbean and the EU. In addition to the political and cultural connections between the UK and many Caribbean states, the UK also has a constitutional responsibility to represent a number of Caribbean territories in their foreign relations. This paper concludes that a close relationship between the United Kingdom and European Union is of considerable importance to Caribbean states, in particular where matters of taxation are concerned, and that without the UK as a moderating influence within Europe, the EU may well be minded to pursue more aggressive policies against tax avoidance and harmful tax competition.

Previous and current efforts at tackling tax avoidance

Although issues of tax avoidance have gained considerable impetus since the financial crisis of 2007–08, concerns had been mounting about perceived harmful tax practices for over a decade beforehand. This stands in sharp contrast to the near-century of international tax policy that preceded these concerns. At the turn of the 20th century, the principal concern was double taxation; however, by the turn of the 21st century, double non-taxation became the focus of states' attention.

In the past two decades, a notable pattern of action has emerged. First, the OECD recognises the existence of a problem, and commissions work at a technocratic level to research the issue and develop proposals. Then the OECD agrees on recommendations, which often go far beyond what might reasonably be expected of a body that works entirely upon consensus and lacks any formal decision-making or enforcement mechanisms. Following the OECD's initiative, and normally in parallel with the work of the OECD that follows, the EU identifies how the issues identified particularly affect its Member States and seeks to pursue measures which reflect those particular concerns, the significantly stronger legal frameworks that exist in the EU to act on those measures, as well as, increasingly, the EU's economic and political power to impose its will on others.

In 1996, in response to a request from the OECD's Ministerial Council Meeting in order to take action to tackle what it perceived to be harmful tax competition, the OECD Committee on Fiscal Affairs commenced a two-year project investigating the effects of harmful tax competition and ways of combating it. This impetus was endorsed by the Group of Seven (G7) states in the communique agreed at their Lyon summit:

> We strongly urge the OECD to vigorously pursue its work in this field, aimed at establishing a multilateral approach under which countries could operate individually and collectively to limit the extent of these practices.[5]

The G7 repeated its endorsement of the OECD's effort at its subsequent summit in Denver in 1997.[6]

The CFA reported in 1998, and their findings were broadly welcomed by member governments. Their report defined a tax haven as those territories or countries with 'no or only nominal taxation which is usually coupled with a reduction in regulatory or administrative restraints'.[7] The report identified four criteria for identifying tax havens: no nor nominal taxation, or a perception that the state or territory offers itself as a place to escape higher taxation; lack of effective information exchange; a lack of transparency; and the absence of a requirement that any taxable activity be substantial.[8]

Although not specifically directed at Caribbean nations, its follow-up report – 'Towards Global Tax Co-operation: Progress in Identifying and Eliminating Harmful Tax Practices' – identified 35 states and territories which, in the view of the CFA, met the 1998 report's criteria to qualify as a tax haven, the preponderance of which were located in the Caribbean.[9] The report was not without its critics. CARICOM loudly protested the inclusion of its members on the

5 G7, 'Economic Communiqué: Making a Success of Globalization for the Benefit of All' (*G7 Information Centre, University of Toronto*, 28 June 1996) <www.g8.utoronto.ca/summit/1996lyon/communique.html>.

6 G7, 'Confronting Global Economic and Financial Challenges: Denver Summit Statement by Seven' (*G7 Information Centre, University of Toronto*, 21 June 1997) <www.g8.utoronto.ca/summit/1997denver/confront.htm>.

7 OECD, *Harmful Tax Competition: An Emerging Global Issue* (OECD Publishing 1998) 21.

8 ibid. 23.

9 OECD, *2000 Progress Report: Towards Global Tax Co-operation: Progress in Identifying and Eliminating Harmful Tax Practices* (OECD Publishing 2000).

OECD's list. Vaughn James was even more scathing in his criticism, arguing that the OECD:

> like the pirates who plied the waters of the Caribbean during the sixteenth through nineteenth centuries, has, through its ill-advised anti-harmful tax competition initiative, effectively robbed fourteen CARICOM nations of their sovereign right to determine their tax and economic policies.[10]

The OECD's early action on tax havens did achieve some success, albeit limited. Progress was made, in particular, with respect to transparency and information exchange, although subsequent scandals betrayed the limitations of what was achieved. Robert Kudrle described the harmful tax competition initiative as a 'damp squib'.[11]

European Union: from code of conduct, to action plan, to blacklist

In 1998, in response to growing concerns about base erosion within the EU, the European Council set up the Code of Conduct Group (Business Taxation). The initial focus of the group's efforts was preferential tax regimes in certain Member States. The work of the Code of Conduct Group did achieve some success in engendering a common approach to harmful tax practices among EU Member States. With consensus emerging, the EU increasingly turned its sights beyond its own members to third states. An early example of the EU's outward focus can be seen in the action against the United States initiated by the EU within the WTO in *Foreign Sales Corporations.*[12] The Appellate Body affirmed the decision of the Dispute Settlement Body that the United States' Foreign Sales Corporations legislation constituted a preferential regime and, therefore, an export subsidy prohibited under arts III:4 and XVI of the GATT, as well as arts 3(a) and (b) of the SCM Agreement.[13]

In 2008, ECOFIN agreed that Member States would seek to export good practice to third states through the inclusion of a clause in bilateral agreements. The clause required parties to 'commit themselves to implement the principles of good governance in the tax area as subscribed to by Member States at the

10 Vaughn E James, 'Twenty-First Century Pirates of the Caribbean: How the Organization for Economic Cooperation and Development Robbed Fourteen CARICOM Countries of Their Tax and Economic Policy Sovereignty' (2002) 34 The University of Miami Inter-American Law Review 1, 5.

11 Robert T Kudrle, 'The OECD's Harmful Tax Competition Initiative and the Tax Havens: From Bombshell to Damp Squib' (2008) 8 Global Economy Journal.

12 US: WTO, Appellate Body Report of 20 February 2000, DS108, *United States Foreign Sales Corporations.*

13 The authorisation of countermeasures up to the value of USD 4043 million per year remains the largest in WTO history.

Community level'.[14] Third countries broadly resisted this move, however, fearing a loss of tax sovereignty. [15]

The EU, therefore, decided to take a more unilateral approach, and in 2012 the Commission published a recommendation regarding measures intended to encourage third countries to apply minimum standards of good governance in tax matters.[16] The 2012 recommendation proposes that Member States should publish blacklists of states that do not conform with certain minimum standards with respect to transparency, exchange of information, and harmful tax practices. The Commission recommends that Member States should renegotiate, suspend, or even terminate double taxation conventions with states that appear on those blacklists. The 2012 recommendation undoubtedly recommends a shift in the EU's approach from collaboration to imposition, which Kalloe has described as 'one sided and punitive'.[17] It transpires, however, that the 2012 recommendation was merely an opening salvo to the more aggressive action that followed.

Following the agreement of the OECD's 15 Base Erosion and Profit Shifting (BEPS) Actions,[18] the European Commission published a communication to both the Council and Parliament, 'A Fair and Efficient Corporate Tax System in the European Union: 5 Key Areas for Action'.[19] Under action 4, on tax transparency, the European Commission proposed 'a more common approach to third country non-cooperative tax jurisdictions',[20] while under action 5 on improving coordination, the Commission proposed reforming the Code of Conduct on Business Taxation. While in 2012 the Commission recommended that Member States maintain individual backlists of uncooperative tax jurisdictions, the 2015 proposal envisaged the EU throwing its collective weight behind a common blacklist of tax havens.

In 2016, ECOFIN agreed on the criteria[21] against which jurisdictions are to be assessed for the purposes of blacklisting. The criteria fall into three categories, the first of which is tax transparency. States should have taken steps to implement automatic exchange of information (the 'Common Reporting Standard') by 2017, with the first exchanges of information taking place by 2018. States should have a 'largely compliant' rating by the Global Forum with respect to

14 ECOFIN, Council Conclusions of 14 May 2008, 8850/08, 23.

15 Vinod Kalloe, 'European Union-EU Tax Haven Blacklist – Is the European Union Policing the Whole World?' (2018) 58 European Taxation 47, 51.

16 Commission Recommendation 2012/771/EU of 6 December 2012 regarding measures intended to encourage third countries to apply minimum standards of good governance in tax matters [2012] OJ L 338.

17 Kalloe (n. 15) 51.

18 OECD, 'BEPS 2015 Final Reports' (2015) <www.oecd.org/ctp/beps-2015-final-reports.htm>.

19 European Commission, *A Fair and Efficient Corporate Tax System in the European Union: 5 Key Areas for Action* (2015).

20 ibid. 12.

21 Council of the European Union, *Criteria and Process Leading to the Establishment of the EU List of Noncooperative Jurisdictions for Tax Purposes* (14166/16, 2016).

OECD exchange of information requests. Sovereign states should have ratified OECD Multilateral Convention on Mutual Administrative Assistance ('the OECD Multilateral Convention') or should have an equivalent network of conventions in place. Non-sovereign territories should be participating in the OECD Multilateral Convention or an equivalent network of conventions. Until 30 June 2019, meeting two out of three of these sub-criteria is sufficient to be regarded as compliant with respect to tax transparency. The Council also agreed that a fourth criteria on beneficial ownership registers should be agreed and adopted at a later date.

The second criterion concerns fair taxation. States and territories should not operate harmful preferential tax regimes as set out in the EU Code of Conduct, nor should they facilitate offshore structures aimed at attracting profit shifting without any real economic activity. Finally, states should have committed to implement to the OECD agreed minimum anti-BEPS standards by the end of 2017. Implementation of the OECD minimum standards will be incorporated as an independent criterion at a later date.

In December 2017, the Council agreed on its initial blacklist.[22] The initial blacklist included the Caribbean states of Barbados, Grenada, Saint Lucia, and Trinidad and Tobago, as well as American Samoa, Bahrain, Republic of Korea, United Arab Emirates, Guam, Macao SAR, Marshall Islands, Mongolia, Namibia, Palau, Panama, Samoa and Tunisia. Furthermore, Belize, Bermuda, Cayman Islands, Curacao, Jamaica, Montenegro, and Saint Vincent and the Grenadines were among those states included on a separate 'greylist' (see Table 8.1). Determinations on Anguilla, Antigua and Barbuda, The Bahamas, British Virgin

Table 8.1 EU Blacklist, 5 December 2017

Blacklist:	*Greylist:*
American Samoa, Bahrain, Barbados, Republic of Korea, United Arab Emirates, Grenada, Guam, Macao SAR, Marshall Islands, Mongolia, Namibia, Palau, Panama, Saint Lucia, Samoa, Trinidad and Tobago, Tunisia.	Albania, Andorra, Armenia, Aruba, Belize, Bermuda, Bosnia and Herzegovina, Botswana, Cabo Verde, Cayman Islands, Cook Islands, Curacao, Faroe Islands, Fiji, Greenland, Guernsey, Hong Kong, Jamaica, Jersey, Jordan, Lichtenstein, Labuan Island, Macedonia, Malaysia, Maldives, Isle of Man, Morocco, Mauritius, Montenegro, Nauru, Niue, New Caledonia, Oman, Peru, Qatar, Saint Vincent and the Grenadines, San Marino, Serbia, Seychelles, Switzerland, Swaziland, Taiwan, Thailand, Turkey, Uruguay, Vanuatu, Vietnam.
Total: 17	Total: 47
Postponed: Anguilla, Antigua and Barbuda, The Bahamas, British Virgin Islands, Dominica, Saint Kitts and Nevis, US Virgin Islands, Turks and Caicos Islands.	

22 Council Conclusions on the EU list of non-cooperative jurisdictions for tax purposes [2017] OJ C 438.

Islands, Dominica, Saint Kitts and Nevis, US Virgin Islands, Turks and Caicos Islands were deferred following the devastation caused by Hurricane Irma.

Together with the Council's decision as to which jurisdictions to include on their blacklist, the Council also agreed that, at a minimum, EU Member States *should* apply at least one of the following defensive measures to blacklisted states and territories:

1 Reinforced monitoring of certain transactions;
2 Increased audit risks for taxpayers benefiting from the regimes at stake;
3 Increased audit risks for taxpayers using structures or arrangements involving these jurisdictions.[23]

The evident objective of these measures is to ensure that non-compliant jurisdictions are perceived by taxpayers as riskier places to do business. The Council also agreed on a number of additional measures which Member States *may* take. These include:

1 Non-deductibility of costs;
2 Controlled Foreign Company (CFC) rules;
3 Withholding tax measures;
4 Limitation of participation exemption;
5 Switch-over rule;
6 Reversal of the burden of proof;
7 Special documentation requirements;
8 Mandatory disclosure by tax intermediaries of specific tax schemes with respect to cross-border arrangements.

While these are actions to be undertaken by Member States, the EU has also begun applying punitive measures against tax havens at a Union-wide level too. Regulation 2017/1601 provides that those entities in receipt of guarantees from the European Fund for Sustainable Development may not enter into new or renewed operations with entities incorporated or established in jurisdictions on the EU blacklist or that 'do not effectively comply with Union or internationally agreed tax standards on transparency and exchange of information'.[24]

The EU's blacklists, as well as the defensive measures being applied to tax havens have, understandably, attracted criticism that the EU is seeking to 'police the whole world'.[25] Nevertheless, it appears that this process has produced a significant measure of success, and fairly quickly. In just over six months, 13 states or territories were moved from the blacklist to the greylist (see Table 8.2). At the time of writing, only one Caribbean state remains on the blacklist – Trinidad and Tobago – as well as the US Virgin Islands territory.

23 ibid.
24 Art. 22, Regulation (EU) 2017/1601 of the European Parliament and of the Council of 26 September 2017 establishing the European Fund for Sustainable Development [2017] OJ L 249/27.
25 Kalloe (n. 15).

Table 8.2 EU Blacklist, 25 May 2018

Blacklist:	*Greylist:*
American Samoa, Guam, Namibia, Palau, Samoa, Trinidad and Tobago, US Virgin Islands.	Albania, Andorra, Anguilla, Antigua and Barbuda, Armenia, Aruba, Bahamas, Bahrain, Barbados, Belize, Bermuda, Bosnia and Herzegovina, Botswana, British Virgin Islands, Cabo Verde, Cayman Islands, Cook Islands, Dominica, Republic of Korea, Curacao, United Arab Emirates, Faroe Islands, Fiji, Granada, Greenland, Guernsey, Hong Kong, Jamaica, Jersey, Jordan, Lichtenstein, Labuan Island, Macao SAR, Qatar, Former Yugoslav Republic of Macedonia, Malaysia, Maldives, Isle of Man, Marshall Islands, Morocco, Mauritius, Mongolia, Montenegro, Nauru, Niue, New Caledonia, Oman, Panama, Peru, Saint Kitts and Nevis, Saint Lucia, Saint Vincent and the Grenadines, San Marino, Serbia, Seychelles, Switzerland, Swaziland, Taiwan, Thailand, Tunisia, Turkey, Turks and Caicos, Uruguay, Vanuatu, Vietnam.
Total: 7	Total: 65

Tax avoidance and the EU: differing approaches and objectives

We have seen an increasingly coordinated and concerted effort at tackling the problems of global tax avoidance – in particular among EU states. While there is, at least, a common recognition of the problems, it is not at all clear that the Member States favour a common approach to tackling these problems. Even less evident is the existence of a common set of objectives from efforts at tackling global tax avoidance. This section seeks to consider the efforts, discussed earlier, that have been taken to tackle the problems of tax avoidance in their domestic and regional political contexts, as well as the limitations of those approaches.

United Kingdom

Since the 1980s, the United Kingdom has been the foremost advocate of a competitive internal market.[26] Sensing an opportunity to export her government's domestic market reforms to Europe, thus entrenching them in the UK's legal order, Margaret Thatcher, together with West German Chancellor Helmut Kohl, forged a consensus amongst European leaders that led to the adoption of the Single European Act in 1986.[27]

In the past decade the UK has also been one of the leading advocates for tackling BEPS through international consensus and rules-based reform. The UK was

26 Geoffrey Garrett, 'International Cooperation and Institutional Choice: The European Community's Internal Market' (1992) 46 International Organization 533, 534.

27 Kenneth Armstrong and Simon Bulmer, *The Governance of the Single European Market* (Manchester University Press 1998) 21.

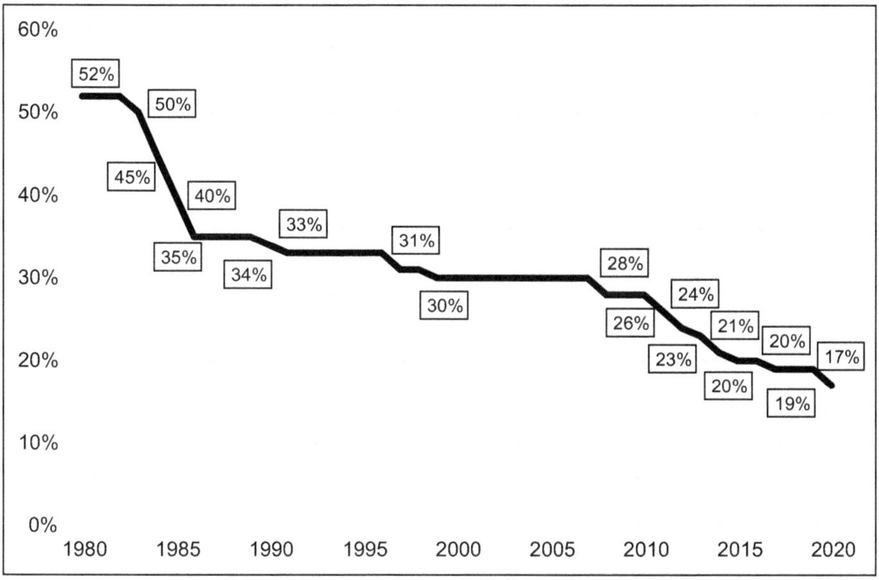

Figure 8.1 UK Standard Rate of Corporation Tax 1980–2020

an early adopter of CFC and General Anti-Avoidance Rules (GAAR), as well as pioneering a new Diverted Profits Tax (the so-called Google Tax). Despite these efforts at tackling what it perceives as harmful tax practices, the UK continues to regard tax policy as a central tool in promoting a competitive economy. While a decade ago the UK's Corporation Tax was levied at a rate of 28%, it presently stands at 19% and is set to fall to 17% by 2020 (see Figure 8.1).[28] These rate reductions come on top of a number of targeted reliefs, such as the Patent Box,[29] although the UK's system of capital allowances is somewhat less competitive than those of many other developed countries.

The UK's objectives when it comes to international tax policy can therefore be summarised as follows: clamping down on tax competition that is opaque and secretive, while continuing to use taxation as a tool for enhancing the UK's competitiveness – quite the balancing act. While it might be tempting to conclude that there is a tension or, worse still, a degree of hypocrisy underlying the UK's approach, a more charitable conclusion is that the UK has no problem with jurisdictions competing on tax provided that all jurisdictions play by the same rules. This stands in contrast to an apparent desire on the part of some states, in particular in the EU, to eliminate tax competition altogether.

28 HMRC, 'Corporation Tax to 17% in 2020' (*HMRC*, 2016) <www.gov.uk/government/publications/corporation-tax-to-17-in-2020>.
29 Part 8A, Corporation Tax Act 2010.

European Union

In recent years, the European Union has given extensive consideration to questions of direct taxation and tax avoidance. This is somewhat remarkable, given the limited competence the EU has over matters of direct taxation.

The principal grant of competence to the EU over matters of taxation can be found in Art. 113 TFEU, which provides that

> [t]he Council [of Ministers] shall, acting unanimously in accordance with a special legislative procedure and after consulting the European Parliament and the Economic and Social Committee, adopt provisions for the harmonisation of legislation concerning turnover taxes, excise duties and other forms of indirect taxation to the extent that such harmonisation is necessary to ensure the establishment and the functioning of the internal market and to avoid distortion of competition.

By far the most significant action the EU has taken in this field is the abolition of turnover taxes and the establishment of a common system of Value Added Tax (VAT) across the EU.

The EU treaties contain no grant of competence over matters of direct taxation to EU institutions, with the only substantive tax rule being Art. 110 TFEU's prohibition on discriminatory tax treatment.[30] Despite this, the EU institutions, in particular the Court of Justice, and the Commission, have successfully used Article 49 TFEU (on freedom of establishment) and, more recently, and more controversially, Art. 107 TFEU (on state aid), to engage with questions of direct taxation. Perhaps somewhat perversely, the Commission's attempt to use Article 107 TFEU is aimed at combating harmful tax avoidance, while the effect of Article 49 TFEU, through a string of cases before the court, has been to vitiate national rules designed to limit opportunities for tax avoidance.[31]

Article 49 of the Treaty on the Functioning of the European Union (TFEU) prohibits restrictions upon freedom of establishment of nationals of Member States in the territory of another Member State including establishment of companies. Article 58 TFEU further prohibits any restrictions on the free movement of capital. National laws, including tax laws, which infringe upon those rights are, in almost all circumstances, not permitted. This has resulted in a number of laws designed to clamp down on tax avoidance being struck down by the ECJ.

The case of *Sandoz* concerned a requirement to pay Austrian stamp duty on loans.[32] Austrian law contained a provision designed to prevent the arrangement

30 Art. 65 TFEU contains an explicit exclusion for tax laws from the scope of Art. 63 TFEU on free movement of capital.

31 Brady Gordon, 'Tax Competition and Harmonisation under EU Law: Economic Realities and Legal Rules' (2014) 39 European Law Review 790.

32 Case C-439/97, *Sandoz* [1999] ECR I-07041.

of loans outside of Austria to avoid paying the tax. In his opinion on the case, Advocate General Leger took the view that:

> [t]he principle of the free movement of capital was introduced inter alia in order to enable Community nationals to enjoy the most favourable conditions for investing their capital available to them in any of the States which make up the Community.[33]

The Court agreed with the Advocate General's position, holding that the measure:

> deprives residents of a Member State of the possibility of benefiting from the absence of taxation which may be associated with loans obtained outside the national territory. Accordingly, such a measure is likely to deter such residents from obtaining loans from persons established in other Member States.[34]

It follows that such legislation constitutes an obstacle to the movement of capital within the meaning of Article 63 TFEU.

If the very purpose of free movement is to ensure the allocation of resources to their most efficient location, it logically follows that measures which inhibit shopping around for the most favourable environment for those resources must surely be unlawful. A more pertinent example is the decision of the ECJ in *Cadbury Schweppes.*[35] At issue in the case was whether the UK's controlled foreign corporation (CFC) rules, an anti-avoidance measure designed to prevent companies from shifting profits outside of the UK to avoid tax, were compatible with the treaties. The Court in *Cadbury Schweppes* reiterated its earlier pronouncement in *Barbier* that:

> a Community national cannot be deprived of the right to rely on the provisions of the Treaty on the ground that he is profiting from tax advantages which are legally provided by the rules in force in a Member State other than his State of residence . . . the mere fact that a resident company establishes a secondary establishment, such as a subsidiary, in another Member State cannot set up a general presumption of tax evasion and justify a measure which compromises the exercise of a fundamental freedom guaranteed by the Treaty.[36]

In other words, under EU law the fact that a company shifts its operations to another EU state (such as Ireland or the Netherlands) to take advantage of more

33 Opinion of AG Leger, ibid., para 47.
34 (n. 32) para 19.
35 Case C-196/04, *Cadbury Schweppes* [2006] ECR I-8031.
36 John A Swain, 'State Income Tax Jurisdiction: A Jurisprudential and Policy Perspective' (2003) 45 Wm. & Mary L. Rev. 319, para 71.

favourable tax treatment cannot be prohibited. Anti-avoidance rules may not be applied, even where there is an explicit intention to avoid tax, where the taxpayer nonetheless carries on genuine economic activities. Such tax rules are only effective where they target wholly artificial arrangements – an extremely low bar. The author has previously argued that the effect of this line of case law on the UK's flagship anti-avoidance measure, the Diverted Profits Tax, is to empty the tax of almost all practical effect.[37]

Brady Gordon argues that such consequences arise not merely as an unintended spillover effect from the application of Art. 49 TFEU. Rather, Gordon argues that the facilitation of competition, not just across the Member States, but between them, is a core objective of European economic integration. According to Gordon, 'the empirical effects of tax competition are demonstrably concomitant with the objectives of EU law and tax policy'.[38]

The tension between the twin objectives of, on the one hand, clamping down on abusive tax avoidance while, on the other, maintaining a competitive economic environment is a familiar one for tax lawyers. While policymakers, ideally, seek to balance these two objectives, when they come into conflict the decision as to which objective to favour is a matter of political choice. It is in this political choice that the divergent objectives of EU Member States play a significant role.

For most of the 20th century, a degree of low-level tax avoidance has been viewed as a price worth paying for a competitive market economy, both within the EU and beyond. In recent years, however, a marked shift towards the objective of tackling that tax avoidance has taken place and is widely recognised. Consequently, and despite its lack of direct competence in the field of direct taxation, the EU has sought to embrace this shift in objective and take the required action.

Despite the supposed lack of competence over matters of direct taxation, the effects of tax avoidance on the functioning of the internal market has led to the EU utilising Art. 115 TFEU to act. Art. 115 TFEU provides that

> the Council shall, acting unanimously in accordance with a special legislative procedure and after consulting the European Parliament and the Economic and Social Committee, issue directives for the approximation of such laws, regulations or administrative provisions of the Member States as directly affect the establishment or functioning of the internal market.[39]

The flagship piece of legislation in this field is the 2016 Anti-Avoidance Directive, which mandates Member States to introduce five anti-avoidance measures where they have not already done so:

1 CFC rules;
2 Switchover rules;

37 Stuart MacLennan, 'The Questionable Legality of the Diverted Profits Tax Under Double Taxation Conventions and European Union Law' (2016) 44 Intertax 903.
38 Gordon (n. 31).
39 Art. 115 TFEU.

3 Interest limitation rules;
4 Exit taxation; and,
5 A general anti-avoidance rule.

The fact that an EU directive mandates Member States to implement CFC rules more than a decade after the Court of Justice so famously limited the effects of the UK's CFC rules in *Cadbury Schweppes* illustrates the shift in the EU's priorities.

However, it is arguable that the EU's approach to tax competition, generally, remains considerably more sceptical than that of the UK. In 2011, the European Commission proposed a directive to harmonise the corporate tax bases of EU Member States – the Common Consolidated Corporate Tax Base (CCCTB). Under this proposal, every Member State's corporate tax base would be identical, while leaving each Member State to decide upon its own corporate tax rates and bands. This, in the opinion of the Commission, retains the positive competitive effects of tax competition, while eliminating its harmful effects:

> [f]air competition on tax rates is to be encouraged. Differences in rates allows a certain degree of tax competition to be maintained in the internal market and fair tax competition based on rates offers more transparency and allows Member States to consider both their market competitiveness and budgetary needs in fixing their tax rates.[40]

However, while the case for CCCTB on grounds of simplification and reducing compliance costs is clear, it is less clear as to why the CCCTB is necessary on competition grounds. The prevailing trend in tax policy in developing countries over the preceding two decades has been of steady but slowly declining tax rates, coupled with targeted reliefs designed to reflect national priorities. The principal economic gain from free competition is specialisation. At a fiscal level, the use of targeted reliefs to facilitate specialisation is entirely consistent with the overall objectives of tax competition.

There has long existed a broad consensus among Member States that the use of targeted reliefs to attract profit shifting without any underlying economic activity does constitute harmful tax competition. The CCCTB, however, seeks to eradicate corporate tax competition on all grounds, bar rate. While the Commission's proposal expressed support for fair tax competition,[41] the CCCTB goes far beyond what is necessary to combat harmful tax competition, thus breaching one of the general principles of the EU: proportionality.

The 2011 proposal did not gain much traction, with the UK, and other, smaller, states firmly opposed. In 2015 the Commission revived the proposal, and it is arguable that without opposition from the UK, the measure stands a greater

40 Commission, 'Proposal for a Council Directive on a Common Consolidated Corporate Tax Base (CCCTB)' COM (2011) 121, at 4.
41 ibid.

chance of adoption.[42] The fact that Brexit might potentially have breathed new life into the proposal illustrates the increasing divergence between the UK and EU on matters of tax avoidance.

Tax, Brexit and the Caribbean

Caribbean states and territories have long viewed the United Kingdom as something of an 'honest broker', in particular where questions of tax and financial services are concerned. This might be explained, in part, by the fact that the UK, as discussed previously, looks more favourably upon tax competition, in general, than other Member States. In addition to this, however, the UK's long-standing constitutional and legal links to numerous Caribbean states and territories should not be overlooked.

The foregoing section identifies the tension between the EU's fundamental pro-competition objective and its more recent aim of tackling tax avoidance. Although Brexit will remove one of the EU's stalwart supporters of the competitiveness agenda, numerous Caribbean states and territories participate in formal dialogue with and decision-making within EU institutions.

There is, arguably, no region in the world with more substantial geopolitical links to the EU than the Caribbean. The islands of Guadeloupe and Martinique are both *Départements d'Outre-mer* (Overseas Departments) of France, making them part of the internal territory of the French Republic and are, therefore, within the territory of the EU. In addition, the French territory of Saint Martin, though a *Collectivité d'Outre-mer* (Overseas Collectivity) since 2007,[43] remains within the territory of the EU.

Beyond those territories that are within the territory of the EU, a number of Caribbean Islands comprising the EU's overseas countries and territories ('OCTs') maintain strong constitutional links with EU Member States, and, consequently, formal institutional links with the EU through the Association of Overseas Countries and Territories ('the Association'). The Association finds its basis in Article 198 TFEU, although its origins can be found in Article 227(3) of the Treaty of Rome.[44]

Although the Association's members are spread across the globe, the majority of its members are situated within the Caribbean. These territories include the former French *Département* of Saint Barthélemy; five British Overseas Territories (Anguilla, British Virgin Islands, the Cayman Islands, Montserrat, and the Turks and Caicos Islands), and six territories (Aruba, Bonaire, Curaçāo, Saba,

42 Dan Neidle, 'The Relaunched Common Consolidated Corporate Tax Base' [2016] Tax Journal 8.

43 Like Saint Martin, the *Collectivité* of Saint Barthélemy also transitioned from *Département* status in 2007, but, unlike Saint Martin, left the territory of the EU at this point.

44 'Les paye et territoires d'outremer dont la liste figure à l'Annexe IV dupèrent Traité font l'objet du régime spécial d'association défini dans la quatrième partie de ce Traité' Art. 227(3) Treaty Establishing the European Economic Community (25 March 1957).

Sint Eustatius, and Sint Maarten) previously comprising the Netherlands Antilles. The broad aim of the Association, as mandated by Art. 198 TFEU, is to 'promote the economic and social development of the countries and territories and to establish close economic relations between them and the Union as a whole'.[45] Institutional cooperation within the Association takes the form of the OCT-EU Forum, trilateral consultations between OCTs, their respective Member States, and the European Commission, and working parties. Among the objectives of the Association is the promotion of

> cooperation in the tax area in order to facilitate the collection of legitimate tax revenues and to develop measures for the effective implementation of the principles of good governance in the tax area, including transparency, exchange of information and fair tax competition.[46]

The association is also intended to promote 'regulatory convergence with recognised international standards on regulation and supervision in the area of financial services',[47] including the OECD Agreement on exchange of information on tax matters, and the G20 'Statement on Transparency' and exchange of information for tax purposes.[48]

It is evident, therefore, that the Association is seen by the EU as a means of bringing the OCTs into alignment with their own objectives. Beyond the Association, however, a number of other Caribbean states have extensive links with the EU through their historical links with the UK. 13 of the 15 full members of the Caribbean Community (CARICOM) are members of the Commonwealth of Nations.[49]

In general terms, these efforts have, thus far, proved successful, with OCTs moving (at times, somewhat grudgingly) into alignment with international standards on taxation. This is evidenced by the number of states – 13 out of 20 – featured on the EU blacklist being quickly shifted to the greylist.[50] These advances have, arguably, been made possible by the 'good cop, bad cop'[51] routine between the UK and the EU with respect to tax cooperation, discussed later. It

45 para 2.
46 Art. 73, Council Decision 2013/755/EU of 25 November 2013 on the association of the overseas countries and territories with the European Union ('Overseas Association Decision') OJ L 344/1.
47 Art. 71, ibid.
48 ibid.
49 One of these members, Montserrat, is a full member though not an independent sovereign state. Two full members of CARICOM are not, strictly, situated in the Caribbean: Belize, in Central America; and Guyana, in South America. A 14th CARICOM member – Suriname – has applied to join the Commonwealth.
50 See tables 1 & 2.
51 Susan E Brodt and Marla Tuchinsky, 'Working Together but in Opposition: An Examination of the "Good-Cop/Bad-Cop" Negotiating Team Tactic' 81 Organizational Behavior and Human Decision Processes 155.

may well be the case, however, that without the UK as a moderating influence on tax matters within the EU, it becomes more difficult to bring Caribbean states, countries, and territories into alignment with the EU on tax matters.

The UK as foreign representative for British Overseas Territories

The power to establish legal frameworks for overseas territories forms part of the crown prerogative.[52] Consequently, the constitutions of each of the Overseas Territories are provided for by Orders in Council – legal instruments enacted by the Queen with the advice of the Privy Council of the United Kingdom, albeit in reality the provider of that advice is the UK government. Although the constitutions of each of the territories differ from one another, every one of those constitutions circumscribes the power of the territories' governments to conduct foreign policy.

For example, the Constitution of Anguilla, Art. 28(2)(a) provides that the Governor is not obliged to act on the advice of the Executive Council on 'any matter that in his opinion relates to defence, external affairs or internal security'.[53] A more recent example can be found in Art. 55 of the Cayman Islands Constitution, which provides for an explicit grant of authority over external affairs to the Governor, subject to the delegation to local ministers on matters relating to:

(a) the Caribbean Community, the Association of Caribbean States, the United Nations Economic Commission for Latin America and the Caribbean, or any other Caribbean regional organisation or institution;
(b) other Caribbean regional affairs relating specifically to issues that are of interest to or affect the Cayman Islands;
(c) tourism and tourism-related matters;
(d) taxation and the regulation of finance and financial services; and
(e) European Union matters directly affecting the Cayman Islands.[54]

These powers, however, remain subject to extensive control by the Secretary of State in the UK. In general, any significant act of foreign policy done by any of the overseas territories requires a form of prior authorisation from the Secretary of State, known as an 'entrustment'.[55]

The international role of the overseas territories has expanded significantly in recent years. Four of the five territories in the Caribbean, as well as Bermuda, participate in CARICOM as associate members, while the sixth, Montserrat, is a full member of CARICOM. Nevertheless, in 2008, the Secretary of State refused

52 *Phillips v Eyre* (1870) L.R. 6 Q.B. 1.
53 Anguilla Constitution Order 1982, Schedule 1.
54 Cayman Islands Constitution Order 2009, Schedule 1.
55 For a more detailed discussion of the constitutional relationship between the UK and its overseas territories, see, in particular, Ian Hendry and Susan Dickson, *British Overseas Territories Law* (2nd edn, Bloomsbury Publishing 2018).

to grant Montserrat an entrustment to join the CARICOM single market and economy (CSME). In a private meeting of the House of Lords EU Select Committee, the Premier of the British Virgin Islands, Dr. Orlando Smith, described the United Kingdom's role in EU discussions as a 'champion for those countries that are properly regulated jurisdictions'.[56] Similarly, the Secretary to the Cabinet of Bermuda 'acknowledged that the UK's membership of the EU provided significant support for Bermuda'[57] and expressed his concern about the loss of the UK's voice at the negotiating table. Judith Freedman hypothesises that 'the fact that the UK is not at the table at the EU may make it more likely that the dependent territories will have to introduce changes or will suffer sanctions introduced at EU level'.[58]

Of course, it should not be inferred from the foregoing that the UK always acts in the interests of its overseas territories. In April 2018, the Sanctions and Anti-Money Laundering Act 2018 ('the 2018 Act') received royal assent, to the near-universal dismay of the UK's Caribbean territories. Of particular concern is the requirement on Overseas Territories under s51 to develop and publish registers of companies' beneficial owners. While s51(1) requires the Secretary of State to assist the Overseas Territories to do so on a voluntary basis, s51(2) of the Act requires the Secretary of State to prepare a draft order to compel compliance on the part of any territory that has not complied by the end of 2020. Commenting on the 2018 Act, Dr. Smith said it 'calls into question our very relationship with the UK',[59] while the Premier of the Cayman Islands, Alden McLaughlin, described the measure as 'a gross affront to the constitutional relationship we currently have with the United Kingdom'.[60] While not a single member of the House of Commons voted against any element of the Sanctions and Anti-Money Laundering Bill, a small minority of peers supported an amendment by Lord Naseby to reject the mandate on British Overseas Territories.[61] The former President of the Supreme Court of the United Kingdom, Lord Neuberger of Abbotsbury, described clause 51 as 'old-style colonialism'.[62]

Tax avoidance and the UK post-Brexit

The UK has, arguably, led the way on combating tax avoidance. At times, the UK's efforts at combating tax avoidance appear to have been stymied by the limitations placed on the UK by EU law, in particular, the jurisprudence of the

56 L Jay of Ewelme, 'Letter from the House of Lords EU Select Committee to the Secretary of State for Exiting the European Union' (*House of Lords*, 13 September 2017) <www.parliament.uk/documents/lords-committees/eu-select/Correspondence-2017-19/11-09-17-Overseas-Territories-letter-to-David-Davis-MP.pdf>.

57 ibid.

58 Judith Freedman, 'Tax and Brexit' (2017) 33 Oxford Review of Economic Policy 79.

59 Madison Marriage and Henry Mance, 'Why British Overseas Territories Fear Transparency Push' (*Financial Times*, London, 3 May 2018).

60 ibid.

61 HL Deb 21 May 2018, vol 791, col 924.

62 HL Deb 21 May 2018, vol 791, col 931.

CJEU. As discussed earlier, the CJEU has substantially curtailed a number of the UK's efforts at combating tax avoidance, in particular in cases such as *Cadbury Schweppes*[63] and *Marks and Spencer*.[64]

Brexit, as discussed in Chapter 2, therefore arguably creates new opportunities to introduce anti-avoidance measures which, at present, are not compatible with EU law. One possibility is lowering the threshold for the application of CFC rules and the DPT to behaviour that is 'harmful', as opposed to the higher standard of 'abusive'. Another possibility might be the removal of loss relief for cross-border losses, or the imposition of new withholding taxes on interest, dividends and royalties. Such approaches, however, would not be consistent with the broad tenor of British government policy in the field of taxation, in particular in the context of Brexit. The UK appears committed to using Brexit to enhance its competitiveness, in particular in the field of taxation. In addition to the planned cuts to corporation tax, there is evidence that government ministers and MPs view Brexit as an opportunity to introduce a litany of new reliefs and incentives.[65]

Nonetheless, the UK remains committed to BEPS and to tackling harmful tax practices, generally. As Judith Freedman rightly argues, '[t]he tension between tax competitiveness and opposition to tax avoidance will not be removed by Brexit'.[66] It seems likely that the United Kingdom will continue to steer the course it has been following for decades: tightening rules on tax avoidance and evasion while enhancing its own competitiveness through reductions in headline rates of tax.

Conclusions

Despite efforts at economic diversification, many Caribbean states and territories remain highly reliant upon inflows of foreign capital. Consequently, Caribbean states and territories are particularly sensitive to the tax policies of capital exporting nations.

There has been a marked shift in attitude, in the EU in particular, away from the view of taxation as a tool for enhancing competitiveness and towards regarding tax competition as a threat to Member States' fiscal bases. The past two decades have seen numerous efforts at clamping down on tax avoidance and the use of tax havens. While many of these efforts, initially, achieved very little by way of results, recent measures, including the EU Action Plan have achieved a modest degree of success. While many of these measures have been met with grudging acceptance by haven states, in particular in the Caribbean, some measures have encountered outright resistance. Consequently, economic muscle has been flexed, and the threat of 'defensive measures' against haven states has been deployed.

63 (n. 35).

64 Case C-446/03, *Marks and Spencer* [2005] ECR I-10837.

65 Edward Malnick, 'Sajid Javid Says No Deal would Be Opportunity for "Tax Incentives" and Attracting Global Talent' (*The Telegraph*, London, 15 September 2018).

66 See n. 58.

Throughout this process, however, the United Kingdom has been demonstrably more sympathetic to Caribbean states and territories. This is likely due, in part, to the constitutional links, both extant and historic, between the UK and numerous Caribbean states and territories. It is possible that the UK's exit from the European Union will result in the Caribbean losing one of its most effective advocates in EU decision-making. Despite this sympathetic view, however, the UK remains willing to impose stricter tax rules upon its unwilling territories and continues to implement sophisticated anti-haven legislation.

The prevailing trend in international tax law is clearly towards tougher anti-haven rules, with the states, both within the EU and beyond, willing to flex their political and economic muscle in order to compel haven states to fall into line. While Brexit may remove the brake on the pursuit of tougher anti-haven rules within the EU, it may be that, given the prevailing trend in international tax policy, movement towards such rules is inevitable either way.

9 Impoverished law

A review of Trinidad and Tobago's Immigration Act

Aschille Clarke-Mendes

In 2014, the Trinidad and Tobago (TT) government published the Phased Approach,[1] a document which reaffirms TT's commitment to the protection of refugees, and "frames the approach that Trinidad and Tobago will adopt to address asylum-seekers and refugees in the country."[2] The document cites numerous international documents to which TT is a party,[3] and outlines the domestic legislation to be used in the interim period between its publication, and the drafting of genuine legislation, in accordance with the Geneva Convention and its 1967 Protocol.[4] These domestic instruments include: the Constitution,[5] a 1979 Cabinet Decision,[6] the Trafficking in Persons Act,[7] The Immigration Act[8] and its subsidiary regulations.[9] Taken as a whole, these comprise a patchwork of procedures for dealing with immigrants, and powers and mandates of government officials, as a makeshift system of protection.

1 National Legislative Bodies/National Authorities, *Trinidad and Tobago: A Phased Approach towards the Establishment of a National Policy to Address Refugee and Asylum Matters in the Republic of Trinidad and Tobago* (June 2014). Hereinafter, "the Phased Approach".

2 ibid. 3.

3 UN General Assembly, *Convention on the Elimination of All Forms of Discrimination Against Women* (United Nations, Treaty Series, vol. 1249, 18 December 1979) 13; UN General Assembly, *Convention on the Rights of the Child* (United Nations, Treaty Series, vol. 1577, 20 November 1989) 3; The 1951 Refugee Convention; its 1967 Protocol; the UDHR; ICCPR; ICESCR; and the UNCRC.

4 *The Geneva Convention* article 36 and *The Protocol* article III, both oblige States to communicate to the UN Secretary-General the national laws and regulations they may adopt to ensure the application of said treaties.

5 *TT Constitution*. The Phased Approach outlines section 4 (Recognition and Declaration of Rights and Freedoms) and section 5 (Protection of Rights and Freedoms).

6 Cabinet in Minute No. 4809 (16 November 1979), pertaining to granting refugee status on 'political or economic grounds' is to be dealt with by the Immigration Act. Furthermore, 'refugees from natural disasters' is to be dealt with on a case-by-case basis and is dependent on the prevailing circumstances in TT as the cases arise.

7 Ministry of the Attorney General and Legal Affairs, *The Trinidad and Tobago Trafficking in Persons Act* (2011) Chapter 12:10 (Act No. 14 of 2011).

8 *Trinidad and Tobago: Immigration Act of 1976* (July 1976) Chapter 18:01, Published by: Ministry of Legal Affairs. Updated to December 31st 2009 ("TT Immigration Act").

9 *Trinidad and Tobago Immigration Regulations*, Chapter 18:01, Published by: Ministry of Legal Affairs. Updated to December 31st 2009 ("Immigration Regulations").

The Immigration Act is the primary device for the determination of not only refugee status, but all other immigration-related matters. However, where said Act's provisions resemble those that would adhere to the internationally recognised standards for protection of vulnerable immigrants, they stand as merely ersatz to comprehensive, refugee-specific legislation. The underlying problems stemming from the Immigration Act are that it grants the Minister of National Security and the Chief Immigration Officer (including any of their delegates)[10] broad discretion with respect to entry and exclusion and results in a deprivation of liberty and a violation of freedom of movement. Immigration authorities are receiving training from the UNHCR, but this is an ongoing process.

Simultaneously, the provisions (especially those relating to the duties and obligations of immigration authorities) are vague and confusing, and furthermore, many of the Act's provisions are obsolete or are contrary to international human rights practices. This observation was made as early as 1981, when Justice KC McMillan contended that the Immigration Act "appears to contain many pitfalls for the unwary."[11]

Several TT High Court cases help to show how, in the absence of comprehensive refugee-specific legislation, immigration authorities have misinterpreted and misapplied its provisions, resulting in undue detention, wrongful execution of deportation orders and the dereliction of due process, the violation of fundamental tenets of natural justice. Where the statute is unelaborate as to procedure, the High Court has had to step in to fill the gap. So far, there have been many instances where judges have had to employ "judicial activism" to remedy human rights violations manifested from Parliament's reluctance to amend the Immigration Act.

Judicial activism

Of greater consequence than the views expressed by the citizenry is the silence of legislation on the matter and the combined effect of both. Professor Rose-Marie Belle Antione, in a 2015 panel discussion at the Hall of Justice, Port-of-Spain, stated that the Commonwealth Caribbean 'is out of sync with many . . . international human rights norms and they can be rendered invisible in our domestic legal systems if we do not make a concerted effort to highlight them'.[12] Antoine suggested that part of the reason why litigation on human rights is sparse is not only because of cultural attitudes but because the citizenry is simply unaware of human rights.[13] Therefore, she called upon courts to introduce meaningful ways

10 TT Immigration Act, section 2.

11 *Francisco Centeno v Chief Immigration Officer* (1981) No. 3092 A (per J McMillan).

12 Rose-Marie Belle Antoine, 'Panel Discussion – Address by Professor Rose-Marie Belle Antoine' in *Who's Afraid of Human Rights? The Judge's Dilemma* (Judicial Education Institute of Trinidad and Tobago Fifth Distinguished Jurist Lecture 2015 by Dame Linda Dobbs, D.B.E.) 78 <www.ttlawcourts.org/jeibooks/books/DJLDobbs_final.pdf>.

13 ibid. 84.

to address social concerns.[14] This paper will now address two provisions, common to common law jurisdictions and to TT in particular: the ouster clause, and the savings law clause, and will explore how judges have been able to overcome them, championing the inherent worth of the person.

Ouster clauses are provisions included in legislation to exclude judicial review of acts and decisions of the executive and may be taken as a limit to the court's role in the balance produced by the separation of powers doctrine. Courts in common law jurisdictions are increasingly challenging these clauses, but Lord Diplock has been clear that judges must be cognizant of when to be modest in their competencies and when to exercise judicial activism.[15] This trend has not evaded TT. Indeed, at the Community level, the CCJ appears to encourage domestic courts of State parties to apply a liberal interpretation so as to harmonise it with Community law, even if it were found in the Constitution itself, and especially where the clause may oust a 'fundamental principle that gives effect to the Rule of Law'.[16]

For example, Section 27(3) of the Immigration Act states that deportation orders are beyond the reach of 'any Court,' unless the persons are citizens or residents.[17] Section 30 is yet another of these clauses which deprives the court from jurisdiction to 'review, quash, reverse, restrain or otherwise interfere' with any decision, proceeding or order from the Chief Immigration Officer, Minister or Special Inquiry Officer concerning detention or deportation, 'on any ground whatsoever', unless the person is a citizen or resident.[18] This section was a preliminary matter in the case of *Ekwedike*, where the Court concluded that section 30 must be read against *Anisminic* principles;[19] where the authority has acted ultra vires, the decision must be void ab initio.[20]

Power to appeal a deportation order is statutorily under the Minister's purview. Section 28 of the Trinidad and Tobago Immigration Act lays out the powers of the Minister responsible for Immigration,[21] as it pertains to dismissing an appeal against a deportation order.[22] Hidden within its subsections are both the provisions for non-refoulement, and humanitarian and compassionate considerations, both incarnated as executive discretionary powers of the Minister to either stay or quash the order, but it is unclear as to procedure.

14 ibid. 85.
15 Lord Diplock, 'The Protection of the Law' (October 1978) *WILJ* 12.
16 *Shanique Myrie v Barbados* [2013] CCJ 3 [81].
17 *Immigration Act*, section 27(3).
18 *Immigration Act*, section 30. The exception also applies where the person has applied for residency under section 31(3).
19 See *Anisminic Ltd v Foreign Compensation Commission* [1968] UKHL 6.
20 *Henry Obumneme Ekwedike v The Chief Immigration Officer and The AG* (2017) HC 2148/2017 [3].
21 "Minister responsible for Immigration" is the verbatim term provided under the interpretation clause (section 2). Today, this person is the Minister of National Security, hereinafter referred to as simply, 'the Minister'.
22 *TT Immigration Act*, section 28.

This issue arose in the case of *Sodiq*, where a Nigerian citizen entered TT illegally and married.[23] He pursued naturalisation at the Immigration Authorities, only to be placed under several consecutive Orders of Supervision and given the opportunity to purchase his own ticket back to Nigeria.[24] When he failed to do so by the stipulated date, a Special Inquiry was scheduled, wherein the Special Inquiry Officer served a deportation order.[25] After Sodiq's initial appeal to the minister was dismissed,[26] he launched a separate appeal under regulation 28 (now section 28 of the Immigration Act); on humanitarian and compassionate (H&C) grounds.[27] However, the deportation order was executed while his H&C application was pending.[28]

The court reasoned that in the absence of legislation specifying a procedure,[29] regulation 28 does not require a special application to be made; the Minister needs only to consider the facts revealed at the Special Inquiry to grant such special relief.[30] The court came to this conclusion upon considering regulation 30 (written representations with respect to regulation 28) in conjunction with two prescribed forms. The court determined that it is only in the interest of fairness that a deportee be given ample opportunity to appeal to the Minister for these grounds; be given the opportunity to present further facts for H&C; and further, that the Minister must consider the application.[31] Otherwise, the Minister will have made an improper exercise of their discretion and a breach of natural justice.

A major hurdle amending the TT Immigration Act is the exhausting endeavour of successfully challenging so-called 'savings law clauses' within the constitution. Savings law clauses are common features of constitutions of former British colonies,[32] included at independence, initially so as to provide continuity of the law by marrying common law rights and constitutional protections.[33] However, these provisions have served to confound jurisprudential construction, as courts have struggled to reconcile their municipal law with their international human rights obligations.[34]

In TT's constitution, there are two such clauses: a 'general savings clause' that saves all law existing prior to the constitution's enactment from judicial challenge,

23 *Sodiq Olalekan v The Minister of National Security* (2010) HC 3671/2009 [2].
24 ibid. [3].
25 ibid. [4].
26 ibid. [8].
27 ibid. [10].
28 ibid. [1].
29 ibid. [33].
30 ibid. [17].
31 ibid. [41]–[42].
32 For instance, *Commonwealth of Australia Constitution Act* [Australia], 9 July 1900 [108]; *Constitution of the Republic of Singapore* Act 8/65, 9 August 1965 [162]; or, closer to home: *Constitution of Barbados* [Barbados], 30 November 1966 [26].
33 Margaret A Burham, 'Saving Constitutional Rights from Judicial Scrutiny: The Savings Clause in the Law of the Commonwealth Caribbean' (2005) 36 U. Miami Inter-Am. L. Rev 249.
34 ibid.

including those laws which are incompatible with the fundamental rights guaranteed by the constitution itself, and includes the Immigration Act;[35] and a 'special savings law clause' which stipulates that if an Act expressly declares itself exempt from the Constitution's sections 4 and 5, it shall have effect regardless of its inconsistency, given that its Bill was passed by both Houses of Parliament by at least a three-fifths majority in each.[36]

This becomes problematic in instances of particular importance for human rights protections. For instance, in the context of the death penalty debate, the Privy Council has made a series of conflicting judgements in Commonwealth Caribbean death penalty cases.[37]

For instance, in the 2003 TT case of *Roodal*, the Privy Council reasoned that whereas the clause in question prohibited "invalidation" of any pre-existing law, section 5(1) of the 1976 Constitution required modifications to bring the law into conformity with the constitution, to alter the mandatory nature of the death penalty without invalidating it.[38] One year later, the Privy Council, in a split decision, rejected *Roodal's* reasoning, leading to an impassioned dissent from Lord Nicholls of Birkenhead, who lambasted the majority's dereliction of international law.[39] In analysing these cases, Jamaican attorney-at-law, Anthony Gifford, reasoned that the savings law clauses are 'most objectionable' and leave the law 'frozen in the mould of the 1960s,' urging that, 'A living constitution must be capable of interpretation according to the developing standards of the day'.[40]

35 *TT Constitution Ch 1, pt II*, section 6 (1): Nothing in sections 4 and 5 shall invalidate – (a) an existing law; (b) an enactment that repeals and re-enacts an existing law without alteration; or (c) an enactment that alters an existing law but does not derogate from any fundamental right guaranteed by this Chapter in a manner in which or to an extent to which the existing law did not previously derogate from that right.

36 *TT Constitution,* section 13: (1) An Act to which this section applies may expressly declare that it shall have effect even though inconsistent with sections 4 and 5 and, if any such Act does so declare, it shall have effect accordingly unless the Act is shown not to be reasonably justifiable in a society that has a proper respect for the rights and freedoms of the individual. (2) An Act to which this section applies is one the Bill for which has been passed by both Houses of Parliament and at the final vote thereon in each House has been supported by the votes of not less than three-fifths of all the members of that House.

37 See the Barbados case of *Boyce v The Queen* [2004] UKPC 32, where the Privy Council reasoned international human rights law notwithstanding, the death penalty was saved by the savings law clause, and the Court could not alter the provision, as that would breach the Separation of Powers [22]; and the Jamaican case of *Watson v The Queen* [2004] UKPC 34, where the Privy Council reasoned that the mandatory character of the death penalty was inhumane [62] and is consequently now within the discretion of a trial judge.

38 *Roodal v State* [2003] UKPC 78 [22].

39 *Matthew v. State* [2004] UKPC 33 [68] (Nichols, L., dissenting): 'Each government justifies its mandatory sentences of death for murder by pointing to a transitional savings clause in the country's constitution in respect of laws in force when the constitution was adopted. Each government seeks thereby to clothe a form of inhuman punishment with continuing constitutional legitimacy and an appearance of human rights respectability'.

40 Lord Anthony Gifford, 'The Death Penalty: Developments in Caribbean Jurisprudence' (2009) 37(2) International Journal of Legal Information 196, 201.

Caribbean legal scholar, Simeon McIntosh, notes that the special savings clause might be one of the most 'disabling' devices in the West Indian Independence constitutions and should be removed.[41]

Just as savings law clauses have obstructed the development of human rights-based law in the arena of the death penalty, so too does it stifle innovation in immigration. As *Valerio* illustrates,[42] the court is precluded from ruling unconstitutional a provision which allows the Minister to revoke permission of entry to any 'inmates', but the categories of persons whom the Minister may expel is more extensive and includes various groups of persons identified in the 'prohibited classes' who would have otherwise been denied entry in the first place.[43] Restriction on several of classes are undoubtedly unchallenged by international human rights law[44] since they go to the heart of State security. However, the provision contains some problematic items, which are anathema to contemporary human rights jurisprudence but are nevertheless cemented by the TT Constitution section 6. For instance, section 8(1)(e) prohibits, 'prostitutes, homosexuals . . . or persons reasonably suspected as coming to Trinidad and Tobago for these or any other immoral purposes'. More curiously, 8(1)(q) contains the vaguely defined catch-all, 'any person who from information or advice which in the opinion of the Minister is reliable information or advice is likely to be an undesirable inhabitant of, or visitor to Trinidad and Tobago'.[45]

The restriction against homosexuals has been unsuccessfully challenged before, on the grounds that the mere existence of the restrictions is inconsistent with Community law governing free movement of CARICOM nationals.[46] Maurice Tomlinson sought declarations that both TT's and Belize's[47] immigration acts are unlawful, and orders to amend them insofar as they purport to restrict entry of homosexuals.[48] Both States of TT and Belize acknowledged that they are bound by the *Shanique Myrie* decision;[49] that homosexuals are not a genuine threat to

41 Simeon CR McIntosh, *Caribbean Constitutional Reform: Rethinking the West Indian Polity* (The Caribbean Law Publishing Company 2002) 252.

42 *Francisco Javier Polanco Valerio and Johan Rodofo Custodio Santana v AG of Trinidad and Tobago* (2018) HC 1766/2017 [43].

43 *TT Immigration Act*, section 9(4)(e).

44 For instance, *TT Immigration Act*, 8(1)(l): persons believed to be involved in governmental overthrow; 8(1)(m): potential spies; and arguably, 8(1)(h): persons likely to be a charge on public funds.

45 Strikingly, these classes of people are grouped alongside 8(1)(i) 'chronic alcoholics'; 8(1)(j) 'drug addicts'; 8(1)(b) 'persons afflicted with any infection or dangerous infectious disease'; 8(1)(a) imbeciles and feeble-minded persons.

46 *RTC*, article 7 prohibits discrimination on grounds of nationality; article 45 governs free movement of CARICOM nationals; article 46 facilitates movement of skilled workers.

47 *Belize Immigration Act CAP 156*, section 5 contains almost facsimile wording as TT's 8(1)(e).

48 *Maurice Tomlinson v The State of Belize & The State of Trinidad and Tobago* [2016] CCJ 1 (OJ) [13].

49 ibid. [33].

the interests of society;[50] and that they should not bar them entry.[51] The CCJ[52] acknowledged the wealth of liberal human rights precedent that should be followed[53] but that state practice must also be taken into account;[54] the provisions have never been known to have been enforced to prohibit homosexuals,[55] and therefore both States still adhered to international principles.[56] However, Tomlinson argued that leaving the provision in place creates legal uncertainty, and there is no guarantee that it would be enforced when practices and polices change.[57] Much can be said about the fact that homosexual immigrants would be at the whims of immigration authorities at ports of entry, therefore not having true 'freedom' of movement, at least not in the 'republican sense',[58] but it is even more cogently argued in *Toonen* that if the laws are not enforced, then they must not be necessary for the protection of society's moral standards in the first place.[59]

This was the main rationale used by The Honourable Justice Devindra Rampersad in a recent case,[60] wherein the TT High Court struck down long-standing anti-buggery laws.[61] First, the Court acknowledged that the impugned provisions discriminatorily imposed criminal sanctions which 'have the potential to

50 ibid. [21].

51 ibid. [43].

52 ibid. [5]. The Caribbean Court of Justice had jurisdiction to hear the claim since it concerned the interpretation of Community law as enshrined within the RTC. This is the case notwithstanding TT not being party to the CCJ. The CCJ conceded: 'this Court is not the final appellate court for Trinidad and Tobago and therefore cannot be as definitive in its remarks concerning interpretation of the national law of Trinidad and Tobago' [39]. See also *Shanique Myrie*.

53 *Maurice Tomlinson v The State of Belize & The State of Trinidad and Tobago* (n 48) at [44], citing the UNDHR; ADRDM; and ICCPR.

54 ibid. at [17].

55 Famously, in 2007 Archdeacon Philip Isaac launched a campaign to oppose Elton John's entry into Tobago, but the Parliament of Trinidad and Tobago ultimately rejected this, and the concert went ahead as planned. Lester Haines, 'Elton John Free to Menace Tobago' (*The Register* 2007) <www.theregister.co.uk/2007/03/28/elton_ban_denied/>.

56 *Maurice Tomlinson v The State of Belize & The State of Trinidad and Tobago* (n 48) at [46]. This was the conclusion notwithstanding the CCJ acknowledging the precedent of *Toonen v Australia* (1994) Communication No. 488/1992, UN Doc. CCPR/C/50/D/488/1992.

57 *Maurice Tomlinson v The State of Belize & The State of Trinidad and Tobago* (n 48) at [53].

58 Philip Pettit, 'Republican Freedom and Contestatory Democratization' in Ian Shapiro and Casiano Hacker-Cordon (eds), *Democracy's Value* (CUP 1999) 168.

59 *Toonen v Australia* (1994) Communication No. 488/1992, UN Doc. CCPR/C/50/D/488/1992 [6.8]. See also, Terry S Kogan, 'Legislative Violence Against Lesbians and Gay Men' (1994) Utah L. Rev. 209, 233: 'Our society exhibits little interest in implementing direct control over sexual activity in private bedrooms. . . . Rather, the purpose of sodomy statutes is to proclaim the message that society hates homosexuals, whoever that category happens to encompass and whatever those people happen to do in bed'.

60 *Jason Jones v AG of Trinidad and Tobago et al* (2018) Claim No. CV2017-00720 [168].

61 *Sexual Offences Act,* 1986, *Chapter 11:28*, section 13 made persons convicted of "buggery" liable to imprisonment for 25 years. This Act replaced the earlier *Offences Against the Person Ordinance No.10* (1925) sections 60 and 62 and was therefore argued (unsuccessfully) to have been saved by the Constitution section 6 (general savings law clause). Furthermore, the Act contains a declaration as to its legitimacy, notwithstanding its inconsistency with the TT

be used oppressively by differently minded citizens as a foundation for hate as condoned by the State'.[62] Then, the court used a purposive approach to determine whether the special savings law clause saved the sections in question in that instance, finding that democratic societies worldwide are decriminalising homosexuality in conformity with international obligations,[63]but more importantly, that the section achieved no legitimate aim, and moreover, 'maintaining an unenforced law on the statutes makes no logical sense and, instead, seems more vindictive than protective or curative in any manner'.[64]

Juxtaposing *Jason Jones* with *Tomlinson* illustrates the similarity between immigration law and criminal law in that they invoke the underlying question of inclusion into society; as Ken Plummer observed: 'Questions concerning intimacy, citizenship and nationalism are deeply embedded in interpersonal, inter-group, national and international tensions and conflicts'.[65] Another question that should be asked is if the laws in question are not enforced, and if they represent a vestige of a previous era,[66] do they still reflect the 'will of the people', and if not, should they be struck out?

Like the anti-buggery laws, the Immigration Act's provision on prohibited classes is guarded by a savings law clause. Therefore, to emulate the *Jason Jones* victory,[67] and successfully challenge section 8(1)(e) of the Immigration Act, it would make sense to examine whether it achieves a legitimate aim, or if it is otherwise, 'more vindictive than protective'. Furthermore, the question should be asked as to whether the exclusionary letter of the Immigration Act, or its enforcement, has the effect of perpetuating oppression of the sort Justice Rampersad cautioned against, by imposing the stigma of criminality.[68]

Constitution, thus being saved by the Constitution section 13 (special savings law clause). Justice Rampersad addressed the latter in detail.

62 *Jason Jones v AG of Trinidad and Tobago et al* (n 60) at [95].

63 ibid. at [145].

64 ibid. at [156].

65 Ken Plummer, 'Intimate Citizenship in an Unjust World' in Eric Margolis and Mary Romero (eds), *The Blackwell Companion to Social Inequalities* (Blackwell 2005) 75.

66 For a discussion of modern changing views on Caribbean sexual expressions, see Toni Holness, 'Same-Sex Marriage in the Commonwealth Caribbean: Is It Possible?' in Macarena Sáez (ed), *Same Sex Couples – Comparative Insights on Marriage and Cohabitation* (Springer 2015) 163, where it is argued that Caribbean heteronormativity, a vestige of British colonialism, is being increasingly challenged in the modern context. For more on historical perspectives on sexuality in the Caribbean generally, see: Tamika Haynes-Robinson, 'The Evolution of Sexual Behaviour in the Caribbean: A Psychological Perspective' in Frederick Hickling et al (eds), *Perspectives in Caribbean Psychology* (Jessica Kingsley Publishers 2012). Haynes-Robinson attributes anti-buggery laws, and associated homophobia, to a combination of colonial-era Christian evangelic indoctrination, and the economics of 'breeding' enslaved people, which have together worked to shape sexual expression within slave-culture, which has led to pervading homophobic sentiments (370).

67 *Jason Jones v AG of Trinidad and Tobago et al* (n 60) at [143]: Justice Rampersad acknowledges that the case is likely to be appealed.

68 For more on how legislation reinforces deeply embedded homophobia in Trinidad and Tobago, and across the Caribbean more broadly, see, Joseph Gaskins Jr, '"Buggery" and

Theoretical perspectives on the phenomenon of 'crimmigration'

The result of placing immigration almost exclusively within the hands of the executive facilitates a system of exclusionary practices in TT, whereby immigration is conflated with criminality, creating a continuum of arrest, detention and deportation, which does not always conform to internationally recognised best practices. Criminalising illegal entry of asylum-seekers in particular has the effect of essentially punishing persons for desperation and further contributes to negative attitudes towards migrants in general. Furthermore, it perpetuates various myths regarding 'the other', the menace from abroad who leeches off the State.

François Crépeau observed this practice as unfounded, particularly with respect to undocumented migrants, since it serves to create a 'hyperbolic putative threat' of 'illegal' ('bad') migrants, in contrast to the 'good' ones, thus externalising complex issues and creating an 'other' to whom the State can attribute its problems.[69] In fact, Crépeau argues that the practice of detention fails to serve its supposed aim entirely, as it fails to address the underlying motivations of its target group; whatever deterrence-measure is erected, it must still be weighed with push-factors of persecution in the State-of-origin for the asylum-seeker, coupled with the persuasive pull-factors of the receiving State's labour market.[70]

Criminalising immigration is becoming a global trend, part of the exclusionary convergence. In Turkey, for instance, the International Crisis Group reports that a 2014 survey showed that there was widespread distrust of Syrian refugees (62 percent of those surveyed) and a belief that they are heavily involved in crime, despite the police reporting that between 2011 and 2014, only 0.33 percent of Syrians had been involved.[71] Further, Juliet Stumpf has coined this phenomenon 'crimmigration', which is a term used to explain the connection between several different topics, all interrelated: the rights of 'irregular' migrants; migrants' detention; the rights of victims of crimes; the criminalisation of migration; the

---

the Commonwealth Caribbean: a Comparative Examination of the Bahamas, Jamaica, and Trinidad and Tobago' in *Human Rights, Sexual Orientation and Gender Identity in The Commonwealth: Struggles for Decriminalisation and Change* (Institute of Commonwealth Studies, School of Advanced Study, University of London 2013) 429–54.

69 François Crépeau, 'Criminalising Irregular Migration: The Failure of the Deterrence Model and the Need for a Human-Rights-based Framework' (January 2014) 28(3) J.I.A.N.L. 213, 215.

70 ibid. 231–33. See also: Alice Edwards, *Back to Basics: The Right to Liberty and Security of Person and "Alternatives to Detention" of Refugees, Asylum-Seekers, Stateless Persons and Other Migrants* (UNHCR Legal and Protection Policy Research Series, PPLA/2011/01.Rev.1, April 2011) 1 ('There is no empirical evidence that the prospect of being detained deters irregular migration, or discourages persons from seeking asylum'.) as restated in United Nations, Report of the Special Rapporteur on the Human Rights of Migrants, François Crépeau, A/HRC/20/24, 2 April 2012, [8].

71 International Crisis Group, 'Turkey's Refugee Crisis: The Politics of Permanence' (2016) *Europe Report N. 241*, 14.

securitisation of borders; and human trafficking.[72] Also, Stumpf contends that the conflation of the two fields of law should come as no surprise, given that they both are, at their centres, 'systems of inclusion and exclusion'[73] and directly concern the relationship between the individual and the State. Exclusion on the grounds of criminality has been part of the Geneva Convention and its Protocol from the beginning.[74] However, the relationship between the two fields, Stumpf contends, has evolved to the criminalisation of immigration violations themselves.[75] The conflation of these two branches of law is in no small part due to what Stumpf refers to as 'membership theory',[76] a term synonymous with Sivitri Taylor's 'particularism'. One implication of particularism (membership theory, for Stumpf) in the context of crimmigration is that it has the effect of shielding the State from moral culpability; if the individual is a 'criminal', then they will likely cause great harm to the State. Then the State is fully justified in their exclusion.

Sheldon Novick writes on crimmigration in the context of the United States in the post 9/11 era, describing the broad utility of plenary powers in blurring the distinction between border control and deportations.[77] This conflation created a new status, 'unlawful presence', which applies to both newly arrived, irregular migrants, and settled long-term residents who had violated some federal provisions which requires their detention and subsequent deportation.[78] The statutes enabling these measures create a class of crimes called 'aggravated felonies' which transformed otherwise state misdemeanours into federal crimes, justifying deportation.[79] Administrators were given broad discretion to retroactively revoke permanent residency status for a broad range of 'aggravated felonies'.[80] These plenary powers of deportation also have the consequence of removing the jurisdiction of the court by creating an avenue for expedited removal, without individualised hearing, judicial review, or the right to appointed counsel.[81] This measure has essentially dissolved constitutional safeguards ostensibly afforded to any 'person within its jurisdiction'.[82] Novick explains that this broad administrative discretion not only deprives individuals of their human rights but invites discriminatory practices based on race or nation of origin.[83] All this was justified

72 Juliet Stumpf, 'The Crimmigration Crisis: Immigrants, Crime, and Sovereign Power' (December 2006) 56(2) American University Law Review 367.
73 ibid. 380.
74 See Article 1(F) of *the Geneva Convention*.
75 Stumpf (n 72) 380.
76 ibid. 396.
77 Sheldon Novick, 'Citizenship Is Not the Only Goal: Reform Should Bring an End to Mass Deportations' (2013) 27 Georgetown Immigration Law Journal 485, 509.
78 8 U.S. Code § 1182(a)(9(B)(2013).
79 Novick (n 77) 548.
80 ibid. 507.
81 ibid. 487.
82 *Constitution of U.S.A*, 1907, Constitution of USA [Constitution of U.S.A], amendment XIV, § 1.
83 Novick (n 77) 507.

under the familiar guise of protection from irregular immigrants who pose an economic burden on the State,[84] despite all evidence to the contrary.[85]

Ingrid Eagly argues that crimmigration within the United States has led to a second-tier system criminal law system for immigrants charged with crimes,[86] which allows for a correspondingly inferior system of rights for immigrants.[87] This results in discriminatory application of procedural safeguards without much public accountability.[88] One feature of the United States' crimmigration phenomenon is an expanded deportation regime, which takes power to appeal a deportation order from the realms of the courts, as well as expanding the grounds for mandatory detention.[89] This expansion and lack of accountability has led to racial profiling and arbitrary arrest, detention and expulsion of Latinos by police, without due process of law, sometimes in expedited removal procedures.[90]

For refugee law in particular, crimmigration has severe ethical repercussions. James Simeon points out that, in the context of Canadian refugee law, the invocation of Article 1F of the Geneva Convention has a lower burden of proof than both civil and criminal trials.[91] This observation was echoed by James Eyster, comparing the standard of review placed on migrants in RSD hearings with that on suspected criminals in criminal matters, submits that whereas society prefers a wrongful acquittal to a wrongful conviction in the criminal arena, the opposite is true for immigration.[92] Hamlin points out that whereas the volume of criminal cases involving citizens has gradually decreased in developed States in the early 2010s, the reverse has been true for non-citizens.[93]

The continuum of arrest-detention-deportation in TT is marred with substantial infringements on the right to liberty, one of the paramount rights in liberal Western democracies. As will be discussed, human rights law has largely supplanted refugee law and informs various aspects of immigration law, State

84 ibid.

85 Francine J Tipman, 'The "Illegal" Tax' (2012) 11 Conn. Pub. Int'l. L. J. 93. Tipman uses a mixed quantitative/qualitative approach to demonstrate that undocumented immigrants within the US pay more taxes as US citizens, contrary to a pervading idea that 'undocumented immigrants do not pay taxes'. In fact, she describes this myth as patently racist and 'inflammatory propaganda' (95), embodying, 'the exploitation of the immigration debate' (93).

86 Ingrid V Eagly, 'Criminal Justice in an Era of Mass Deportation: Reforms from California' (2017) 20 New Crim. L. Rev. 12, 38.

87 ibid. 18.

88 David Alan Sklansky, 'Crime, Immigration, and Ad Hoc Instrumentalism' (2012) 15 New Crim. L. Rev. 157, 158.

89 Eagly (n 86) 19–20.

90 ibid. 14.

91 James C Simeon, 'Ethics and the Exclusion of Those Who are "Not Deserving" of Convention Refugee Status' in Satvinder Singh Juss and Colin Harvey (eds), ***Contemporary Issues in Refugee Law*** (Edward Elgar Publishing, Inc. 2013) 284.

92 James P Eyster, 'Searching for the Key in the Wrong Place: Why Common Sense Credibility Rules Consistently Harm Refugees' (2012) 30(10) Boston University International Law Journal 29.

93 Rebecca Hamlin, 'International Law and Administrative Insulation: A Comparison of Refugee Status Determination Regimes in the United States, Canada, and Australia' (2012) 37 Law & Soc. Inquiry 933 at footnote 20.

sovereignty notwithstanding. To fully understand the breadth of human rights violations enabled by the vaguely guided administrative actions, it is imperative to first examine some key international safeguards to determine whether TT's violations are justified when balanced with considerations for national sovereignty.

International stance on detention

According to international human rights norms and laws, detention of irregular migrants or asylum seekers – whether upon entry to the State or pending deportation – must not be performed arbitrarily and must be predicated on law.[94] The UNHCR has emphasised that the State should only resort to detention once other, less restrictive, alternatives have been exhausted; it should be conducted only 'if absolutely necessary for reasons of national security or public order', and even still, such detention 'should not be unduly prolonged'.[95] In summary, detention must follow principles of necessity, proportionality, non-arbitrariness and with procedural safeguards in place – particularly, making judicial review and reparations for unjustified detention available to the detainee.[96] These safeguards are necessary especially where the individual has suffered deprivation of their liberty beyond the period which detention was necessary.

TT courts have pointed out that the State has not been consistently honouring these international obligations. For instance, in the 2018 case of *Eze*, the TT High Court ruled that a Nigerian national was detained without due process of law. She had not been informed of her right to legal representation and had been detained for an excessive length of time.[97] In granting damages, the High Court reasoned: 'The Constitution protects the fundamental rights of human beings even when they run afoul of our immigration laws'.[98] Then, whereas the State is granted a breadth of independence with respect to what it may consider 'national security or public order', the practice of detention is nevertheless circumscribed by interests of fairness for the individual as reflected within international human rights law.[99]

Immigration detention and deportations in Trinidad and Tobago

The powers to detain are laid out within sections 14 and 15 of the Immigration Act, which provide broad discretion to immigration authorities. Section 15 in

94 ACHR art7; ArCHR art14; ICCPR art9.

95 Executive Committee of the High Commissioner's Programme, *Expulsion*, Conclusion No.7 (XXVIII), UNHCR, 28th Session, UNGA Doc. 12A, A/32/12/Add.1 (1977), (e).

96 International Commission of Jurists, *Migration and International Human Rights Law: Practitioner's Guide No. 6* (Geneva 2011) 147.

97 *Isioma Loveth Eze v The Chief Immigration Officer & The Attorney General of Trinidad and Tobago* (2018) HC 4426/2016 [34].

98 ibid. [41].

99 *Ashingdane v United Kingdom*, ECtHR, Application No. 8225/78, Judgement of 28 March 1985 [44]; *Abdolkhai and Karimnia v Turkey*, ECtHR, Application No. 30471/08, Judgement of 22 September 2009 [127].

particular is problematic, as it enumerates many classes of persons who may be arrested or detained, without warrant.[100]

At the Privy Council, the Law Lords admitted to having considerable difficulty with its interpretation, calling it 'uncertain' and that it must therefore be 'resolved in favour of the liberty of the individual. The governing principle is that a person's liberty should not be curtailed or interfered with except under clear authority of law'.[101] Notably, the Privy Council in *Naidike* conceded that whereas individuals' liberty must be 'jealously' safeguarded by the courts, they must do so bearing in mind other considerations, such as those of national security: 'Proper consideration should be had to the maintenance of public order and other aspects of the public interest and powers conferred by Parliament should not lightly be rendered ineffective'.[102]

In a more recent case, Justice Kokaram echoed Justice McMillan's concern.[103] This case concerned the substantive question, whether the power to detain was lawfully excised by the first defendant, the Chief Immigration Officer. Mr Odikagbue, a Nigerian citizen, entered TT irregularly in 2007 via Venezuela.[104] He was detained by immigration authorities in 2015 after being arrested on drug-related offences, pending deportation proceedings.[105] In this case, he launched judicial review to challenge the authority to detain him, and also to detain him for an excessive length of time (one year), contrary to his right to liberty and to be deprived thereof without due process.[106]

The judge concluded that although detention was properly exercised, the length of time was unreasonable, confusing the lawful authority of the Chief Immigration Officer under the Immigration Act to detain for the purposes of holding an inquiry, with an authority to detain suspicious persons for criminal offences.[107] This infringed on the claimant's constitutional right to liberty.

Of importance for administrative law purposes is the fact that the court found that the powers to detain under sections 14 and 15 of the Immigration Act are subject to an implied limitation, whereby the detention must be for such a period that is reasonably necessary for its purposes; namely, for either to effect the purpose of convening a special inquiry, or to execute a deportation order.[108] The

100 *TT Immigration Act*, section 15: 'Every police officer and every immigration officer may, without the issue of a warrant, order or direction for arrest or detention, arrest and detain for an inquiry or for deportation, any person who upon reasonable grounds is suspected of being a person referred to in section 9(4) or section 22(1)(i), and the Chief Immigration Officer may order the release of any such person'.

101 *Naidike v Attorney General of Trinidad and Tobago* [2004] UKPC 49 [48].

102 ibid. [49].

103 *Odikagbue v Chief Immigration Officer and the Attorney General* (2017) TT HC 80 [60] (per J Kokaram).

104 ibid. [2].

105 ibid.

106 ibid. [4].

107 ibid. [9].

108 ibid. [47].

overriding considerations for this were observed as being: rationality, fairness, reasonableness, proportionality, and whether conducted with a legitimate aim.[109] Therefore, applying the Hardial Singh Principles, it was found that where a statute does not explicitly prescribe a length of administrative detention, the court is to assume that the legislature must have intended that such power could only be exercised reasonably and with a sui generis approach to safeguarding individual liberty.[110]

The case of *Valerio* likewise shows that the global trend of criminalising illegal entry has not eluded TT immigration authorities. There, the claimants were permitted entry to TT for a period not exceeding three months.[111] During this time, they were arrested and detained for suspicion of possession of firearms and ammunition, but those charges were dismissed.[112] The claimants were subsequently arrested by Immigration Authorities.

Section 9(4)(c) of the Immigration Act permits the Minister to revoke the status of "permitted entry" to any person who has become an 'inmate'.[113] The court noted that the Immigration Act has no definition for the term, instead deriving meaning from the Prison Act, which is interpreted literally.[114] The section therefore allows the Minister to declare 'inmates' as prohibited entrants, even where the person is awaiting trial and is presumed innocent, contrary to the provisions of the constitution.[115] Although the Minister neglected to make the declaration, the claimants were still arrested, only to be released on Orders of Supervision when the prison authorities recognised that there was no Order of Detention issued for them.[116] They were subsequently placed on consecutive Orders of Supervision, requiring them to return to Immigration Authorities on a weekly basis, therefore confining them to the country beyond their date of departure.

The claimants argued that in effect they were being retried by the Immigration Division for the same offences which the criminal court had already dismissed.[117] In the end, the court declared the actions of the Immigration Authorities to be unconstitutional but that the provision in question (section 9(4)) was in place

109 Ian Macdonald, *Macdonald's Immigration Law and Practice* (6th edn, Butterworth's Law 2014) 17:40.

110 *R v Governor of Durham Prison ex parte Singh* [1984] 1 All ER 983 at 985 (per Woolf J). See also *Tan Te Lam v Superintendent of Tai A Chau Detention Centre* [1997] AC 97 111.

111 *Francisco Javier Polanco Valerio and Johan Rodofo Custodio Santana v AG of Trinidad and Tobago* (n 42) at [2].

112 ibid at [4].

113 *TT Immigration Act*, section 9(4)(c).

114 *TT Prison Act Chapter 13:01* [2]: 'every inmate of any prison detained therein under sentence or conviction for any offence or under committal or remand pending trial or investigation on a charge of any offence'.

115 *TT Constitution*, section 6.

116 *Francisco Javier Polanco Valerio and Johan Rodofo Custodio Santana v AG of Trinidad and Tobago* (n 42) at [4]–[6].

117 ibid. at [8].

before the proclamation of the Constitution and was therefore saved as pre-existing law.[118]

Conclusions

The imprecision of the Immigration Act has made reality the promulgation of the phenomenon of crimmigration within Trinidad and Tobago, enabling severe deprivations of liberties by State actors against non-members. The courts have had to intervene in order to clarify discrepancies between statute and common law principles. But for sustainable change, amending this legislation is necessary for Trinidad and Tobago to realise the principles of non-discrimination. This is most pertinent, as Trinidad and Tobago is grappling with fallout of the Venezuelan Refugee Crisis. In a time marked by increased migration worldwide, Trinidad and Tobago is a case study for the EU and beyond on the consequences of statutory imprecision.

118 ibid. at [43].

Part IV

Sustainable development and regional governance issues in the EU-CARICOM

10 CARICOM regional integration and challenges in maritime law – a case study of Guyana's offshore energy developments

Alicia Elias-Roberts

In a world where the majority of our energy continues to be derived from petroleum resources, control of the territory in which these resources are located is important and directly connected to the upstream operations[1] from which everything else in the energy-value chain flows. The following quote from Judge Stephen Schwebel articulated this point when he said:

> Energy is at the heart of modern life. Industry, agriculture, transport, home, light, and heat, cannot function without it. The industrial revolution was fuelled by coal, which remains a vital if polluting resource. Since petroleum displaced whale oil in the 19th century, it has been the energy source of choice. Investments in the finding, production, transport, refining, and marketing of petroleum . . . remain huge. [These] complex and expensive arrangements require contracts and concessions.[2]

Petroleum development, if properly managed, has the potential to rapidly transform the economy of many developing countries through the various sources of income that the government will receive.[3] For developing countries like Guyana, maximising the benefits that can be derived from rents through sovereignty over prospective hydrocarbon deposits is particularly important. Many maritime boundary disputes are often fuelled by the suspected or confirmed presence of hydrocarbon deposits in maritime areas.[4] According to Justice Ndiaye,[5] '[t]he

1 The upstream operations include exploration, for, and extraction and production of oil and gas.
2 Judge Stephen Schewbel, 'Foreword to P.D. Cameron' in *International Energy Investment Law – The Pursuit of Stability* (OUP 2010).
3 These usually include licensing fees from exploration, then development, followed typically by production share, royalties and taxes on successful production on a recurring basis over what is hoped will be a long-term project.
4 Jan Paulsson, 'Boundary Disputes into the Twenty-First Century: Why, How . . . And Who?' (2001) 95 ASIL 122, 123. See *Oceans and the Law of the Sea: Report of the Secretary General*, UN General Assembly Fifty-sixth session UN Doc A/56/58 (9 March 2001) para 42 where in 2001 the United Nations noted that '100 maritime boundary delimitations throughout the world still await some form of resolution by peaceful means'.
5 Judge of the International Tribunal for the Law of the Sea, Hamburg, Germany. Updated list of judges <www.itlos.org/the-tribunal/members/>.

total number of potential maritime boundaries is 420, yet there are only about 200 boundary agreements to date'.[6] This figure from 2015 naturally excludes territorial boundary disputes and more recent maritime disputes awaiting resolution. A number of boundary disputes are renowned internationally, and many are significant sources of political tension, such as the maritime disputes in the South China Sea and the continuing dispute between the United Kingdom and Argentina over the Falklands/Malvinas. Even though the law has recently clarified several matters in this area, there are still several grey areas.

This chapter examines the approach of the Guyana government towards its legal maritime dispute with Venezuela. The application filed on 29 March 2018 in which Guyana asked the International Court of Justice (ICJ) 'to confirm the validity and binding effect of the Award regarding the Boundary between the Colony of British Guiana and the Unites States of Venezuela of 3 October 1899'[7] and the response of the Caribbean Community to the *Guyana v Venezuela* international dispute is discussed. This chapter also explores how regional integration might influence and impact this dispute.

Background of the Guyana-Venezuela border controversy[8]

Guyana is at the embryonic stage of becoming a petroleum exporting country, and it is interesting to analyse its approach to developing its energy sector. The disputed maritime zones in the Guyana-Venezuela case have their roots in a historical arbitral award.[9] On 29 March 2018 Guyana filed an application against Venezuela before the ICJ 'to confirm the validity and binding effect of the Award regarding the Boundary between the Colony of British Guiana and the Unites States of Venezuela of 3 October 1899'.[10] The dispute between Venezuela and Guyana concerns the legal title to the Essequibo region. Directly linked to the territorial dispute is the dispute over legal rights to the maritime zones connected to the Essequibo region. Venezuela calls the Essequibo area and the bordering sea a 'reclamation zone'[11] while Guyana regards the area as part of its territory and currently exercises effective possession over the territory.[12]

6 Tafsir Malick Ndiaye, 'The Judge, Maritime Delimitation and the Grey Areas' (2015) 55(4) Indian Journal of International Law 493–533 at 494.

7 *Cooperative Republic of Guyana v Bolivarian Republic of Venezuela (Application Instituting Proceedings in the ICJ)* (29 March 2018) <www.icj-cij.org/files/case-related/171/171-20180404-PRE-01-00-EN.pdf>.

8 For a detailed account of the history behind the border dispute between Guyana and Venezuela see Alicia Elias-Roberts, 'Legal Reflections on the Guyana-Venezuela Maritime Issue' (2014) 2(1) Caribbean Journal of International Law and Diplomacy 1–23.

9 *United Kingdom v Venezuela (British Guiana v. Venezuela Boundary Arbitration)* (1899) 92 BFSP 160.

10 *Guyana v Venezuela (Application Instituting Proceedings in the ICJ)* (n 7).

11 Venezuelan Foreign Office, Public Record Office (London), 'Exhibition of the National Congress of Dr Ignacio Iribarren Borges, Minister of Foreign Affairs, on the Geneva Agreement of March 17, 1966' (*Ministerio del Popular para Relaciones Exteriores*) <https://web.archive.org/web/20170914180942/http://esequibo.mppre.gob.ve/index.php/capitulo-i>.

12 See *Minquiers and Ecrehos* (1953) ICJ Reports 47, 55–57, the ICJ stated that the issue of possession and effective occupation was equated with sovereignty.

According to the statement of facts submitted by Guyana to the ICJ, during the 19th century, the United Kingdom and Venezuela were at the brink of war because of the conflicting territorial claims over the Essequibo area.[13] Subsequently, the parties agreed to resolve their dispute by an amicable settlement. As a result, an Arbitral Tribunal was empanelled to determine the borders in 1897.[14] The Tribunal consisted of five jurists: two on the part of Great Britain, two on the part of Venezuela (who were US nationals); and the president, the fifth jurist, was nominated by the four persons nominated.[15] A Russian jurist was selected as the President of the Tribunal.[16] The Tribunal issued the Arbitral Award on 3 October 1899. The 1899 Arbitral Award ruled that the Essequibo territory belonged to the British.[17] Venezuela was awarded the entire mouth of the Orinoco River and the land on both sides. According to contemporaneous evidence, it appears that at the time of the award, Venezuela treated the Arbitral Award as a success because the mouth of the river was considered to be more valuable, and the Essequibo territory was considered less valuable.[18] A few years after the Award a Joint Boundary Commission made up of representatives from Great Britain and Venezuela agreed on the specific demarcation between Venezuela and British Guiana.[19] A concrete marker was erected soon after. At this time all parties agreed that the matter was permanently settled, and in 1905 the Commission drew up an Official Boundary Map which was signed by the parties.[20]

Venezuela's change of position and the 1966 Geneva Agreement

According to the statement of facts, only in 1962, 63 years after the 1899 Award, Venezuela for the first time indicated that it changed its position. Venezuela issued a statement that 'there is a dispute between my country and the United Kingdom concerning the demarcation of the frontier between Venezuela and

13 *Guyana v Venezuela (Application Instituting Proceedings in the ICJ)* (n 7) para 26; See P K Menon, 'The Guyana-Venezuela Boundary Dispute' 6 (1972) Encyclopedia of Public International Law 212.

14 ibid. paras 26–31. See *Treaty between Great Britain and the United States of Venezuela Respecting the Settlement of the Boundary between the Colony of British Guiana and the United States of Venezuela*, signed at Washington (2 February 1897) <www.icj-cij.org/files/case-related/171/171-20180329-APP-01-01-EN.pdf> as Annex 1 of the *Guyana v Venezuela (Application Instituting Proceedings in the ICJ)* (n 7).

15 ibid. para 28.

16 ibid. para 29.

17 See *Award Regarding the Boundary between the Colony of British Guiana and the United States of Venezuela* (Reports of International Arbitral Awards, Vol. XXVIII, 3 October 1899) 331–40 <http://legal.un.org/riaa/cases/vol_XXVIII/331-340.pdf>.

18 *Guyana v Venezuela (Application Instituting Proceedings in the ICJ)* (n 7) paras 33 and 34.

19 ibid. para 35.

20 ibid. See also *The Agreement between the British and Venezuela Boundary Commissioners with regard to the Map of the Boundary* (10 January 1905) <www.icj-cij.org/files/case-related/171/171-20180329-APP-01-01-EN.pdf> as Annex 3 of the *Cooperative Republic of Guyana v Bolivarian Republic of Venezuela (Application Instituting Proceedings in the ICJ)* (n 7).

British Guiana'.[21] Venezuela based its change of position on a 'secret memorandum' purportedly written in 1944 by a Venezuelan junior counsel who assisted with the 1899 arbitration.[22] The memorandum alleged that there was some form of collusion between the Russian President of the Arbitral Tribunal and the British arbitrators.[23] Venezuela claimed that the decision of the Arbitral Tribunal had not been based on a fair arbitral process, and as a result it declared that the 1899 Award was null and void and that it would no longer abide by it.

At a meeting in Geneva in 1966, right before Guyana became independent, Great Britain and Venezuela adopted the Geneva Agreement and agreed to receive recommendations from a representative of the United Nations Secretary-General on ways to settle the dispute peacefully.[24] The Geneva Agreement was signed on 17 February 1966, and Guyana became an independent country on 26 May 1966.

It was unfortunate that in addition to the transformation that Guyana had gone through during the decolonisation process that, as a newly independent State, it was saddled with the border controversy. The timing of the change of position by Venezuela and the Geneva Agreement which the British signed leads to speculations that it was not a mere coincidence that this occurred while Guyana was preparing for independence.[25] Note that the Vienna Convention on the Succession of States in respect of Treaties[26] provides protection to newly independent States during the transition period and provides in Article 10 (2) that '[i]f a treaty provides that, on the occurrence of a succession of States, a successor State shall be considered as a party to the treaty, that provision takes effect as such only if the successor State expressly accepts in writing to be so considered'. However, this Convention does not apply to the Guyana and Great Britain situation.

According to Article VIII of the Geneva Agreement, Guyana became a party to the treaty when it gained independence in 1966. The Geneva Agreement provided for the establishment of a mixed commission, tasked with the duties of

21 *Guyana v Venezuela (Application Instituting Proceedings in the ICJ)* (n 7) para 40.

22 ibid. para 42. On 8 February 1944, Severo Mallet-Prevost, a Venezuelan junior counsel before the Arbitral Tribunal, wrote a letter which was posthumously published in the American Journal of International Law in 1949 ((1949) 43 AJIL 523).

23 ibid.

24 ibid. para 45. See *Agreement to Resolve the Controversy between Venezuela and the United Kingdom of Great Britain and Northern Ireland over the Frontier between Venezuela and British Guiana*, signed at Geneva (*Geneva Agreement*, 17 February 1966) <www.icj-cij.org/files/case-related/171/171-20180329-APP-01-01-EN.pdf> as Annex 4 of the *Cooperative Republic of Guyana v Bolivarian Republic of Venezuela (Application Instituting Proceedings in the ICJ)* (n 7).

25 ibid. para 41.

26 The *Vienna Convention on the Succession of States in Respect of Treaties*, 23 August 1978, United Nations Treaty Series, Vol. 1946, p. 3 acknowledges in the preamble 'the profound transformation of the international community brought about by the decolonization process' and sets out several provisions that would give the newly independent State or successor State the freedom and opportunity to consent and accede to treaties entered into by the predecessor State.

seeking 'satisfactory solutions for the practical arrangement' of the dispute.[27] In the event that the mixed commission failed to reach a solution after four years, Article IV of the Agreement provided that the parties would be required to select the means of peaceful dispute settlement under Article 33 of the Charter of the United Nations to resolve the controversy.

From 1966 to 2013 attempts at mediation and amicably resolving the border controversy between Guyana and Venezuela has been going on. Both countries agreed to the establishment of the mixed commission provided for in Article I of the Geneva Agreement. The mixed commission was established in 1966 and expired in 1970 after holding 16 sessions and without a resolution to the conflict. In 1970 the parties agreed to the Protocol of Port-of-Spain, which suspended the operation of Article IV of the Agreement for 12 years. The Protocol of Port-of-Spain expired in 1982. In 1990 both parties agreed to utilise Good Officer Process of the United Nations Secretary-General[28] in accordance with Article IV (2) of the Geneva Agreement.

Petroleum exploration and the *RV Teknik Perdana* incident

Diplomatic relations between the two countries took a drastic change in 2013. Venezuela's approach to the border dispute took a more forceful and aggressive tone following the *RV Teknik Perdana* incident in 2013. The *RV Teknik Perdana* was conducting petroleum explorations in the disputed waters[29] and was contracted by the US Texas-based Anadarko Petroleum Inc. to search for oil off the Essequibo coast. The Government of Guyana awarded Anadarko Petroleum an exploration license which authorised the vessel to conduct seismic research in the area. According to the Government of Guyana, Ministry of Foreign Affairs, an armed Venezuelan Navy vessel, the *Yekuana*, used force and detained the seismic research vessel *RV Teknik Perdana* on 10 October 2013.[30] The Venezuelan authorities instructed the *RV Teknik Perdana* to sail to an area in Venezuela where the ship's captain was charged with violating Venezuela's exclusive economic zone. Shortly after the charges were laid, the crew and vessel were released.[31]

27 Article I of the 1966 Geneva Agreement, as Annex 4 of the *Guyana v Venezuela (Application Instituting Proceedings in the ICJ)* (n 7).

28 The Good Office process under the United Nations is traditionally used around the world to encourage mediation and conciliation among disputing parties.

29 'Guyana, Venezuela Maritime Boundary Issue . . . Technical Team to Meet within Four Months' (*Kaieteur Newspaper*, 18 October 2013) <www.kaieteurnewsonline.com/2013/10/18/guyana-venezuela-maritime-boundary-issuetechnical-team-to-address-matter-within-four-months/>; and 'Oil Search in Disputed Guyana/Venezuela Waters Halted' (*Kaieteur Newspaper*, 20 October 2013) <www.kaieteurnewsonline.com/2013/10/20/guyanas-oil-search-halts-until-venezuelan-dispute-is-resolved/>.

30 ibid. The Ministry of Foreign Affairs reported in 'Oil Search in Disputed Guyana/Venezuela Waters Halted' (*Kaieteur Newspaper*, 20 October 2013).

31 ibid. Note that the captain was Ukrainian, the vessel had 36 crew members and included five Americans and a number of Russians. The vessel was Panamanian-flagged.

After this incident Guyana and Venezuela severed diplomatic ties. The Government of Guyana argued that as a sovereign State, Guyana has the right to explore for and exploit natural resources in its sovereign territory.[32] The Government of Guyana also initially argued that there is no 'disputed' territory but rather the matter is settled.[33] As a result, the Government of Guyana stated that Venezuela's claim to the Essequibo territory and the adjoining maritime area has no legal basis.[34] On the other hand, Venezuela argued that it has a legal claim to the Essequibo territory and that Guyana granted the permit for exploration in 'disputed waters'. While the arbitral award was agreed to be final and binding in international law,[35] the maritime delimitation was never formally settled. This situation is common, and the provisions of UNCLOS regarding the obligations of States with opposite or adjacent coasts to enter into agreements on the basis of international law is relevant. Later chapters will examine whether this specific obligation can be considered part of customary international law.

Guyana as a new frontier in the petroleum production countries

In 2015, immediately following the announcement about the discovery of oil in the disputed area, Venezuela laid claim to the waters where the oil was found. On 6 May 2015 ExxonMobil and its partners Hess and CNOOC Nexen announced a significant discovery at the Liza-1 well in the Stabroek Block.[36] Ten days later, on 16 May 2015 David A. Granger was sworn in as the 8th Executive President of the Cooperative Republic of Guyana. Ten days after the new President took office, on 26 May 2015 Venezuela issued a Presidential Decree No.1787 claiming all the territorial waters in the Atlantic Ocean off the Essequibo Coast within a 200-mile range belong to that State.[37] According to the ExxonMobil Guyana Project information website, the gross recoverable resources for the Stabroek Block are estimated to total more than 4 billion recoverable oil-equivalent barrels, based on discoveries at Liza, Liza Deep, Payara, Snoek, Turbot and other wells drilled in the Stabroek Block.[38] The resolution of this maritime dispute

32 The Ministry of Foreign Affairs report in *Kaieteur Newspaper*, 20 October 2013 (n 31).

33 See Statement made by Prime Minister of Guyana, Hon. LFS Burnham in 1966, Venezuelan Foreign Office, Public Record Office (London) (n 11); and Statement made by the Attorney General of Guyana, the Hon. Mr Basil Williams at the *Oil and Gas in the Caribbean: Training and Development Conference*, organised by the IMPACT, Improved Access to Justice in the Caribbean Project, Christ Church, Barbados, 30 September 2015.

34 "Guyana-Venezuela Border Dispute" as reported in *Keesing's Record of World Events Online* (1960–Present) Vol. 45; Menon (n 13).

35 ibid. See also Article XIII of the *1897 Treaty between Great Britain and the United States of Venezuela. . .* as Annex 1 of the *Guyana v Venezuela (Application Instituting Proceedings in the ICJ)* (n 7).

36 The initial reports stated that the discovery had about 1.8 barrels of high-quality crude oil.

37 See<http://energynow.tt/blog/venezuelan-president-blames-exxonmobil-for-tensions-with-guyana>.

38 See ExxonMobil Guyana Project overview <http://corporate.exxonmobil.com/en/company/worldwide-operations/locations/guyana/about-us/project-overview>. According to some

between Venezuela and Guyana will have major economic implications for both parties as billions of barrels of petroleum are involved.

In late 2015,[39] the new Government in Guyana took the controversy between Venezuela and Guyana to the United Nations. Outgoing Secretary-General, Ban Ki-moon, had committed to have the matter looked at. In 2016, the United Nations Secretary-General announced that if there was failure towards a solution of the controversy by the end of 2017, and unless both parties jointly request that he refrain from doing so, he would choose the International Court of Justice (ICJ) as the next means of settlement.[40] In February 2017 the new Secretary-General, António Guterres, appointed Norwegian ambassador, Dag Nylander, as his personal representative to mediate on the territorial controversy. Both Guyana and Venezuela agreed that they would attempt, until the end of 2017, to reach a resolution, failure of which the matter would be sent to the ICJ. After a series of unsuccessful attempts to resolve the dispute between the parties, the United Nations Secretary-General announced his decision to submit the dispute to the ICJ in January 2018.

However, it was reported that Venezuela 'back pedalled' on its recognition of the UN's authority to determine the next step on territorial controversy with Guyana.[41] In a statement made by the Venezuelan Foreign Minister, Jorge Arreaza, he said that his State does not recognise the jurisdiction of the ICJ and that Venezuela prefers political dialogue to resolve this dispute. The statement related that Venezuela signed the Geneva Agreement in 1966, which 'recognized' the sovereignty of Venezuela over the Essequibo and declared the Arbitral Award issued in 1899 in Paris as 'null and void'.[42] The Venezuelan Foreign Minister also said 'that is the treaty that governs the territorial controversy',[43] and

> the Government of Venezuela, faithful to its historical tradition and in accordance with the Bolivarian Diplomacy of Peace, reiterates its willingness to defend the territorial integrity of our homeland and maintain political negotiation based on the 1966 Geneva Accord, as the only way to reach a peaceful solution, practical and satisfactory for both parties and in favor of our Peoples.[44]

---

commentators, the latest oil discovery puts the estimates at 10 billion barrels, see 'Latest Guyana discovery opens the way to a new 10 billion barrel oil province and transformation for one of South America's smallest countries' <www.westwoodenergy.com/news/westwood-insight/latest-guyana-discovery-opens-the-way/>.

39 'Venezuela Rejects Referral of Border Controversy to Int'l Court' (*Kaieteur Newspapers*, 1 February 2018) <www.kaieteurnewsonline.com/2018/02/01/venezuela-rejects-referral-of-border-controversy-to-intl-court/>.

40 See letter from UNSG, 15 December 2016, Annex 6 of the *Guyana v Venezuela (Application Instituting Proceedings in the ICJ)* (n 7).

41 See 'Venezuela Rejects Referral' (*Kaieteur Newspapers*, 1 February 2018) (n 39).

42 ibid.

43 ibid.

44 ibid.

Application before the International Court of Justice: *Guyana v Venezuela* (Application Instituting Proceedings in the ICJ), 29 March 2018

Guyana made several requests in its application against Venezuela before the ICJ. Guyana asked the ICJ 'to confirm the validity and binding effect of the Award regarding the Boundary between the Colony of British Guiana and the Unites States of Venezuela of 3 October 1899'. Guyana also requested the court to adjudge and declare that: Guyana enjoys full sovereignty over the territory between the Essequibo River and the boundary established by the 1899 Award and the 1905 Agreement; that Venezuela shall immediately withdraw from and cease its occupation of the eastern half of the Island of Ankoko, and each and every other territory which is recognised as Guyana's sovereign territory in accordance with the 1899 Award and 1905 Agreement; that Venezuela shall refrain from threatening or using force against any person and/or company licensed by Guyana or engage in economic or commercial activity in Guyanese territory; and that Venezuela is internationally responsible for violations of Guyana's sovereignty and sovereign rights, and for all injuries suffered by Guyana as a consequence.[45]

It must be highlighted that while Guyana asked the court to confirm the validity of the 1899 Arbitral Award, its application would require the court to decide other matters, such as the use of force and the violation of Guyana's sovereignty and sovereign rights on the basis of customary international law. Since the Geneva Agreement does not provide for several of the requests made by Guyana, the application goes beyond the interpretation of the obligations under the 1966 Geneva Agreement.

There is the requirement to establish a dispute in the first instance before states can implement the mechanisms dealing with the obligations to resolve disputes by peaceful means under international law. The ICJ defined a dispute in *Mavrommatis Palestine Concessions* (jurisdiction) case [46]as 'a disagreement over a point of law or fact, a conflict of legal views or of interest between two persons'. Whether or not an international dispute exists is a matter for objective determination. This was pointed out in the *Interpretation of Peace Treaties* case[47] in which the ICJ noted that in the instant case 'the two sides hold clearly opposite views concerning the question of the performance or non-performance of certain treaty obligations' so that 'international disputes have arisen'.[48]

Sometimes a distinction is made between legal and political disputes, or justiciable and non-justiciable disputes.[49] However, it is extremely difficult to determine the objective criteria to clearly differentiate between the different categories. The role of political influences and considerations in inter-state disputes is obvi-

45 *Guyana v Venezuela (Application Instituting Proceedings in the ICJ)*(n 7) para 55.

46 PCIJ, Series A No 2 (1924) 11.

47 ICJ Reports (1950) 74.

48 ibid.

49 See H Lauterpacht, *The Function of Law in the International Community* (London 1933), especially 19–20; See also Malcolm N Shaw, *International Law* (7th edn, CUP 2014) 773–75.

ously a vital one, and many settlements can only be properly understood within the broader international political context. Further, how a state proceeds in a dispute will be often be conditioned by political factors. This is a subtle but very important distinction between a legal dispute as described in the *Mavrommatis Palestine Concessions* (jurisdiction) case and a situation that falls short of meeting the requirements of a legal dispute in international law. For the latter to be satisfied and for the process of peaceful settlement of disputes to operate successfully, there has to be a specific issue or issues readily identifiable to be resolved.

In fact, the parties disagree as to whether a territorial dispute exists in the first place. The current issue turns on the interpretation and application of the 1966 Geneva Agreement. Venezuela contends that under the Geneva Agreement, there is an implicit acknowledgement by the parties that the 1899 Award is invalid, with the result being that the dispute between the two countries concerning sovereignty over the Essequibo area remains unresolved.[50] In contrast, Guyana argues that the Geneva Agreement carries no implications concerning the validity or nullity of the 1899 Award. Guyana initially contended that the only subject in dispute between the parties is whether the 1899 Award is, as Venezuela contends, null and void.[51]

The British government and later the Guyana government initially argued that a legal dispute did not exist between Guyana and Venezuela because the matter was settled by a binding arbitral award several years ago. If this is the case, then an important question is, if this is not a dispute, how should this situation between Guyana and Venezuela be classified? Was this situation a political and diplomatic agreement that didn't rise to the level of a legal dispute? While this means unclear, this is now a moot point since, as indicated earlier, the controversy between Venezuela and Guyana was recently referred to the ICJ. By taking this course of action, Guyana therefore conceded that there is a dispute between the two States. The Ministry of the Presidency in Guyana in a press release stated that Guyana has recommended that the Secretary-General refer the matter for juridical settlement, 'which is the only remaining option'.[52]

It is submitted that submitting the matter for judicial settlement before the ICJ is not the only remaining option that Guyana has. Under Article 65(1) of the Statute of the ICJ, the court 'may give an advisory opinion on any legal question at the request of whatever body may be authorised by or in accordance with the

50 Official Statement by the Bolivarian Government of Venezuela, 'Venezuela Ratified Commitment to the Geneva Agreement on Essequibo' (*Ministerio del Poder Popular para la Comunicacion e Informacion*, 17 February 2018) <http://minci.gob.ve/2018/02/venezuela-ratifica-compromiso-acuerdo-ginebra-solventar-controversia-esequibo/>; and *El Nacional*, 17 February 2016 'Keys to Understanding the Geneva Agreement' <www.el-nacional.com/noticias/mundo/claves-para-entender-acuerdo-ginebra_11164>.

51 ibid.

52 Department of Public Information, 'Guyana Pleased with UN Secretary-General's Efforts to Resolve Border Controversy – President Granger' (Press Release, 19 September 2017), <http://dpi.gov.gy/guyana-pleased-with-un-secretary-generals-efforts-to-resolve-border-controversy-president-granger/>.

Charter . . . to make such a request'.[53] Article 96 of the UN Charter empowers the General Assembly and Security Council to request and provides that the General Assembly may authorise other organs and specialised agents to do so. Questions that can be submitted to the ICJ for advisory opinion to provide legal clarity on the situation between Venezuela and Guyana include: what is the legal status of Venezuela's Presidential Decree No.1787 of 26 May 2015 claiming all the territorial waters in the Atlantic Ocean off the Essequibo Coast within a 200-mile range belong to that State? Or what are the legal consequences of Guyana authorising oil exploration and production in the 'disputed maritime zone' in light of the claims made by Venezuela? However, the option to use the Advisory Opinion of the ICJ is now moot since Guyana has conceded that it now has a contentious dispute with Venezuela by agreeing that the matter be settled by the ICJ.

Looking at the dispute procedurally, it is unclear whether the ICJ would accept the unilateral application by Guyana and find that it has jurisdiction over the dispute.[54] The reason why this is unclear is because, while the Geneva Agreement delegates to the UN Secretary-General the power to refer the dispute to 'judicial settlement' and provides that he 'shall choose another of the means stipulated in Article 33 of the Charter of the United Nations', there are doubts about whether this broad interpretation of the delegation power of the Secretary-General will be binding. In the letter from the UN Secretary-General[55] to the President of Guyana, there is reference to Article IV of the 1966 Geneva Agreement and Article 33 of the UN Charter as the basis for his power to decide the dispute settlement mechanism. The letter from the UN Secretary-General stated that

> if by the end of 2017, the Secretary General concludes that significant progress had not been made toward arriving at a full agreement for the solution of the controversy, he will choose the International Court of Justice as the next means of settlement, unless your Government and the Government of Venezuela jointly request that he refrain from doing so.

In the *Corfu Channel* case,[56] there was a similar referral to the ICJ. The UN Security Council (SC) recommended the referral of the dispute between Albania and the UK to the ICJ. The United Kingdom argued that the ICJ could exercise jurisdiction based on the Security Council resolution which recommended that the UK and Albania submit their dispute to the ICJ. In the judgment rendered on 25 March 1948, the ICJ rejected the preliminary objections raised by Albania concerning

53 1945 *Statute of the International Court of Justice* (ICJ), 59 Stat.1031; T.S. 993; 39 AJIL Supp. 215 (1945).

54 See Julian Ku, 'Does the ICJ Have Binding Jurisdiction over the Guyana-Venezuela Border Controversy? Probably, But Maybe Not' (*Opinio Juris*, 12 February 2018) <http://opiniojuris.org/2018/02/12/does-the-icj-have-jurisdiction-over-the-guyana-venezuela-border-controversy-probably/#comments>.

55 See letter from UNSG, 15 December 2016, Annex 6 of the *Cooperative Republic of Guyana v Bolivarian Republic of Venezuela (Application Instituting Proceedings in the ICJ)* (n 7).

56 *Corfu Channel* (UK v Albania) Preliminary Objection, (1947) ICJ Reports 15.

jurisdiction and admissibility of the application.[57] However, the court did not find the SC referral binding because the SC resolution was non-binding. In contrast, in the dispute between *Guyana v Venezuela* the Geneva Agreement can be argued to be a binding treaty which allows the UNSG to make the referral which he did.

Another issue that the ICJ will have to determine is whether as one of those means, the UN Secretary-General can choose judicial resolution by the ICJ. Article IV (2) Geneva Agreement does not expressly state that the ICJ is a means of dispute settlement, but instead it provides that:

> If, within three months of receiving the final report, the Government of Guyana and the Government of Venezuela should not have reached agreement regarding the choice of one of the means of settlement provided in Article 33 of the Charter of the United Nations, they shall refer the decision as to the means of settlement to an appropriate international organ upon which they both agree or, failing agreement on this point, to the Secretary-General of the United Nations. If the means so chosen do not lead to a solution of the controversy, the said organ or, as the case may be, *the Secretary-General of the United Nations shall choose another of the means stipulated in Article 33 of the Charter of the United Nations*, and so on until the controversy has been resolved or until all the means of peaceful settlement there contemplated have been exhausted[58] (emphasis mine).

It is submitted that even though Article 33 of the UN Charter[59] does not expressly refer to the ICJ either, it mentions 'judicial settlement' as one of the means for the pacific settlement of disputes, and the ICJ would be classified under 'judicial settlement' in this list. Further, it is submitted that Article IV of the Geneva Agreement could be read as Guyana has submitted in its application to the ICJ, as a compromissory clause which confers jurisdiction on the ICJ indirectly.

Uncertainty and unanswered questions

The dispute between Guyana and Venezuela includes both substantive and procedural elements.[60] From a substantive viewpoint, there are several unanswered

57 On the issue of jurisdiction, the ICJ found, inter alia, that a communication dated 2 July 1947, addressed to it by the Government of Albania, constituted a voluntary acceptance of its jurisdiction. It recalled on that occasion that the consent of the parties to the exercise of its jurisdiction was not subject to any particular conditions of form and stated that, at that juncture, it could not hold to be irregular a proceeding not precluded by any provision in those texts.

58 Article IV of the 1966 Geneva Agreement, as Annex 4 of the *Guyana v Venezuela (Application Instituting Proceedings in the ICJ)* (n 7).

59 1945 Charter of the United Nations (San Francisco) I UNTS xvi, Article 33 lists 'negotiation, enquiry, mediation, conciliation, arbitration, judicial settlement, resort to regional agencies or arrangements, or other peaceful means of their own choice' as options for 'pacific settlement of disputes'.

60 See Frederica Paddeu and Brendan Plant, 'The Dispute between Guyana and Venezuela over the Essequibo Region' (*EJIL Talk*, 11 April 2018) <www.ejiltalk.org/the-dispute-between-guyana-and-venezuela-over-the-essequibo-region/>.

questions that arise under this dispute. Is there a 'dispute' in the first place? Does the government of Guyana have the right to undertake unilateral action with exploration in the 'disputed' area in light of Venezuela's claim? Procedurally, will the ICJ find that it has jurisdiction in this case?

Venezuela has rejected that the ICJ has jurisdiction of the dispute, and several of the arguments to support its position are worth noting.[61] The first argument is that the broad interpretation of the delegation power of the Secretary-General is not supported by the Geneva Agreement. As a consequence, the referral by the UNSG exceeds its competence as a 'good officer' as agreed by the parties.[62] The second argument is that in interpreting Article IV of the Geneva Agreement in isolation without reference to the whole of the agreement contravenes the spirit, purpose and object of the treaty. There is strength in this argument. It is submitted that the preamble of the agreement, while not binding, is still relevant in interpreting the obligations under the treaty. The preamble under the Geneva Agreement provides that the controversy should be 'amicably resolved in a manner acceptable to both parties'. This means that Guyana's unilateral application to the ICJ may not be in conformity with the Geneva Agreement.[63] The third and final argument is that the nature of the dispute settlement mechanism is unacceptable to Venezuela. It appears that Venezuela has a long-standing reservation about third-party dispute settlement.[64] It does not recognise the jurisdiction of the court either generally or for this dispute specifically.

It is therefore submitted that it is uncertain whether the ICJ will exercise jurisdiction in this matter because, while the 1966 Geneva Agreement delegates to the UN Secretary-General, the power to refer the dispute to 'judicial settlement' provides that he 'shall choose another of the means stipulated in Article 33 of the Charter of the United Nations'. As stated previously, it is doubtful whether this broad interpretation of the delegation power of the Secretary-General will be binding.

The response of CARICOM to the *Guyana v Venezuela* border controversy

Shortly after Guyana's oil announcement in 2015, the Government of Venezuela issued a Presidential Decree No: 1787 on 26 May 2015. Two months later, at a

61 See ibid.

62 ibid. See Comunicado Oficial, 'Venezuela Proposes to Guyana to Restart Diplomatic Contacts to Resolve Territorial Controversy' (*Vice Presidencia, Bolivarian Government of Venezuela*, 30 March 2018) <www.vicepresidencia.gob.ve/index.php/2018/03/30/venezuela-propone-a-guyana-reiniciar-contactos-diplomaticos-para-solucionar-controversia-territorial/>.

63 See *Maritime Delimitations and Territorial Questions between Qatar v Bahrain Case (Jurisdiction and Admissibility No. 1)* (1994) ICJ Rep 112, where similar issues were raised.

64 See Paddeu and Plant (n 60) stating that 'Venezuela's distrust of international dispute settlement (it has recently withdrawn from the ICSID convention and the jurisdiction of the Inter-American Court of Human Rights), it would be unsurprising if it decided not to appear before the ICJ in the proceedings unilaterally commenced by Guyana'; and Denis Charbol, 'Guyana, Venezuela Must Abide World Court Ruling on Border Controversy: Greenidge' (*Demerara Waves*, 31 March 2018) <http://demerarawaves.com/2018/03/31/guyana-venezuela-must-abide-world-court-ruling-on-border-controversy-greenidge/>.

July 2015 CARICOM Heads of Government meeting,[65] the Heads made a statement in response to the Venezuelan Decree and emphasised 'the need for peace and stability' as the basis for enhancing regional cooperation and the development of both countries. The Heads noted the negative implications which the decree has for the peace, security and development of the Cooperative Republic of Guyana and the negative implications for several other CARICOM countries.[66] The CARICOM Heads of Government called for adherence to accepted principles of international law in relation to the delineation and delimitation of the Exclusive Economic Zone and Continental Shelf in the region. Four CARICOM Member States were affected by the Presidential Decree by Venezuela. Not only was Guyana affected, but Suriname, Barbados and Trinidad and Tobago were also affected. The CARICOM Heads of Government called on Venezuela to withdraw those elements of Decree 1787 insofar as they affected the maritime space of CARICOM members, and Venezuela subsequently amended the decree.[67]

The CARICOM States issued a statement which indicated that they do not accept any unilateral proclamation which is inconsistent with international law. They emphasised that CARICOM States have legitimate territorial and maritime entitlements that conform to international law and that must be respected.[68] The statement issued by CARICOM noted that Guyana's pursuit of a peaceful settlement by the ICJ was supported by the CARICOM grouping. The Heads of Government noted that

> if by the end of 2017, the Secretary-General [of the United Nations] concludes that significant progress has not been made toward arriving at a full agreement for the solution of the controversy, he will choose the International Court of Justice as the next means of settlement,

unless the Governments of Guyana and Venezuela 'jointly request that he refrain from doing so'.[69]

The attempt to have the dispute settled by peaceful means is supported by one of five pillars which underpin the CARICOM integration and is also one of eight strategic priorities in the Caribbean Community's Strategic Plan (2015–2019). The Council for Foreign and Community Relations (COFCOR), an

65 See, Guyana/Venezuela Controversy, <www.caricom.org/guyana-venezuela-border-dispute> and Statement on The Decree 1787 of Venezuela; Guyana Venezuela Border Dispute, <https://caricom.org/media-center/communications/press-releases/statement-on-the-decree-1787-of-venezuela-guyana-venezuela-border-dispute>.

66 ibid.

67 ibid. Note that as a result of these concerns, and in an effort to have the rights and entitlements of the affected Community Member States fully respected, a delegation of Heads met with the Vice President and Foreign Minister of Venezuela to express the Community's grave concern about Decree 1787.

68 ibid. Speaking on the issue at the Thirty-Sixth Regular Meeting of Heads of Government, in Barbados, the Rt. Hon. Freundel Stuart, then Chair of CARICOM, reiterated CARICOM's position of 'total support for the integrity of Guyana's territory and maritime space'.

69 2017 (July): Twenty-Ninth Intersessional Meeting of Heads of Government, Guyana.

entity established under Article 16 of the Revised Treaty of Chaguaramas to promote the development of friendly and mutually beneficial relations among Member States and to establish measures to coordinate the foreign policies of the Member States of the Community, including proposals for joint representation, and seek to ensure, as far as practicable, the adoption of Community positions on major hemispheric and international issues, among other issues, issued a statement in relation to the *Guyana v Venezuela* dispute.[70] The COFCOR noted that the Government of Guyana had filed its application with the ICJ on 29 March 2018 in keeping with the decision by the Secretary-General of the United Nations issued on 30 January 2018, within the framework of the Geneva Agreement of 1966, to choose the ICJ as the means that is now to be used for the settlement of the controversy between Guyana and Venezuela. The Ministers noted that the decision of the Secretary-General, which was in accordance with the principles and purposes of the United Nations Charter, was intended to bring a peaceful and definitive settlement to a long-standing controversy and the COFCOR reiterated its unequivocal support for the maintenance and safeguarding of Guyana's sovereignty and territorial integrity. This regional response is therefore supportive of the ICJ exercising jurisdiction over the case.

Conclusions

The earlier discussion highlights that CARICOM is a work in progress that aims to promote unity, regionalism and integration. The Caribbean community needs to develop capacity and expertise in the areas of maritime delimitation and oil and gas law. The Caribbean community should also adopt measures to promote the effective management of water resources and conservation and utilisation of living resources in the exclusive economic zone and other maritime areas under the national jurisdiction of the Member States. At the moment there is a regional Caribbean Energy programme, within the Directorate of Trade and Economic Integration at CARICOM and the Caribbean Centre for Renewable Energy and Energy Efficiency (CCREEE), which is an institution of CARICOM with a mandate to promote renewable energy and energy efficiency investments, markets and industries in the Caribbean. While these types of institutions and programmes help to provide oversight for government regulation of activities that have the potential to significantly harm the marine environment in the context of renewable energy, there is no entity nor system dedicated in the region to respond to the challenges of new petroleum developments, not maritime disputes involving petroleum resources. The *Guyana v Venezuela* incident is one example that highlights the need to strengthen the capacity of the CARICOM Community to respond to the challenges of maritime disputes, and in particular, those disputes involving petroleum resources.

70 See Communique: Twenty-First Meeting of the Council for Foreign and Community Relations (COFCOR), Nassau, The Bahamas, 7–8 May 2018 <https://caricom.org/media-center/communications/communiques/communique-twenty-first-meeting-of-the-council-for-foreign-and-community-relations-cofcor-nassau-the-bahamas-7-8-may-2018>.

11 SDGs and their impact on African, Caribbean and Pacific (ACP) group of states and CARICOM – soft law on its way through the legal order

Winfried Huck

It seems to be unlikely that the process of a neo-liberal-driven globalisation will come to a halt. Following economists like Joseph E. Stiglitz,[1] Angus Deaton,[2] Thomas Piketty[3] and UN Special Rapporteur Philip Alston,[4] a flagrant inequality in many directions as a major consequence remains still in place and will unfold its unjust potential unbridled in the future. Inequality should be confronted with the notion and content of capability approach, as observed by Amartya Sen,[5] M. Nussbaum,[6] in particular for women and girls, thoroughly good and better governance based on a strict rule-of-law principle, corruption free, and from a legal perspective underpinned with enforceable rights of individuals and or groups to get in possession of better existential conditions. Globalisation is not defined in a straight, logical way, and it is not only to be reflected in the present. It can be neither accounted

1 M Doyle and J Stiglitz, 'Eliminating Extreme Inequality: A Sustainable Development Goal, 2015–2030' (2014) 28(1) Ethics & International Affairs 5–13.; Joseph E Stiglitz, 'Inequality, Stagnation, and Market Power' (Working Paper 2017, Roosevelt Institute) <https://www8.gsb.columbia.edu/faculty/jstiglitz/sites/jstiglitz/files/Roosevelt%20Inequality-Stagnation-and-Market-Power.pdf>.

2 Angus Deaton, *The Great Escape* (Princeton University Press 2013) 5, 'Economic Growth has been the engine of international income inequality'.

3 Jenmana, Thanasak, Facundo Alvaredo and Thomas Piketty, 'Income Inequality Political Instability and the Thai Democratic Struggle' (Master thesis, Paris School of Economics, September 2018), 'The results suggest that the rise of income inequality stabilised at least from 2001 but remains at a formidable level contrasting all prior claims that inequality has been decreasing', p. 9.

4 Philip Alston, 'The Human Rights Implications of Extreme Inequality', *United Nations, General Assembly, 'Report of the Special Rapporteur on Extreme Poverty and Human Rights, A/HRC/29/31 (27 May 2015)* (NYU School of Law, Public Law Research Paper No. 18–06, February 2018) <https://ssrn.com/abstract=3117156>.

5 Amartya Sen, *Ökonomie für den Menschen* (5. Auflage, Deutscher Taschenbuchverlag, München 2011) 110 f., 134, 143, 148.

6 Marta C Nussbaum, 'Women and Equality: The Capabilities Approach' (1999) 138 International Labour Review 227–245. <https://doi.org/10.1111/j.1564-913X.1999.tb00386.x>; Martha C Nussbaum, 'The Capabilities Approach and Ethical Cosmopolitanism: A Response to Noah Feldman' (2007) 117 Yale L.J. Pocket Part 123 <http://yalelawjournal.org/forum/the-capabilities-approach-and-ethical-cosmopolitanism-a-response-to-noah-feldman>.

by mathematics, and the current process is definitely not to be owned and discharged solely by the West.

The vivid shadows of the past

Sometimes current and even future inequality has its roots in the past. The human memory in the Caribbean contains and reflects blatant inequality that starts to emerge after an Atlantic passage in the triangular trade, a former way of globalisation, in which over 10 million African men, women and children were cruelly transformed from free human beings to slaves.[7] This was a former expression of globalisation, and for nearly 400 years a trade scheme which was linked with genocide of the indigenous people living originally in the Caribbean like the Island Caribs, the Tainos, Arawaks, Guanahatabeys,[8] Siboney and other groups.[9] This memory of the Caribbean people also contains that the end of slavery does not mean a fresh start staffed out with all rights and possibility on a normative concept of equality, but for more the persistence of a long-lasting inequality,[10] which can be demonstrated even today in the condition of illiteracy.[11]

Illiteracy is the lack of education (SDG 4), which is quite often detected in the group of indigenous people. One of most frequent critiques against the conception of the SDGs can be seen in the absence to address explicit the unique rights

7 CARICOM Reparations Commission, No. 3; Indigenous Peoples Development Program <www.caricom.org/caricom-ten-point-plan-for-reparatory-justice>; Andreas Buser, 'Colonial Injustices and the Law of State Responsibility: The CARICOM Claim to Compensate Slavery and (Native) Genocide' (2017) ZaöRV 409, pointed out, that 'In 1838, the British State paid £ 20 million (today: £ 200 billion) to the last (official) British slave owners as a compensation for "expropriation" of those enslaved due to the abolition of slavery in the British Empire and in particular in the British Caribbean'. At the same time, the formerly enslaved got nothing, except the (formal) freedom which they should have enjoyed from the beginning.

8 W Keegan, 'Creating the Guanahatabey (Ciboney): The Modern Genesis of an Extinct Culture' (1989) 63(239) Antiquity 373–379.

9 Juan de Dios Simón Sotz, 'Indigenous Peoples and Education in Central and South America and the Caribbean' in *State of the World's Indigenous Peoples* (3rd Vol, S. 109 ff., UN 2017); A Strecker, 'Indigenous Land Rights and Caribbean Reparations Discourse' (2017) 30(3) Leiden Journal of International Law 629–646; 'Traces of Indigenous "Taíno" in Present-day Caribbean Populations: Researchers Have Produced the First Clear Genetic Evidence that the Indigenous People Whom Columbus First Encountered in the New World Still Have Living Descendants Today', *ScienceDaily* <www.sciencedaily.com/releases/2018/02/180219155009.htm>.

10 Warren Benfield, *The Changing Nature of Poverty and Inequality in the Caribbean: New Issues, New Solutions* (Caribbean Development Bank 2016) 130; Susan Nicolai, Tanvi Bhatkal, Chris Hoy and Thomas Aedy, *Projecting Progress: The SDGs in Latin America and the Caribbean* (Overseas Development Institute 2016), S. 16; Michael DaCosta, 'Colonial Origins, Institutions and Economic Performance in the Caribbean: Guyana and Barbados' (IMF Working Papers, February 2007) 1–37 <https://ssrn.com/abstract=967884>.

11 CARICOM Reparations Commission, 'No. 6 Illiteracy Eradication' <http://caricomreparations.org/caricom/caricoms-10-point-reparation-plan/>.

and vulnerabilities of indigenous people.[12] The UN Declaration on the Rights of Indigenous Peoples is not explicitly mentioned, and the UN Special Rapporteur on Human Rights and the Environment has stated that the SDGs failed to address the indigenous rights targets.[13] However, the global agenda is generally grounded in the Universal Declaration of Human Rights, international human rights treaties. Does that mean that all treaties are integrated and no treaty left behind? Therefore, it may not be surprising that the SDGs are viewed as a continuation of a universal Western vision that privileges the West and will favour stakeholders from the West.[14] This is one perspective but probably is not convincing. Worldwide another answer bringing so many together is missing. The SDGs can be seen as a worldwide accepted normative concept and a framework which was adopted by all heads of states in New York on 25 September 2015.

Not only that, but the aspects have changed in the last years of the ongoing evolutionary pathway of globalisation. Only some of those aspects I would like to recall as a factual basis, which at present heralds a shift of a new direction of the pathway of globalisation. The shift comes from and will be further spurred by digitalisation, artificial intelligence and megaprojects like the One Belt, One Road Initiative of China, and the Raise Africa supported by China. Here are more of the impacts shaping the current way of globalisation:

- Climate change, the need for more green and blue economy (even when the US president denies it)
- Withdrawal of the basic understanding in international law that multilateralism is based on equality and sovereignty as well
- Erratic US policy
- Economic and political impact of China, OBOR, also in South- and Middle America (Nicaragua)
- EU in a "Polycrisis" (*Juncker*), Brexit
- A constant growth of immense wealth for a small percentage of people (raising inequality)
- steady growth of people living in the world
- Migration
- Organised crime, corruption
- SDGs of the UN, as a new multi-layered normative concept based on and enshrining human rights

These major impacts are forging a new framework which is up to now not spelled out properly but still influencing the global agenda in many ways.

12 Lynda M Collins, 'Sustainable Development Goals and Human Rights: Challenges and Opportunities' in D French and LJ Kotzé (eds), *Sustainable Development Goals* (Edward Elgar Publishing 2018) 66, 87 f.

13 ibid.

14 Nigel O M Brissett, 'Sustainable Development Goals (SDGs) and the Caribbean: Unrealizable Promises?' in *Progress in Development Studies* (SAGE Publishing, December 2017), S. 19, 'is still a deeply Westernized version of social change that is embedded in the SDGs, in which change takes place on the terms of the power of Western ideas and practices', p. 28.

The Caribbean pathway of CARICOM,[15] ACP,[16] CARIFORUM,[17] CELAC[18] and the new attempt of bridging to the Spanish-speaking Caribbean is obviously one of the consequences. The EU and CELAC both are backing the Agenda 2030 for Sustainable Development. They have also been prime movers of the Paris Agreement on climate change.[19] What is needed today is a more normative concept, leaving policies behind, and addressing inequalities to shape a deeper humanised future. But are the SDGs heralding a new and better world? Or are they, as Adelman has put it, a 'neoliberal incarnation of green capitalism',[20] contesting and breaking the natural limits of biological inherent eco-systems of the world.[21]

The normative oriented concept of SDGs

The UN General Assembly adopted the 2030 Global Agenda for Sustainable Development on 25 September 2015 as a resolution[22] which is not legally binding[23] and entered into force on 1 January 2016.[24] Its scope, objectives and targets

15 The Caribbean Community (CARICOM) is an international organisation of 15 Caribbean nations and dependencies whose main objective is to promote economic integration and cooperation among its members, to ensure that the benefits of integration are equitably shared and to coordinate foreign policy. The organisation was established in 1973; see Francesco Seatzu, 'The Caribbean Community (CARICOM)' in Marco Odello and Francesco Seatzu (eds), *Latin American and Caribbean International Institutional Law* (Asser Press 2015) 219 ff.

16 The African, Caribbean and Pacific Group of States (ACP) is an organisation created by the Georgetown Agreement in 1975.

17 Economic Partnership Agreement between the CARIFORUM States, of the one part, and the European Community and its Member States, of the other part; from 30.10.2008, Official Journal of the EU, L 289/I/3 <http://trade.ec.europa.eu/doclib/docs/2008/february/tradoc_137971.pdf>.

18 Community of Latin American and Caribbean States: represent 61 countries – around one third of the UN membership – and over a billion people – 15% of the world's population.

19 <www.consilium.europa.eu/en/meetings/international-ministerial-meetings/2018/07/16-17/>.

20 Sam Adelman, 'The Sustainable Development Goals, Anthropocentrism and Neoliberalism' in D French and Louis J Kotzé (eds), *Sustainable Development Goals – Law, Theory and Implementation* (Edward Elgar 2018) 15.

21 Louis J Kotzé, 'The Sustainable Development Goals: An Existential Critique alongside Three New-Millennial Analytical Paradigms' in D French and Louis J Kotzé (eds), *Sustainable Development Goals – Law, Theory and Implementation* (Edward Elgar 2018) 57 ff.

22 Entered into force on 1 January 2016 and is valid until 2030, see UNGA Res. A/RES/70/1, 7, No. 21 <www.un.org>. For the development of the 3 1/2 year-long negotiations of the 2030 Global Agenda and the SDGs, see M Kamau, P Chasek and D O'Connor, *Transforming Multilateral Diplomacy, The Inside Story of the SDGs* (Routledge 2018).

23 E Klein and S Schmahl, 'Article 10' in B Simma, D-E Khan, G Nolte and A Paulus (eds), *The Charter of the United Nations, A Commentary* (3rd edn., Oxford University Press 2012), Vol. 1, 479, marginal no. 46. For a list of individual members admission date, see: Mitteilung des Regionalen Informationszentrums der Vereinten Nationen für Westeuropa <www.unric.org>. Liesa (n 46) 94, who defines SDGs as somewhere between soft law and hard law.

24 UN,A/RES/70/1, 7, No. 21.

are regarded as universal.[25] In terms of content, the 17 goals and 169 more concrete targets encompass their respective sustainable economic, social and environmental development.[26] Attempts have been made since the 1980s to bridge the divide between developed and underdeveloped countries by way of promoting sustainable development in international law. In this regard, the International Law Association (ILA)[27] adopted the 'New Delhi Declaration of Principles of International Law Relating to Sustainable Development' in 2002.[28] This is cited by the 'Sofia Guiding Statements on Sustainable Development Principles'[29] of the ILA, which were designed to assist courts of law in applying principles and homogeneous interpretation criteria using a methodically well-founded approach.[30]

The Sofia Guiding Statements play a contributing role in ensuring that with the Global Agenda and the SDGs a 'need to build peaceful, just and inclusive societies that provide equal access to justice . . . on effective rule of law and good governance at all levels and on transparent, effective and accountable institutions'[31] may be given concrete expression in judicial practice. The integration of judicial interpretation standards in international and national law reflects the contents of the resolution at least to the extent 'that the Agenda is to be implemented in a manner that is consistent with the rights and obligations of States under international law' is accorded due emphasis.[32] Historically, the SDGs are

25 Winfried Huck and Claudia Kurkin, 'The UN Sustainable Development Goals (SDGs) in the Transnational Multilevel System' (2018) 2 Heidelberg Journal of International Law (HJIL)/Zeitschrift für ausländisches öffentliches Recht und Völkerrecht (ZaöRV) 375–424 at 379 <https://ssrn.com/abstract=3273899>.

26 General Assembly Economic and Social Council, A/72/75 – E/2017/56, 5.4.2017: Mainstreaming of the Three Dimensions of Sustainable Development Throughout the United Nations System, Report of the Secretary-General No. 6.

27 ILA <www.ila-hq.org/>.

28 Nico Schrijver, 'Advancements in the Principles of International Law' in M-C Cordonier Segger and H.E. Judge C G Weeramantry (note 2) 99 ff.; Nico Schrijver, 'ILA New Delhi Declaration of Principles of International Law Relating to Sustainable Development' (Routledge 2002) 49 NILR 299 ff.; M-C Cordonier Segger, 'Commitments to Sustainable Development Through International Law and Policy' in M-C Cordonier Segger and H.E. Judge C G Weeramantry, 86.

29 2012 Sofia Guiding Statements on the Judicial Elaboration of the 2002 New Delhi Declaration of Principles of International Law relating the Sustainable Development are reproduced in: Duncan French, 'The Sofia Guiding Statements on Sustainable Development Principles in the Decisions of International Tribunals' in M.-C. Cordonier Segger and H.E. Judge C G Weeramantry (eds), *Sustainable Development Principles in the Decisions of International Courts and Tribunals 1992–2012* (Routledge 2017) 239 ff.

30 For sustainable development in the case law of international courts, see inter alia the ICJ ruling *Gabčíkovo-Nagymaros* in which the necessity 'to reconcile economic development with protection of the environment' was emphasised, cf. French (n 29) 177; L Trevisan, 'The International Court of Justice's Treatment of "Sustainable Development" and Implications for Argentina v. Uruguay' (Fall 2009) 40(85) Sustainable Development Law & Policy 15.

31 UN, A/RES/70/1, 9, No. 35.

32 UN, A/RES/70/1, 6, No. 18; 18, SDG5.a: 'Undertake reforms to give women equal rights to economic resources . . . in accordance with national laws'; SDG 16.3: " . . . ensure access to justice for all".

built upon the Millennium Development Goals (MDGs)[33] and are aimed at overcoming inequality, defending human rights for all and empowering all women and girls.[34] To ensure funding for the SDGs, the development financing architecture was further developed[35] at the Third International Conference on Financing for Development, which took place in Addis Ababa on 13–16 July 2015 and explicitly integrated into the UN resolution as Addis Ababa Action Agenda (AAAA).[36]

Above all, the SDGs are designed to put intermediate linkages into practice in the economic, environmental and social dimensions of sustainable development.[37] In addition to the ongoing development priorities such as eradicating poverty, as well as fostering health, food security and nutrition, the Agenda sets out a wide range of economic, social and environmental objectives to promote more peaceful and inclusive societies.[38] The global framework that is required is being developed first and foremost in the area of human rights through a gradual legal condensation of corporate social responsibility policies.[39] The Guiding Principles on Business and Human Rights of *John G. Ruggie*[40] are a key point of reference for the realisation of the SDGs.[41] It seems questionable at the very least as to whether the relationship between human rights and SDGs can still be expressed

33 Bundestag Printed Paper 18/7361, Antrag der Fraktionen der CDU/CSU und SPD, UN-Ziele für nachhaltige Entwicklung – 2030-Agenda konsequent umsetzen v. 26.1.2016, 1; for Open Working Group; see also F Dodds, Ambassador D Donoghue, and J L Roesch, *Negotiating the Sustainable Development Goals: A Transformational Agenda for an Insecure World* (Routledge 2017) 31 ff.

34 Bundestag Printed Paper 18/7361 (n 33).

35 ibid.

36 UN, A/RES/70/1, No. 40; The final text of the outcome document adopted at the Third International Conference on Financing for Development (Addis Ababa, Ethiopia, 13.–16.6.2015) and endorsed by the General Assembly in its Resolution 69/313 of 27.7.2015 <https://sustainabledevelopment.un.org>.

37 Report of the German Federal Government, 'Eine Agenda für den Wandel zu nachhaltiger Entwicklung weltweit. Die deutsche Position für die Verhandlungen über die Post 2015-Agenda für nachhaltige Entwicklung' <www.bmz.de>.

38 UN, A/RES/70/1, 6, No. 17.

39 Cf. for instance EU Commission, Leitlinien für die Berichterstattung über nichtfinanzielle Informationen, ABl. 2017/C 215/01 zur RL 2014/95/EU; see also (e.g. K Sopp and J Baumüller, 'Die Leitlinien der EU-Kommission für die Berichterstattung über nichtfinanzielle Informationen: Orientierungshilfe ohne Orientierung') (2017) 12 Zeitschrift für Internationale Rechnungslegung 377; see B Spießhofer, *Unternehmerische Verantwortung* (2017) 61 ff.; B Spießhofer, 'Wirtschaft und Menschenrechte – rechtliche Aspekte der Corporate Social Responsibility' (Nomos Verlagsgesellschaft, Baden - Baden 2014) 67 NJW 2479 und in Deutschland: Gesetz zur Stärkung der nichtfinanziellen Berichterstattung der Unternehmen in ihren Lage- und Konzernlageberichten (CSR-Richtlinie-Umsetzungsgesetz [CSRRLUmsG]) vom 11.4.2017, BGBl. I, 802.

40 A/HRC/17/31, Annex: Report of the Special Representative of the Secretary General on the Issue of Human Rights and Transnational Corporations and Other Business Enterprises; J Ruggie, 'Guiding Principles on Business and Human Rights: Implementing the United Nations "Protect, Respect and Remedy" Framework'.

41 UN, A/RES/70/1, 29, No. 67 footnote; see also N Schönherr, F Findler and A Martinuzzi, 'Exploring the Interface of CSR and the Sustainable Development Goals' (2017) 24(3) Transnational Corporations (UNCTAD) 33 ff.

in metaphorical terms as 'ships passing in the night',[42] particularly since the 2030 Agenda calls for the elimination of inequality, as well as discrimination,[43] and was explicitly predicated on the absolute respect for international law, the Universal Declaration of Human Rights and international human rights treaties.[44] For example, the Working Group on Business and Human Rights within the Office of the High Commissioner for Human Rights (OHCHR) stresses that human rights need to be embedded in policies and practices once States begin to translate the SDGs into concrete measures.[45]

It is also easily possible for the discussion largely taking place within the realm of public law to obscure our perception of the privatisation phenomenon[46] and the contextual dimension of civil law on issues of contract and liability.[47] The dimension of human rights and consequently also that of the SDGs are increasingly encroaching on civil law, particularly in the areas of trade,[48] investment,[49] labour rights,[50] gender equality[51] and transnational companies,[52] as well as general private law.[53] Inasmuch as the SDGs refer to the private sector, the transnational approach[54] becomes directly discernible.[55] In the global context of supply

42 Philip Alston, 'Ships Passing in the Night: The Current State of the Human Rights and Development Debate Seen Through the Lens of the Millennium Development Goals' (2005) 27 HRQ 755 ff.

43 Key Message OHCHR: Human Rights and the 2030 Agenda <www.ohchr.org>. I Saiz and K Donald, 'Tackling Inequality Through the Sustainable Development Goals: Human Rights in Practice' (2017) 21 The International Journal of Human Rights 1029 ff.

44 UN, A/RES/70/1, 4, No. 10. I T Winkler and C Williams, 'The Sustainable Development Goals and Human Rights: A Critical Early Review' (2017) 21 The International Journal of Human Rights 1023 ff.

45 In this connection, the OHCR has developed a ten-point programme, see OHCR, The Business and Human Rights Dimension of Sustainable Development: Embedding 'Protect, Respect and Remedy' in SDGs implementation Geneva, 30 June 2017 <www.ohchr.org>.

46 C R F Liesa, 'Sustainable Development in International Law: General Issues' in C R F Liesa, C M Díaz Barrado and P Durán y Lalaguna (eds), *International Society and Sustainable Development Goals* (ARANZADI S.A.EDITORIAL 2016) 86 f.

47 Explicitly referring to contractual obligation, B Spießhofer, *Unternehmerische Verantwortung* (n 42) 419.

48 UN, A/RES/70/1, 29, No. 68, 1: 'International trade is an engine for inclusive economic growth and poverty reduction, and contributes to the promotion of sustainable development'.

49 SDG 8.7, 8.8; UN, A/RES/70/1, 29, No. 67, 3: 'Private business activity, investment and innovation are major drivers of productivity, inclusive economic growth and job creation'.

50 UN, A/RES/70/1, 29, No. 67, 1: 'protecting labour rights'.

51 SDG 5.2; 5.4; 5.5.

52 A Kolk, A Kourula and N Pisani, 'Multinational Enterprises and the Sustainable Development Goals: What Do We Know and How to Proceed?' (2017) 24(3) Transnational Corporations (UNCTAD) 9 ff.

53 Perhaps necessary for SDG 10.4 'equality'; 12.6 'Encourage companies, especially large and transnational companies, to adopt sustainable practices and to integrate sustainability information into their reporting cycle' and SDG 16 B 'Promote and enforce non-discriminatory laws and policies for sustainable development'.

54 O Dilling and T Markus, 'Transnationalisierung des Umweltrechts' (2016) 27 Zeitschrift für Umweltrecht 3, 4.

55 UN, A/RES/70/1 (e.g. 10, No. 39; 30, No. 70).

chains[56] and the global value chain generally used in a development nexus,[57] private law is linked to national and international public law on the basis of the 10 Principles developed by *John G. Ruggie*.[58] In this way, hybrid legal structures are bringing about a soft law with hard sanctions[59] or metaphorically represent rather 'ships in a convoy'.[60] The Danish Institute for Human Rights estimates that more than 90% of the Sustainable Development Goals (SDGs) targets are linked to international human rights and labour standards.[61]

Impact of the international economic law on the SDGs

Financing is considered as the major prerequisite of the success of the SDGs.[62] In order to provide financial security for the SDGs, an additional financing architecture was developed at the Third Conference on Financing for Development held in Addis Ababa on 13–16 July 2015, which has been explicitly integrated into the UN resolution as the Addis Ababa Action Agenda (AAAA).[63] The AAAA supports, complements and helps to contextualise the 2030 Agenda's means of implementation targets.[64] Countries also agreed to work together to fund infrastructure for energy, transport, and water and sanitation and to align private investment in agriculture and nutrition. The special development challenges faced by the Least Developed Countries (LDCs), Landlocked Least Developed Countries and Small Island Developing States (SIDS) are well recognised in the document, although the AAAA falls short of committing any new resources to these countries.[65]

Most of the SDGs are linked to human rights which are the fundamental approach of the SDGs. The worlds (dis-) order must seek for legal provisions to reach 'full realization of rights and capabilities' for all people. Against this background and related to my research in the last years concerning the impact of SDGs (e.g. with respect to CARICOM, ASEAN,[66] Cuba,[67] Europe[68]), it is open

56 B Spießhofer, *Unternehmerische Verantwortung*, 416.

57 G Gereffi and F Stacey, 'The Global Apparel Value Chain, Trade and the Crisis: Challenges and Opportunities for Developing Countries (1.4.2010)' World Bank Policy Research Working Paper No. 5281.

58 Cf. B Spießhofer, *Unternehmerische Verantwortung*, 2017, 87, 91 ff.

59 B Spießhofer, 'Wirtschaft und Menschenrechte – rechtliche Aspekte der Corporate Social Responsibility' (2014) 67 NJW, 2479.

60 Huck and Kurkin (n 25) 383.

61 <www.humanrights.dk/our-work/sustainable-development/human-rights-sdgs>.

62 <www.un.org/esa/ffd/ffd3/press-release/countries-reach-historic-agreement.html>.

63 <www.un.org/esa/ffd/wp-content/uploads/2015/08/AAAA_Outcome.pdf>.

64 UN GA A /70/1, No 62.

65 Gail Hurley, 'The Addis Ababa Action Agenda: A Step Forward on Financing for Development?' (21 July 2015) <www.undp.org/content/undp/en/home/blog/2015/7/21/The-Addis-Ababa-Action-Agenda-A-step-forward-on-financing-for-development-.html>.

66 Winfried Huck, 'ASEAN und EU: Vertrauen, Konsultation und Konsens statt „immer engerer Union"' (2018) EuZW 886–891.

67 Winfried Huck, 'EU und Kuba: Wirtschafts- und Nachhaltigkeitsdimensionen im ersten Political Dialogue and Cooperation Agreement' (2017) EuZW S. 249 ff.

68 Huck and Kurkin (n 25) 397.

as to whether the shifting paradigm of the international landscape under the auspices of climate change will lead under the legal order of international law to a specific rights of groups or individuals who may be legally entitled to claim on the basis of modern renewed Free Trade (FTA) and Investment Agreements (IPA).

Impact of the SDGS on the EU

The EU has stated on several occasions to implement the 2030 Agenda across all internal and external policies and address the interlinkages between the different SDGs.[69] Pursuant to Art. 3 para. 5 of the Treaty on European Union (TEU), under primary law the EU is committed to the goal of achieving global sustainable development, as well as contributing to free and fair trade, eradicating poverty and protecting human rights, in addition to strictly complying with and further developing international law.

Under the impression of its sustainability goals and its current investment and trade policies, the EU is beginning to incorporate the contents of the resolution into current negotiated international treaties in the form of free trade and investment agreements.[70] This development can be seen as an effect deriving from Article 13 (1) (a) of the UN Charter, under which the General Assembly makes recommendations to facilitate the codification of international law. In this respect too, it can be seen that with the global approach of the SDGs, a legally relevant integration effect is achieved, which is based on the knowledge of the necessary change and objectively penetrates into existing legal systems through various stages in an evolutionary process.

Although the UN Resolution on the Global Agenda 2030 cannot be classified as an international treaty, the Member States and the EU, which is usually the negotiating mandate, remain free to integrate the contents of the resolution into international treaties. This approach is characterised by the modern layout of numerous bilateral and multilateral free trade agreements (FTAs). The objectives put forward by the EU Commission are concerned with how and to what extent employee work conditions, environmental protection and other cross-cutting issues of the sustainability goals should be incorporated, for example, into the Transatlantic Trade and Investment Partnership (TTIP).[71] The proposal can be read as a follow-up to the MDGs and as a new basis for the inclusion of sustainability goals in the EU's trade and investment agreements; for example, with Colombia, Peru and Ecuador[72] in the Comprehensive Economic and Trade

69 European Commission – Joint public statement: Adoption of the new European Consensus on Development Brussels, 7 June 2017, STATEMENT/17/1547, No 7.

70 See EU-Commission, 'Trade and Sustainable Development' <http://ec.europa.eu/trade/policy/policy-making/sustainable-development/>.

71 EU Commission, 'EU to Pursue the Most Ambitious Sustainable Development, Labour and Environment Provisions in TTIP' (Press Release, 2015).

72 EU Commission, 'Trade Agreement between the European Union and Its Member States, of the One Part, and Columbia and Peru, of the Other Part' (2010) 321 ff.; Ecuador joined the Agreement on 11 November 2016, the Protocol to the Agreement became effective on

Agreement (CETA) with Canada[73] and the Japan Economic Partnership Agreement (JEFTA)[74] recently negotiated with Japan, each containing a chapter on sustainable development. This clearly demonstrates the extensive influence of sustainability goals on trade policy.

New European consensus on development

The EU and its Member States respond to current global challenges and opportunities in the light of the 2030 Agenda. They will implement the 2030 Agenda across all internal and external policies of the EU, integrating the three dimensions of sustainable development. One of the outcomes of the implementation of the SDGs is the new European consensus (NEC). The NEC is the cornerstone of the new development policy and constitutes an important part of the EU's overall response to the 2030 Agenda and the SDGs. For the first time a shared framework applies to all EU Institutions and Member States, providing a common approach to development policies in the next decades.[75] This NEC frames the implementation of the 2030 Agenda in partnership with all developing countries, taking due account of the framework provided by the Lisbon Treaty.[76]

The impact of the SDGs is clearly to be seen in different international trade and investment agreements. But it also has a strong impact on the agreement between ACP. The ACP is an organisation created by the Georgetown Agreement in 1975.[77] It is composed of 79 African, Caribbean and Pacific states, with all of them, without Cuba, signatories to the Cotonou Agreement, also known as the 'ACP-EC Partnership Agreement'. There are 48 countries from Sub-Saharan Africa, 16 from the Caribbean and 15 from the Pacific.[78] The EU-ACP partnership focuses on the eradication of poverty and inclusive sustainable development for ACP and EU countries. It is divided into three key action areas: development cooperation, political dialogue and trade.[79] The world has changed considerably since the Cotonou Agreement was adopted almost two decades ago. Global and

---

1 January 2017; PM EU Commission from 11 November 2016, R Zimmer, 'Das Nachhaltigkeitskapitel im bilateralen Freihandelsabkommen der EU mit Kolumbien und Peru, Gutachten' (2011) 4 ff. <www.fdcl.org>.

73 EU Commission, 'Consolidated CETA Text (2014)' <http://trade.ec.europa.eu>.

74 Huck and Kurkin (n 25) 402.

75 European Commission – Joint public statement: Adoption of the new European Consensus on Development Brussels, 7 June 2017, STATEMENT/17/1547.

76 ibid. No 5.

77 Georgetown Agreement on the Organisation of the African, Caribbean and Pacific Group of States (ACP) [*] Done at: Georgetown, Date enacted: 1975–06–06, In force: 1976–02–12.

78 African, Caribbean and Pacific Group of States <www.acp.int/content/secretariat-acp>.

79 J Kenner, 'Labour Clauses in EU Preferential Trade Agreements – An Analysis of the Cotonou Partnership Agreement' in K Bagwell and P Mavroidis (eds), *Preferential Trade Agreements: A Law and Economics Analysis* (Cambridge University Press 2011) 180–209; S Kingah, 'The Revised Cotonou Agreement between the European Community and the African, Caribbean and Pacific States: Innovations on Security, Political Dialogue, Transparency, Money and Social Responsibility' (2006) 50(1) Journal of African Law 59–71.

regional contexts (in Europe, Africa, the Caribbean and the Pacific) have evolved. Therefore, the core objectives of the partnership have to be reviewed to adapt to the new realities.[80]

The Cotonou Partnership Agreement (CPA) is one of the oldest and most comprehensive frameworks of cooperation between the EU and third countries. Signed in 2000 for a period of 20 years, the Cotonou Partnership Agreement unites more than 100 countries (28 EU Member States + 79 ACP countries), represents over 1.5 billion people and governs relations between the EU and 79 members of the African, Caribbean and Pacific (ACP) group of States and is due to expire in February 2020 in light of existing provisions and negotiations between the parties from August/October 2018. The achievement of the Sustainable Development Goals and the implementation of Agenda 2030 are universally seen as key priorities.[81]

Three different sub-options are considered from the EU perspective:

1 a common agreement with all ACP countries;
2 three distinct regional agreements with respectively the countries in Africa, the Caribbean and the Pacific; and,
3 an agreement consisting of three distinct regional partnerships under a common umbrella.

Based on a thorough analysis, the preferred option of the EU is option 3: a new partnership agreement that includes an overarching umbrella that lists shared principles, values and goals and identifies avenues for cooperation between the EU and the ACP countries in international contexts and incorporates three regional partnerships set respectively for African, Caribbean and Pacific countries, which will integrate existing regional strategies. Finally, it is expected that the new partnership will be legally binding, and many arguments will support this view.[82]

The position of the ACP-States on relations with the EU after 2020 regarding the post-Cotonou Agreement[83] is highlighted with three key messages in

80 EU Commission, 'Factsheet: European Commission Ready to Start Negotiations for a New Ambitious Partnership with 79 Countries in Africa, the Caribbean and the Pacific' (Memo 17/5225, 22 June 2018).

81 EU Commission & High Representative of the Union for Foreign Affairs and Security Policy, Executive summary of the Impact Assessment, accompanying the document Joint Communication to the European Parliament and the Council, 'A Renewed Partnership with the Countries of Africa, the Caribbean and the Pacific' Strasbourg 22.11.2016, SWD (2016) 381 final, S. 3.

82 EU Commission, High Representative of the Union for Foreign Affairs and Security Policy, Joint Staff Working Document Impact Assessment, accompanying the document Joint Communication to the European Parliament and the Council, 'A Renewed Partnership with the Countries of Africa, the Caribbean and the Pacific' Strasbourg 22.11.2016, SWD (2016) 380 final, S. 66 f.

83 Keijzer Bartels, *Assessing the Legal and Political Implications of the Post-Cotonou Negotiations for the Economic Partnership Agreements* (Bonn 2017) 4 ff.

the Waigani Communiqué of the Papua New Guinea Summit.[84] The specific objectives that should underpin a Cotonou partnership agreement with the EU from the ACP perspective include, in particular, the adaptation to the Agenda 2030 as the overarching development framework, explicitly incorporating the Addis Ababa Agenda for Action and the Paris Convention on Climate Change, the United Nations Declaration on the Right to Development and continental and regional agendas such as Agenda 2063[85] in Africa as well as the deepening and broadening of regional integration in the Caribbean and the Pacific.[86] At its annual meeting on 23 and 24 May 2019, the EU Council of Ministers for Africa, the Caribbean and the Pacific (ACP) decided[87] to delegate its powers to the ACP-EU Committee of Ambassadors to adopt transitional measures pending the entry into force of a new ACP-EU Partnership Agreement. This may be necessary if no new agreement can be reached before the expiry of the existing Cotonou Agreement on 20 February 2020.[88]

On 22 June 2018, the EU Council adopted the negotiating mandate for the future agreement between the EU and ACP. Formal negotiations will start by the end of August 2018, as provided by the current agreement, the Cotonou Agreement.[89]

EU, Brexit and ACP

The EU must face Brexit, which will have an impact on the ACP's future trade relations with the UK outside the EU regime, in particular for ACP importers and exporters.[90] The ACP countries are more engaged with emerging world powers such as China, among others due to the Belt and Road Initiative[91] also

84 Full text available at <www.acp.int/content/waigani-communique-future-perspectives-acp-group-states>; on this also European Parliament, EN E-007675/2017 Answer given by Mr Mimica on behalf of the Commission.
85 The African Union Commission, 'Agenda 2063, The Africa We Want: A Shared Strategic Framework for Inclusive Growth and Sustainable Development, First Ten-Year Implementation Plan 2014–2023' (September 2015) <www.un.org/en/africa/osaa/pdf/au/agenda2063-first10yearimplementation.pdf>.
86 ACP Group, Mandate, No. 21.
87 <www.consilium.europa.eu/en/policies/cotonou-agreement/>.
88 Council, 'Meeting Information, Brussels 23–24/05/2019' <www.consilium.europa.eu/en/meetings/international-ministerial-meetings/2019/05/23-24/?utm_source=dsms-auto&utm_medium=email&utm_campaign=ACP-EU+Council+of+ministers%2c+23-24%2f05%2f2019'.>
89 Council of the EU PR 375, 22/06/2018.
90 ACP Group, Mandate, adopted on 30 May 2018 by the 107th Session of the ACP Council of Ministers, held in Lomé, Togo, No 4.
91 Heng Wang, 'China's Approach to the Belt and Road Initiative: Scope, Character and Sustainability' (2019) Journal of International Economic Law 49 ff; Julien Chaisse and Mitsuo Matsushita, 'China's "Belt and Road" Initiative – Mapping the World's Normative and Strategic Implications' (2018) 52(1) Journal of World Trade 163–185 <https://ssrn.com/abstract=3134429>.

with a view to a desired better and faster development.[92] The EU must face competition from China, which announced at the China-Africa Summit on 3 September 2018 that it would invest USD 60 billion in Africa, mainly in support of the belt and road initiative. In the Port Moresby Declaration, ACP Heads of State and Government recognised that SDGs are crucial for poverty eradication, inequality reduction, growth and sustainable development.[93]

ACP negotiating mandate for a post-Cotonou Partnership Agreement with the EU

At the ACP Summit in 2012, the ACP Heads of State and Government have affirmed that they are determined to 'stay united as a group' (Sipopo Declaration). [94] The view of the ACP on the relation with the EU after 2020 is particularly addressed in the Waigani communiqué of Papua Neuguinea Summit with three key messages. The communiqué states that the ACP-EU partnership provides a good basis that should be consolidated through an established, comprehensive, and legally binding framework. It further expresses specific commitment to the principles of subsidiarity, complementarity and proportionality, regional integration organisations in the pursuit of sustainable development.[95]

The Cotonou Partnership Agreement will expire on 29 February 2020. In preparation for the negotiations, the highest-level decision-making organs of the Summit of Heads of State and Government and Council of Ministers of the ACP Group of States have adopted the core principles, a common approach and a policy framework document to underpin preparations and execution of the negotiating process for a successor agreement[96] and described their view in the ACP Negotiating Mandate for a post-Cotonou partnership agreement with the EU.[97]

> Many economic and geopolitical realities have changed since the first Lomé Convention was signed between then 9 EEC States and 46 countries from Africa, the Caribbean, and the Pacific.[98] EU has to face the BREXIT, causes

92 ACP Group, Mandate, No. 5.
93 ibid. No. 136.
94 Sipopo Declaration of the 7th Summit of the ACP Heads of State and Government, December 2012.
95 EU Commission, High Representative of the Union for Foreign Affairs and Security Policy, Joint Staff Working Document Impact Assessment (see quote 82), S. 23.
96 See the Waigani Communique of the 8th Summit of ACP Heads of State and Government, Port Moresby, Papua New Guinea, May 2016 [ACP/28/046/16 FINAL]; Towards the ACP We Want, Brussels, May 2017 [ACP/1/1/11/(Vol.1) 17 Rev. 3] and Decision No. 2 / CV/17 of the 105th Session of the ACP Council of Ministers, May 2017 [ACP/25/012/17] on the Three Strategic Pillars on which a Post-Cotonou Agreement should be based.
97 ACP Group, ACP Negotiating mandate for a post-Cotonou Partnership Agreement with the EU [Mandate], Adopted on 30 May 2018 by the 107th Session of the ACP Council of Ministers, held in Lomé, Togo, ACP/00/011/18 FINAL.
98 ACP Group, Mandate, adopted on 30 May 2018 by the 107th Session of the ACP Council of Ministers, held in Lomé, Togo, No. 2.

an impact on the future trade relations of ACP countries with the UK outside the EU regime, in particular for ACP importers and exporters.[99] ACP Countries also are more engaged today directly with emerging global powers such as China in the purpose of a better and quicker development.[100] EU has to face a severe competition from China, which announced recently at the China-Africa Summit on 3 September 2018 to invest in Africa 60 Billions USD (56 Billions €), mainly to support the Belt and Road Initiative. And there could be another reason, to make China's cash so attractive to Africa, it comes with no political conditions, compared to the financing from the EU, the IMF, World Bank and other development finance institutions.[101]

The position of the ACP-States on relations with the EU after 2020 regarding the Post-Cotonou Agreement[102] is highlighted with three key messages in the Waigani Communiqué of the Papua New Guinea Summit.[103] The specific objectives that should underpin a Cotonou partnership agreement with the EU from the ACP perspective include, in particular, the adaptation to the Agenda 2030 as the overarching development framework, explicitly incorporating the Addis Ababa Agenda for Action and the Paris Convention on Climate Change, the United Nations Declaration on the Right to Development and continental and regional agendas such as Agenda 2063[104] in Africa as well as the deepening and broadening of regional integration in the Caribbean and the Pacific.[105] At its annual meeting on 23 and 24 May 2019, the EU Council of Ministers for Africa, the Caribbean and the Pacific (ACP) decided[106] to delegate its powers to the ACP-EU Committee of Ambassadors to adopt transitional measures pending the entry into force of a new ACP-EU Partnership Agreement. This may be necessary if no new agreement can be reached before the expiry of the existing Cotonou Agreement on 20 February 2020.[107]

SDGS as overarching development framework

The specific objectives should underpin a post-Cotonou Partnership Agreement with the EU and include in particular the Alignment to Agenda 2030 and the

99 ACP Group, Mandate, adopted on 30 May 2018 by the 107th Session of the ACP Council of Ministers, held in Lomé, Togo, No. 4.
100 ACP Group, Mandate, No. 5.
101 Benjamin Fox, 'China's Investment Largesse May Dwarf EU in Africa' (*Euractice*, 4 September 2018).
102 Bartels (n 83) 4 ff.
103 Full text available at <www.acp.int/content/waigani-communique-future-perspectives-acp-group-states>; on this also European Parliament, EN E-007675/2017 Answer given by Mr Mimica on behalf of the Commission.
104 The African Union Commission (n 85).
105 ACP Group, Mandate, No. 21.
106 <www.consilium.europa.eu/en/policies/cotonou-agreement/>.
107 Council (n 88).

SDGs as the overarching development framework, which has integrated explicitly the Addis Ababa Action Agenda and the Paris Agreement on Climate Change, the UN Declaration on the Right to Development, as well as continental and regional agendas such as Agenda 2063 in Africa and the deepening and widening regional integration in the Caribbean and the Pacific.[108]

There are the identified cross-cutting themes that the ACP will include in the post-Cotonou Agreements, such as:

1 Capacity Building (SDG 17.8,9)[109];
2 Vulnerability and Resilience Building (SAMOA Pathway, AAAA, Paris Agreement on Climate Change)[110];
3 Ocean and Seas (SDG 14)[111]
4 Climate Change (SDG 13)[112]
5 Gender Equality (SDG 5)[113]
6 Health (SDG 3)[114]
7 Youth and Demographic Dividend (SDG 8)[115]
8 Culture and Development[116];
9 Peace, Security and Democracy (SDG 16).[117]

Furthermore, the ACP has built its mandate for the negotiations on three pillars:

Pillar 1: Trade, Investment, Industrialisation and Services[118]

According to this pillar, it is an objective to strengthening institutional arrangements necessary to build and scale up the capacity of the private sector and governments to take advantage of trade arrangements, including the Economic Partnership Agreements (EPAs), as well as other ACP regional and continental trade arrangements such as the CARICOM Single Market and Economy (CSME) and the African Continental Free Trade Agreement (AfCFTA).[119] Policies for investment promotion and facilitation should be aligned with SDGs and designed to minimise the risk of harmful competition for investment.[120]

108 ACP Group, Mandate, No. 21.
109 ACP Group, Mandate, No. 29.
110 ACP Group, Mandate, No. 31.
111 ACP Group, Mandate, No. 32–36.
112 ACP Group, Mandate, No. 38.
113 ACP Group, Mandate, No. 40.
114 ACP Group, Mandate, No. 42.
115 ACP Group, Mandate, No. 46.
116 ACP Group, Mandate, No. 27.
117 ACP Group, Mandate, No. 58.
118 ACP Group, Mandate, No. 59.
119 ACP Group, Mandate, No. 65.
120 ACP Group, Mandate, No. 70 viii.

Pillar 2: Development Cooperation, Technology, Science, Innovation and Research[121]

The main objective of the African, Caribbean and Pacific Group of States is the achievement of sustainable economic growth and sustainable development in a peaceful, secure, and stable political environment.[122]In particular Remittances from the Diaspora have shown continued growth and have attained high volumes in recent years. Prospects remain positive, which make them one of the major sources of external financial flows for poverty reduction and development finance in ACP countries.[123]

Pillar 3: Political dialogue and advocacy[124]

The areas of cooperation should be the SDGs, corruption and money laundering by organised crime,[125] terrorism and extremism[126] and proliferation of small arms and light weapons.[127] Further the mandate will cover further in this regard that the Agreement should have specific provisions for Landlocked Developing Countries (LLDCs), Least Developed Countries (LDCs), Small Island Developing States (SIDS), Middle-Income Developing Countries (MICs) and Highly Indebted Middle-Income Countries (HIMICs).[128]

Conclusions

Globalisation in its present form is subject to political, economic and legal forces that are constantly evolving. The history has not been completed; it underlies the collective memory also of the Caribbean people and determines the current political and legal agenda regarding historical injustice and inequality (Ten Points/CARICOM Reparations Commission).

The progressing open and hidden agenda of the political and economic power fields (3000 FTAs reshaping the field of trade and investment, OBOR, RCEP, Influence of China, Made in China 2025, AB of the WTO) requires an acknowledgement and improvement of the legal position of an individual also in international law in the interest of fairness and equality. The UN resolution on Global Agenda 2030 and the 17 SDGs and 169 sub-goals are not legally binding as soft law. However, this does not neutralise the effect of the SDGs through conviction. The tasks of states and of the private sector (through CSR) is to integrate the three dimensions of sustainable development (social, economic, and

121 ACP Group, Mandate, No. 77.
122 ACP Group, Mandate, No. 78.
123 ACP Group, Mandate, No. 111.
124 ACP Group, Mandate, No. 130.
125 ACP Group, Mandate, No. 142.
126 ACP Group, Mandate, No. 145.
127 ACP Group, Mandate, No. 146.
128 ACP Group, Mandate, No. 162.

environmental) based on the Human Rights Treaties and by advancing a universal approach (UN Global Compact).

Further, there are beginnings in international law for the development of legal principles of sustainable development. The content and scope of the principles have demonstrable effects; however, the crystallisation process is not yet complete. Sustainable Development is not yet confirmed as customary law by the ILC. Numerous effects of SDGs through adoption in international, interregional, European, national and transnational law are clearly visible. The EU has incorporated the SDGs into its internal and external policies and integrates them in many ways. This transforms the SDGs into directly applicable law and has a legally binding effect between the parties involved.

Finally, the new European consensus on development is a cornerstone of the new EU's global challenges and opportunities in the light of the United Nations' Sustainable Development Goals and Global Agenda 2030. The EU and its Member States have to implement a human rights-based approach to development cooperation covering all human rights. The Cotonou Partnership Agreement expires in 2020 and therefore has to be renegotiated starting in 2018. It is the legal framework ruling relations between the EU and 79 countries in Africa, the Caribbean and the Pacific (ACP). The achievement of the Sustainable Development Goals and the implementation of Agenda 2030 are universally seen as key priorities which are to be integrated. It can be observed that there is a shift from the A[C]P States to China and a reluctant approach regarding the EU caused by Brexit and other dissensions internally. Accordingly, the CARIFORUM-EU Political Agreement (EPA) is the first and the only comprehensive EPA concluded by the ACP States. The Parties of EPA agree that the Cotonou Agreement and this Agreement shall be implemented in a complementary and mutually reinforcing manner. To CARICOM the SDGs and related questions of inequality are in the centre of interest.

12 National Champions and their impact on trade, trade policy and SDGs

Fabian Stancke[1]

When it comes to UN Sustainable Development Goals (SDGs), discussions tend to focus on trade policy in the form of tariffs and regulation. However, more indirect policies must not be forgotten because they may also have significant impacts on trade, trade policy and thus on SDGs. This is particularly true for the non-tariff trade barrier of the formation and preservation of state-backed market-dominant undertakings, better known as "National Champions". National Champions, whether in the form of public corporations or private corporations, may harm the free movement of goods and services within economic areas like the European Union (EU) and CARICOM or on the world market, constitute a barrier to free entry into markets and may impede innovation and sustainability.

National Champions

National Champions or 'European Champions' can be described as large companies that, not least through political support, should promote the interests of a state or a political grouping like the EU by assuming a particularly favourable and competitive position in international markets.[2] In return, the government sets policies that favour these companies by giving certain unfair advantages which work against other market players – or more generally speaking, against competition itself. All in all, such companies can be labelled as 'state-backed'. However, a distinction must be made between National Champions that can have a dominant or even monopolistic market position and 'state'- or 'national monopolies'. The latter means that the state reserves or grants to itself or an entity certain exclusive rights that relate to or affect trade in goods.[3]

1 Prof. Dr. Fabian Stancke teaches Competition Law at the Brunswick European Law School as well as at the Europa-Kolleg of the Hamburg University. This paper is based on a presentation held at EU-CARICOM Law Conference, 26–27 September 2018 at the University of Western Indies, St. Augustine Campus / Trinidad. I have to thank Mr. Tobias Böttcher for his valuable contributions to this paper.

2 Whish and Bailey, *Competition Law* (8th edn) 814.

3 Hochbaum and Berg in von der Groeben, Schwarze and Hatje, *Europäisches Unionsrecht, AEUV* [European Union Law, TFEU] (7th edn), Art 37, para 12; Leible and T Streinz in Grabitz, Hilf and Nettesheim, *Das Recht der Europäischen Union, AEUV*, [The Law of the

While such a policy that supports National Champions insofar as it contradicts principles of open and liberal economies, it fits perfectly into a concept of economic nationalism that strives for protected national markets and pre-eminence abroad – in contrast to open and free markets. The forms of, justifications for and effects of state-backed monopolies will be examined later. Thereafter, the question will be addressed as to how international and supranational agreements deal with National Champions and how they positively or negatively affect SDGs. This chapter will deal with the question of whether there are efficient factual or legal instruments for public bodies or private enterprises or organisations to support or to challenge National Champions and will set out brief proposals for the effective implementation of rules and the effective enforcement of existing rules on them.

Examples of National Champions

The creation of National Champions that dominate national or regional markets, factually, may lead to state-backed monopolies. An undertaking is considered to be a 'monopolist' if it – as a supplier or buyer of a certain type of goods or commercial services in the relevant product and geographic market – is without a competitor.[4] An oligopoly consists of two or more corporations that collectively have a dominant market position in a certain market.[5] True monopolies are very rare in a liberal economy because each undertaking normally faces a certain competitive threat. However, today we also refer to the term 'monopoly' in cases of overwhelming market dominance. 'Market dominance' is defined as 'the ability of an undertaking to behave to a significant degree independently from its competitors, customers and consumers'.[6] While overwhelming strong market positions, in the past, were often held only by formerly state-owned enterprises in network industries (e.g. postal services, railway, telecommunication), in the digital economy – and in particular in the platform industry – 'natural monopolies' become more common due to the 'the winner takes it all' principle that results from data-pooling, log-in effects and leveraging.[7] In addition, in many countries, the public sector is quite active economically, holding stakes in private

European Union, TFEU], Art 37 recital. 12; see also ECJ, Case C-393/92, OJ 1994, I-1477 recital. 30 – Almelo.

4 See, for this definition, for example, Art. 18 para. 1 (1) German Act Against Restrictions of Competition.

5 Bunte and Stancke, *Kartellrecht* [Antitrust Law] (3rd edn, 2016) 181 et seqq.; Bellamy and Child, *European Union Law of Competition* (7th edn), recital 10.047 with further references.

6 ECJ, Case *C-85/76, Hoffmann-LaRoche*, para. 70, ECLI:EU:C:1979:36.

7 See, for example: Haucap and Heimeshoff, 'Google, Facebook, Amazon, eBay: Is the Internet Driving Competition or Market Monopolisation?' (DICE Discussion Paper No. 83, January 2013) 2; Evans and Schmalensee, 'The Industrial Organisation of Markets with Two-Sided Platforms' (2007) 3(1) Competition Policy International 151, 165; Kerber, 'Digital Markets, Data and Privacy: Competition Law, Consumer Law and Data Protection' (*GRUR International* 2016) 639, 642.

undertakings[8] or trying to achieve certain political goals by means of direct influence on market structures.[9] So monopolies regularly are the product of government regulation and intervention. In terms of National Champions, respectively state-backed monopolies, typically, undertakings operating in the 'old economy' like financial institutions, airlines and energy corporations are focused on. However, protectionist tendencies can also be observed in the digital economy. For example, antitrust law enforcers in the US tend to tolerate digital monopolies like those of Google in the search engine market,[10] which could also be seen as a form of protecting a National Champion.[11]

The strengthening of National Champions and protecting them against competition from alien enterprises can be achieved in multiple ways. The most efficient method seems to be actively supporting national undertakings by way of granting a shield against political and regulatory threats, actively promoting external growth, particularly by supporting mergers of national competitors and granting an advantageous tax environment. In terms of mergers, National Champions can be created by government support for a combination of undertakings that would either enable a national undertaking to compete effectively in international markets or enhance this ability.[12] At the same time, activities of foreign undertakings may be harmed by way of hostile regulation, political obstruction of mergers and acquisitions, opposition to a takeover of a domestic undertaking by a foreign company and so on.[13] Recent examples from the German market may be the efforts of German politicians to form a national airline champion by promoting a takeover of the legacy business of Air Berlin by Lufthansa and persistent rumours of the combination of the two biggest German private banks, Deutsche Bank and Commerzbank.[14] On a European level, one prominent example of the creation of a (supra-) National Champion is Airbus, which was heavily promoted by subsidies.[15]

8 See, for example: Scott Cendrowski, 'China's Global 500 Companies are Bigger than Ever – And Mostly State-owned' (*Fortune Magazine*, 22 July 2015).

9 Schepp and Wambach (IFO, magazine 20/2017, 26 October 2017) 3.

10 'Deputy Assistant Attorney General Barry Nigro Delivers Remarks at The Capitol Forum and CQ's Fourth Annual Tech, Media & Telecom Competition Conference, New York' 13 December 2017 <www.justice.gov>.

11 Even though most recently the DOJ tends to question the market position and the use of market power and alleged political censorship by the GAFA group of companies (Google, Amazon, Facebook, Apple) and Twitter.

12 Galloway, 'The Pursuit of National Champions: The Intersection of Competition Law and Industrial Policy' (2007) 8(3) ECLR 172 <https://ssrn.com/abstract=1767865>.

13 See for Börner in: KSE Bd. 32, 137; Cremer in: Calliess, Ruffert and Cremer, *EUV/AEUV, Das Verfassungsrecht der Europäischen Union mit Europäischer Grundrechtscharta* [TEU/TFEU, The Constitutional Law of the European Union with the Charter of Fundamental Rights of the European Union] Art. 107, recital 5; see also for the OECD Global Forum on Competition, 'Competition Policy, Industrial Policy and National Champions' (2009) 11.

14 See, most recently, the call of the German finance minister Olaf Scholz for the creation of a national banking champion, Olaf Storbeck, 'German Finance Minister Calls for Industrial Policy Revival' (*Financial Times*, 30 August 2018).

15 This led to a major WTO dispute with the US side trying to protect Boeing. See, for more information on the dispute and the WTO-case: Kienstra, 'Cleared For Landing: Airbus,

Reasoning for National Champions

In the first place, to a broader audience, the intention of politicians to create or protect National Champions seems to be reasonable. The formation and preservation of National Champions is an important tool for industrial politics,[16] which means the potential for (ideally) elected bodies to exercise decisive influence on the way the undertakings and markets work. It may be argued that, through political influence, political goals like workplace safety, worker participation, environmental protection and the prevention of a sell-off of national intellectual property or 'national crown-jewels' can be achieved. Governments often encourage firms to collaborate or to merge where this would lead to economies of scale or to achieve more effective research and development.[17] When National Champions operate in foreign markets, a government may be motivated to protect the existent share in the foreign markets or to increase the market share.[18] Also 'key industries' may be strengthened through targeted aid. In particular, strong national banks are seen as a question of national sovereignty.[19] This is where populist policy and SDGs seem to unite, while free trade and free trade agreements like CETA and TTIP, and a free and global competitive economy are seen as obstructive to labour rights, environmental and democratic principles/governance and participation.

Besides populism and ideology, in times of 'nation first' policies in China, Europe, the US and elsewhere, the question is whether the formation or preservation of National Champions really do have beneficial effects on SDGs or, on the contrary, may have the effect of harming SDGs.

Impact of National Champions on SDGs

Sustainable development is seen as an objective of global and regional trade law and policy[20] and can be significantly influenced by the creation, prevention and actions of National Champions. While dominant market positions and temporary monopolies can be harmless as long as they are vulnerable,[21] stable monopolies may have significant negative effects on SDGs. This is particularly true in cases of National Champions that may leverage their strong position in domestic markets to expand to other markets with less competitive market players. This may apply to smaller countries and, foremost, to developing countries whose companies do

---

Boeing, and the WTO Dispute over Subsidies to Large Civil Aircraft' (2012) 32(3) Northwestern Journal of International Law & Business 569 et seqq.

16 Mundt (IFO, magazine 20/2017, 26 October 2017) 14; see also the recent call by the German finance minister for a 'revival' of industrial policy: Storbeck (n 14).

17 Whish and Bailey (n 2) 14.

18 OECD Global Forum on Competition (n 13) 208.

19 Storbeck (n 14).

20 Cordonier Segger, *Regional Trade Agreements and the WTO Legal Systems*, 336 with further references.

21 Körber, *Die Macht der Monopole* [The Power of Monopolies] (NZKart 2018) 105.

not have the skills and capacities to compete worldwide, or even with powerful and state-backed foreign companies domestically. This may result in economic injustice, lower quality of goods for consumers and higher prices.[22] So a monopoly leads to a loss of welfare for the entire society.

For reasons of political economy, the inherent danger for the economy itself is that the competitive conditions will be shaped by political influence and lobbying.[23] In the first place, it may be accepted that politicians primarily create National Champions in order to support policies that are in line with SDGs,[24] like decent work and economic growth, industry, innovation and infrastructure, affordable and clean energy. However, it is questionable whether the creation of National Champions actually leads to increased competitiveness and sustainable development and whether these goals really can be achieved by the creation and preservation of monopolies or whether, on the contrary, such policies may be detrimental to these goals. This question becomes particularly important because the concept of National Champions unifies the effects of economic nationalism and protectionism with the allegedly negative effects of monopolies on the economy, customers, innovation and governance.

With good reason, competition advocates propose that by improving economic governance, competition law, in itself, indirectly supports sustainable development.[25] There are several areas where enforcement of competition law has a positive effect on, for example, environmental goals.[26] One may also conclude that competition law seeks to support greater equality by facilitating economic growth while helping to eradicate poverty.[27] This is because the economic and socio-political power of strong market players is limited and remains transparent if a functioning competition law regime is in place. In addition, mergers, abusive practices and cooperation of companies can be blocked if specific SDGs are under threat as a result of a given project, while SDG-compliant projects may be supported by antitrust laws. Most recent examples are actions of antitrust authorities in the field of data protection (against allegedly market-dominant

22 Jenny in: Gehring and Cordonier Segger, *Sustainable Development in World Trade Law*, 356.

23 Haucap (IFO, magazine 20/2017, 26 October, 2017) 11.

24 See, for more information of UN SDGs, World Bank, 'Atlas of Sustainable Development Goals 2017, From World Development Indicators' (*World Bank Atlas* 2017); French and Kotzé, *Sustainable Development Goals, Law, Theory and Implementation* (1st edn, 2018); Campagnolo, Carraro, Eboli and Farnia, 'Assessing SDGs: A New Methodology to Measure Sustainability' (FEEM Working Paper No. 89.2015, 2016) <https://ssrn.com/abstract=2715991> or <http://dx.doi.org/10.2139/ssrn.2715991>; Kolk, Kourula and Pisani, 'Multinational Enterprises and the Sustainable Development Goals: What Do We Know and How to Proceed?' (2017) 24(3) Transnational Corporations 9–32 <https://ssrn.com/abstract=2988607>.

25 Karl M Meessen, 'Competition in the Doha Round of WTO Negotiations' in N Schrijver and F Weiss (eds), *International Law and Sustainable Development*, 217, 227.

26 Gehring in: Cordonier Segger and Khalfan, *Sustainable Development Law, Principles, Practices and Prospects*, 292.

27 Jenny (n 22) 356.

Facebook) in Germany[28] and a case of alleged tax evasion by Apple by the European Commission,[29] the latter handled as a state aid case because tax reductions may be seen as prohibited subsidies.

This, relatively new, view on benefits of unimpeded competition by advocates of SDGs perfectly fits with the traditional reasoning of antitrust laws. In a free liberal economy, a high degree of market concentration and especially monopolies are generally viewed critically.[30] In fact, the monopolisation of the oil market in the US by Standard Oil led to the 'invention' of antitrust laws.[31] Monopolistic markets eliminate competition, whilst competition is the key element of a functioning market economy.[32] The thinking behind this is that competition has to fulfil economic and social functions in a free market economy.[33] Of particular importance here are control or regulatory functions, the market performance function, the innovation and efficiency function, the distribution function (reward for competitive success) and the selection function, as well as the socio-political function (the creation of a reasonably even distribution of power in the economy and society through 'open' markets).[34] The task of competition is to prevent the creation of final positions of power that threaten or eliminate the freedom of other market participants. Thus, it is assumed that functioning competition in an economy provides not only for an efficient and successful economy but also serves customers and acts as a shield against bad governance and the monopolisation of socio-political power.

28 See for Bundeskartellamt, 'Facebook's Collection and Use of Data from Third-Party Sources is Abusive' (Press Release, 19 December 2017) <www.bundeskartellamt.de>; Paal, *Daten und Kartellrecht* [Data and Antitrust] (NZKart 2018) 157, 158.

29 See Commission Decision (EU) 2017/1283 of 30 August 2016 on State aid SA.38373 (2014/C) (ex 2014/NN) (ex 2014/CP) implemented by Ireland to Apple (notified under document C (2017) 5605); CJEU (Vice-President), Decision of 17.05.2018 – CJEU C-12/18 P (I), Unlawful state aid by Ireland to Apple off-shore subsidiaries affect the economic situation of the US.

30 Whish and Bailey (n 2) 7 with further references.

31 Tucker, *Microeconomics for Today* (6th edn), chapter 13, 333; Lamaj, 'The Evolution of Antitrust Law in USA' (2017) 13 European Scientific Journal 156; Foer and Lande, 'The Evolution of United States Antitrust Law: The Past, Present, and (Possible) Future', (1999) 16 Nihon U. Comparative L.J. 149; Schmidt and Haucap, *Wettbewerbspolitik und Kartellrecht* [Competition Policy and Antitrust Law] (10th edn, 2013) 277 et seqq.

32 Emmerich and Hofmann in: Dauses and Ludwigs, *Handbuch des EU-Wirtschaftsrechts* [Handbook of EU Commercial Law], Chapter H. II., recitals 1, 4.; Farah and Ötvös, 'Competition Law and Trade in Energy vs. Sustainable Development: A Clash of Individualism and Cooperative Partnerships?' (2018) 50(2) Arizona State Law Journal 511; OECD Global Forum on Competition (n 13) 11 et seq. Bellamy and Child (n 5), recital 1.014.

33 Wiedemann in: Wiedemann, *Handbuch des Kartellrechts* [Handbook of Antitrust Law] (3rd edn, 2016) section 1 recital 2; Bunte and Stancke (n 5) 8 et seqq.

34 Wiedemann in: Wiedemann (n 33) section 1 recital 2; see for the function of competition (protection) also Bunte and Stancke (n 5) 8 et seq.; as well as in detail Schmidt and Haucap, *Wettbewerbspolitik und Kartellrecht* [Competition Policy and Antitrust Law], (10th edn, 2013) 35; Whish and Bailey (n 2) 4 et seq. with further references.

Besides these fundamental considerations, the creation of National Champions has direct effects on consumers who, in fact, subsidise their strong position on the world market by paying higher prices and, at the same time, suffer from reduced availability. Additionally, National Champions that are free from the disciplining effect of competition on their domestic markets may lack the skills necessary to succeed in the wider world.[35] If a firm has been assisted at a national level and has not been exposed to substantial competition, then it may become inefficient and lack the motivation to innovate.[36] In addition, negative effects on other key players in the domestic market may arise. For example, the establishment of Deutsche Post AG as one of the world's leading logistics companies, at the cost of competition in the German market, allegedly burdened the competitiveness of German companies in other areas (e.g. the automotive industry).[37] In any case, the one-sided support given to individual companies or sectors of the economy always puts other companies or sectors at a disadvantage.[38]

In addition, the social cost of supporting specific industries can be significant.[39] Conflicts of interest may also arise, in particular, in the case of investments by the government in state-regulated companies, as in this case the state assumes a dual role as shareholder on the one hand and regulator on the other.[40] Since the state benefits as (co-) owner from the positive economic development of companies in the form of higher dividend payments, it has an incentive to shape the regulatory framework in favour of the companies in which it participates. Not least, uncontested power also almost always has the potential to degenerate to cases of serious misuse of power and misallocation of resources. This, in turn, is contrary to the SDGs, as recently shown by corruption cases in the oil sector (e.g. Petrobras)[41] or the environmental scandal that originated in the German state-backed automotive company Volkswagen.

However, the creation and preservation of National Champions may indeed also have positive effects on the economy, consumer, innovation and on socio-political goals if interests and implications are carefully balanced out.[42] Thus, it is obvious that the creation and preservation of National Champions require diligent consideration and decision-making prior to their implementation and

35 Whish and Bailey (n 2) 814 with further references.

36 Galloway (n 12) 173.

37 15. Hauptgutachten der Monopolkommission, Wettbewerbspolitik im Schatten „Nationaler Champions“ [Fifteenth Main Report of the German Monopolies Commission, Competition policy in the shadow of "National Champions"] 78, BT-Drucks. 15/3610.

38 ibid.

39 OECD Global Forum on Competition (n 13) 14.

40 Schepp and Wambach (n 9) 4.

41 'Operation Car Wash', see for details (e.g. 'Brazil corruption scandals: All you need to know', <www.bbc.com>, 8 April 2018).

42 See for an econometrical calculation formula that considers several success factors and that may enable decision-makers to anticipate the likelihood of future positive effects of the establishment of a National Champion: Jens Sedekum, 'National Champion versus Foreign Takeover' (IZA Discussion Paper No. 2960, July 2007) <http://ssrn.com/abstract=1010595>.

careful supervision with regard to their market behaviour once established. This means that a positive future projection should be a prerequisite for the creation of National Champions, which needs to be supported by diligent structuring that ensures that the proposed undertaking will be compliant with laws, socio-political goals and SDGs and will not have initial or even significant negative impacts.

Dealing with National Champions

Within the EU and abroad, there are rules and institutions that constitute a political and economic checks and balances system against the driving forces behind state-backed mergers.

EU

In Europe, a key policy of the European Commission and the affiliate national competition authorities within the European Competition Network[43] is to protect free competition within the Union.[44] Thus, it is evident that the European Commission, in the past, has resolutely opposed the creation of National Champions by Member States.[45] A recent example is the prohibition of the state-backed attempted takeover of certain parts of Air Berlin by Lufthansa in merger control proceedings that would have increased the market-dominant position of Lufthansa in a highly regulated market.[46]

In order to be able to assess the admissibility of the respective governmental behaviour, it is essential to examine any imminent distortion of competition which, according to the case law of the European Court of Justice, applies whenever a public intervention improperly reinforces the position of a company in comparison to other competitors in community trade.[47] The benchmark used for this purpose is the 'normal market conditions' test.[48]

Competition law provides several tools to safeguard competitive market structures even when facing state-backed merger activities or abusive market behaviour by market-dominant National Champions. European competition law does not impose a flat prohibition on acts that lessen the intensity of competition but rather makes distinctions based on the way in which such effects are generated.[49]

43 The European Commission and the national competition authorities cooperate with each other through the European Competition Network (ECN), <http://ec.europa.eu/competition/ecn/>.

44 Immenga and Mestmäcker, *EU-Wettbewerbsrecht* [EU-Competition Law], recitals 17 et seq.

45 Whish and Bailey (n 2) 814, footnote 38 with further references.

46 European Commission, Case M.8633, OJ 2017/C 379/08 – Lufthansa/Certain Air Berlin Assets.

47 ECJ, 17.9.1980, Case 730/79, OJ 1980, S. 2671, recital 11 – Phillip Morris Holland/Commission.

48 Immenga and Mestmäcker (n 44) recitals 41 et seq.

49 Rosenthal and Thomas, *European Merger Control* (1st edn, 2010) A. recital 1; Bellamy and Child (n 5) recital 1.023.

In particular, the creation or the strengthening of a position of dominance is not prohibited if it is merely the result of a company's 'internal growth' (e.g. achievement of a technological advance, growth in financial resources, strategic advantages obtained through expansion of a distribution network). This is because the positive result of a company's own commercial success should not and will not be punished under European competition law.[50] However, if a company holds a dominant position in a given market, it must not misuse its market power, for example, by setting abusive prices or by discriminating against market participants (Art. 102 TFEU). If the strengthening of the company's market position, however, takes place through the concentration of previously independent companies (i.e. through 'external growth'), the effects on competition may raise concerns.[51] Therefore, the Council Regulation on the control of concentrations between undertakings (hereinafter 'Merger Regulation' or 'EUMR')[52] prohibits concentrations that meet certain jurisdictional thresholds if they 'would significantly impede effective competition in the common market or in a substantial part of it, in particular as a result of the creation or strengthening of a dominant position'.[53] In recent practice, the proposed acquisition of Air Berlin by Lufthansa, an attempt to create a German National Champion in the airline market, was cleared by the European Commission,[54] while the planned acquisition of Nikki and LGW by Lufthansa as part of the liquidation of the Air Berlin Group was terminated because the European Commission signalled its opposition to such plans.

Even in cases of state-owned enterprises, there are some limiting rules on a European level. Member States are, in principle, prohibited from taking measures that are contrary to European competition law and other policies of the EU. Article 106 (1) TFEU sets out the principle of non-preference of public and other state-related undertakings.[55] By contrast, Article 106 (2) TFEU pursues the objective of ensuring that services of general interest are safeguarded and, for that purpose, makes it possible to refrain from applying European law provisions.[56] Such a privilege will only be considered in a small number of cases.

50 Rosenthal and Thomas (n 49) A. recital 2.
51 ibid. A. recital 3.
52 Council Regulation (EC) No. 139/2004 on the control of concentrations between undertakings, OJ L 24, 29. 1. 2004, p. 1.
53 Rosenthal and Thomas (n 49) A. recital 5; Bellamy and Child (n 5) recital 8.191.
54 European Commission, Case M.8633, OJ 2017/C 379/08 – Lufthansa/Certain Air Berlin Assets.
55 Bechtold, Bosch and Brinker, *EU-Kartellrecht* [EU-Antitrust law], Art. 106 TFEU, recital 2; Bellamy and Child (n 5) recital 11.001.
56 Knauff in: Loewenheim, Meessen, Riesenkampff, Kersting and Meyer-Lindemann, *Kartellrecht* [Antitrust law], recitals 6 et seq.; Bellamy and Child (n 5) recital 11.046 et seqq. with further references.

In addition, Article 107 TFEU formulates a broad basic prohibition on state aid.[57] However, subsidies can be notified to and cleared by the European Commission if they are likely to have positive economic and other effects, and negative effects do not prevail.

CARICOM

Likewise, in Europe, a key policy of the CARICOM and the affiliate national competition authorities within its Member States is to protect free competition within the CARICOM Single Market and Economy (CSME). While the formation of this Single Market is a strategy to better respond to the challenges and opportunities presented by globalisation, the primary focus is on the Caribbean market.[58] Similar to EU regulations, the key elements[59] of the CSME include free movement of goods and services, free movement of people and capital and the Right of Establishment to permit the establishment of CARICOM-owned businesses in any Member State without restrictions.[60] Obviously, anti-competitive activities and structures may harm these principles. For example, National Champions that create market-dominant or monopolistic positions may foreclose national markets and prevent efficient competition within CARICOM. Thus, in addition to these basic principles of a common market, different antitrust rules are laid down to prevent any distortion or restriction of competition and the creation of monopolies.

Generally accepting monopolies, Article 31 of the Revised treaty of Chaguaramas[61] establishing the Caribbean community including the CARICOM single market and economy (RTC) requires that any state monopoly of a commercial nature does not discriminate against nationals of other Member States. In addition, Member States may determine that the public interest requires the exclusion or restriction of the right of establishment of state-backed monopolies in any

57 Despite the fact that the wording is ambiguous, Article 107 (1) TFEU is a prohibition fact, so the prevailing opinion; Wallenberg and Schütte, in: Grabitz, Hilf and Nettesheim, *EU*, Art. 107, recital 15; Mederer, in: GSH, *EU-Recht* [EU law], Art. 107, recital 2; Pache, NVwZ 1994, 318 (319); Calliess, Ruffert and Cremer, *EUV/AEUV, Das Verfassungsrecht der Europäischen Union mit Europäischer Grundrechtscharta* [TEU/TFEU, The Constitutional Law of the European Union with the Charter of Fundamental Rights of the European Union] Art. 107, recitals 8–9, Bellamy and Child (n 5) recital 17.001 with further references.

58 Turner, 'Caribbean Community (CARICOM)' in Turner (ed), *The Statesman's Yearbook* (2013) 63.

59 Secretariat Publications, CARICOM Single Market and Economy Free Movement and Competitiveness,2014/10/02<https://caricom.org/images/publications/9422/caribook-comepetitiveness.pdf>.

60 <https://caricom.org/our-work/the-caricom-single-market-and-economy-csme/>.

61 The Treaty of Chaguaramas was signed in 1973 and created the Caribbean Community. In 2001, a revised treaty was signed by the heads of government <https://caricom.org/documents/4906-revised_treaty-text.pdf>.

industry or in a particular sector of an industry."[62] On the other hand, according to Article 31 (2) (b) RTC, a Member State may determine that the public interest requires the continuation, or creation, of a private sector monopoly.[63] When granting exclusive rights to a private undertaking to pursue commercial activities,

> the Member State shall adopt appropriate measures to ensure that national treatment is accorded to nationals of other Member States in terms of participating in its operations.

Article 179 RTC aims for the prevention of the abuse of a dominant position and determines that an enterprise abuses its dominant position in a market if it prevents, restricts or distorts competition in the market. According to Article 174 (4) (c) RTC, the CARICOM Competition Commission (CCC) directs the enterprise to cease anti-competitive business conduct and to take such steps to overcome the effects of abuse of its dominant position in the market inconsistent with the principles of fair competition. Under Article 175 RTC, a Member State may approach the CCC[64] where it has reason to believe that business conduct by an enterprise located in another Member State prejudices trade and prevents, restricts or distorts competition. A common merger control regime on the Caribbean market is not subject to the treaty, but single Member States have merger control regimes that may apply to efforts to create National, respectively 'Caribbean', Champions.

Most of the CARICOM Member States (except The Bahamas and Montserrat) are also members of the World Trade Organisation (WTO).[65] As a result, they are subject to provisions contained in the General Agreement on Tariff and Trade (GATT) and the General Agreement on Trade in Services (GATS). Whether these provisions are suitable for preventing state-backed monopolies remains to be clarified next.

Trade and free trade agreements

In addition to the EU's rules, there are a variety[66] of free trade agreements between individual states or groups of countries that share the common goal of reducing tariffs and duties on imports from partner countries and eliminating the priority of domestic companies and products. Free trade is commonly understood to mean an

62 See for Article 31 (1) RTC: Treatment of Monopolies.

63 Kaczorowska and Ireland, *Competition Law in the CARICOM Single Market and Economy* (2015) 238.

64 The CARICOM Competition Commission (CCC) is the main body to enforce CSME competition law established on the basis of article 171 RTC; Kaczorowska and Ireland (n 63) 242.

65 See for the Caribbean Community Regional Aid for Trade Strategy 2013–2015, Caribbean Community Secretariat, p. 12 <https://caricom.org/documents/5269-caribbean_community_aft_strategy_final.pdf>.

66 <http://rtais.wto.org/UI/PublicMaintainRTAHome.aspx>.

alliance between two or more states or parts of a state's territory to create a zone where tariffs and other measures that restrict the trade between two partners are abolished.[67]

A free trade zone is generally created through an international law contract between participating states. The question is whether these arrangements have any means at their disposal to counteract the creation and promotion of National Champions.

The following is an example of the provisions of the WTO and the free trade agreement CETA, which may be capable of influencing the future possibility of creating or promoting state-backed monopolies.

WTO

The World Trade Organization (WTO) was established with the aim of reducing trade barriers and creating binding rules for international trade for all Member States.[68] Through the use of underlying multilateral international law contracts, the WTO has sought to create a form of global legal system for the principles of international trade.[69]

In addition to customs duties, technical regulations, standards and sanitary measures may create significant barriers to trade and may be abused to protect domestic products from competition.[70] Thus, two agreements, General Agreement on Tariffs and Trade (GATT) and General Agreement on Trade in Services (GATS) deal with a multitude of barriers to trade. The purpose of the multilateral agreement is to promote world economic development and prosperity by removing trade barriers and mediating trade conflicts. Barriers to trade shall be prevented by three basic principles laid down in the GATT:[71]

- the most-favoured-nation treatment (Art. I),
- the non-discrimination principle (Art. III Clause 1)
- the limitation of protective measures as regards tariffs (general elimination of quantitative restrictions and other trade barriers with respect to import and export, Art. XI)

67 Bergmann in: Bergmann, *Handlexikon der Europäischen Union, Stichwort: Freihandel* [Dictionary of the European Union; Entry: Free Trade] (5th edn, 2015); Grützner and Jakob in Grützner and Jakob, *Compliance A-Z, Stichwort: Zollunion* [Entry: Tariff Union] (2nd edn, 2015).

68 See for Bundesministerium für Ernährung und Landwirtschaft [Federal Ministry of Food and Agriculture] <www.bmel.de/DE/Landwirtschaft/Markt-Handel-Export/_Texte/Welthandel.html?docId=381122>.

69 This must be distinguished from private law rules that are internationally agreed on and govern the legal relationships of private persons in international trade, see (e.g. Ferrari, Kieninger, Mankowski et al., *Internationales Vertragsrecht*) [International Contract Law] (2nd edn, 2011).

70 Van der Bossche and Prevost, *Essentials of WTO Law*, Chapter 6, 178.

71 Krajewski, *Wirtschaftsvölkerrecht* [Economic International Law], Chapter section 2, 85, recitals 302 et seq.

The provision of non-discrimination applies not only to state-owned enterprises but also to those to which the state grants special or exclusive rights, in particular, state-protected monopolies.[72] While monopolies or exclusive service suppliers can obviously impede trade, WTO law does not generally prohibit them.[73]

To date, the WTO agreements do not include any separate or in any way extensive rules concerning antitrust law.[74] This is mainly due to the fact that the stipulation of national or supra-national provisions on antitrust law requires an approach adjusted to the respective developmental status and the set of political priorities of each contracting party.[75] Therefore, the provisions of WTO law, GATT and GATS are mostly not suitable to deal with state-backed monopolies. However, global regulators recommend a 'common approach' in closely scrutinising deals that would create National Champions to compete on the global stage but harm domestic competition.[76]

CETA

The CETA agreement[77] between the EU and Canada formulates common trade objectives, which in addition to the economic sector also permeate into social and environmental areas. The agreement removes customs duties between the EU and Canada. The agreement integrates strict control of sustainability strategies to ensure a high degree of transparency. In general, the provisions in CETA correspond to the UN SDGs.[78]

Agreements like CETA or NAFTA typically do not create a stand-alone antitrust system which is directly applicable and equipped with an independent enforcement mechanism.[79] Instead, principles and rough minimum standards are stipulated. Therefore, the influence of CETA on the formation of state-backed monopolies and National Champions will be minimal.

Conclusions

The creation or prevention of National Champions may or may not have negative or positive effects on trade, trade policy and SDGs. The recent past proves

72 Weiß in: Hermann, Weiß and Ohler, *Welthandelsrecht* [World Trade Law] (2nd edn), section 16, recital 775.

73 Bossche and Zdouc, *The Law and Policy of the WTO*, 537.

74 Stancke, 'TTIP, CETA und die Rolle des Wettbewerbsrechts in internationalen Freihandelsabkommen' [TTIP, CETA and the Role of Competition Law in International Free Trade Agreements] (EuZW 2016) 567.

75 Meessen, 'Competition in the Doha Round of WTO Negotiations' in Schrijver and Weiss (eds), *International Law and Sustainable Development* (2004) 217 et seq.

76 Carles Esteva Mosso at the 7th China Competition Policy Forum, University of International Business and Economics Competition Law Center, Beijing, 31 July August, 2018.

77 Comprehensive Economic and Trade Agreement (CETA) <http://ec.europa.eu/trade/policy/in-focus/ceta/ceta-chapter-by-chapter/index_en.htm>.

78 Huck and Kurkin, 'Die UN-Sustainable Development Goals (SDGs) im transnationalen Mehrebenensystem' [The UN Sustainable Development Goals (SDGs) in the Transnational Multi-Level System] (ZaöRV 2018) 375 (401).

79 Stancke (n 74) 567.

that the liberalisation of the markets will bring down prices and create new jobs. Technological progress will be much faster in a competitive environment than under a sluggish monopolist. Effectively enforced competition rules can provide incentives for companies to improve their efficiency, avoiding wasteful practices and ensuring the sustainable use of natural resources.[80] If governments decide to take measures to favour individual companies, this should only be temporary. Such support has to be consistent with long-term goals and should not lay the basis for future structural problems.[81]

The principles of transparency and non-discrimination serve to depoliticise antitrust law and policy, removing the possibility of including industrial policy considerations within the competition framework and ensuring the independence of antitrust authorities.[82] In general, rather than building up National Champions, it is more fruitful if government action is limited to setting the framework conditions for effective competition and socio-political goals. Good competition law policy enforcement requires a high degree of accountability, openness and monitoring.[83] The best way to keep companies competitive is to ensure they operate in open and dynamic markets.[84] Only in markets that remain vulnerable can consumers be protected from excessive prices and inappropriate terms, as well as benefit from quality products, new ideas and services.[85] Interventionist industrial policies that give preference to established undertakings should therefore be avoided.[86] There are also ways to integrate the concept of sustainable development into policy and antitrust law by accepting efficiencies and consumer benefits reflected in the SDGs through the substantive analysis of cases.

80 Jenny (n 22) 356; Farah and Ötvös (n 32) 511.
81 OECD Global Forum on Competition (n 13) 15.
82 Galloway (n 12) 180; Farah and Ötvös (n 32) 502.
83 Jenny (n 22) 356.
84 Mosso (n 76).
85 Mundt (n 16) 14.
86 To reduce the potential for conflict between competition policy and industrial policy one could adopt an industrial policy that promotes National Champions only in sectors where it is indispensable for improving the competitiveness of the economy in question. However, this would require that there actually be a market failure, that the aid is necessary and proportionate to eliminate it, and that these positive effects are not offset by the negative effects of the distortion of competition; see OECD Global Forum on Competition (n 13) 14 et seq.

13 Charting a path to sustainable development

Goals of CARICOM and the EU

Cherisse Francis

The Caribbean Community was aimed at 'full integration of the national markets of all Member States into a single unified and open market area'.[1] Ideally, it was to become 'an area without internal frontiers' similar to the EU.[2] The CARICOM Skilled Nationals Certificate,[3] the removal of trade restrictions and the region's various trading arrangements[4] have all pursued this objective.[5] These initiatives seek to create economic and trading unities potentially facilitating the 'sustained growth of mutually beneficial intra-community and international trade'.[6] Notwithstanding these efforts, the region continues to face several internal and external challenges.

Internal challenges

Internally, CARICOM's development is hindered by challenges including: nationalistic attitudes by Member States and social, cultural and geographic constraints. Harsh economic conditions and declining inter-regional trade in the 1970s and 1980s made nationalism a priority for Caribbean islands. This attitude persists as CARICOM Heads of State repeatedly reject the idea of a common currency and delay the harmonisation of domestic laws to reflect regional goals. On one hand, regional institutions have made great strides underscoring the endless possibilities of 'homegrown' solutions. On the other, they face great financial turmoil and societal rejection. Without characteristics such as a common currency and harmonised laws, a fully integrated Caribbean common market remains an ambitious vision.

1 Revised Treaty of Chaguaramas establishing the Caribbean Community including the CARICOM Single Market and Economy (adopted 5 July 2001, entered into force 1 January 2006) 2259 UNTS 293 (RTC), art 78(2)(a).
2 Consolidated Version of the Treaty on the Functioning of the European Union [2016] OJ C 202/59, art 26(2).
3 RTC (n 1) art 46.
4 The region has agreements with Costa Rica, Colombia, Cuba, the Dominican Republic, the EU and Venezuela.
5 RTC (n 1).
6 ibid. art 78(1).

This paradox is exemplified through the Caribbean Court of Justice (CCJ). This court has proven invaluable in setting regional precedents on a wide range of topics from electoral to immigration matters and even import tariffs and duties. Notwithstanding this, only four Member States have accepted its Appellate jurisdiction[7] with Antigua and Grenada rejecting this move by referendum in 2018.[8] Periodically, there has also been dissention by the signatory jurisdictions with the leaders threatening to withdraw.[9] These threats often arise during times of political instability, reflecting the uncertainty in developing CSME and other CARICOM institutions. Thus, the situation exists that while Caribbean political leaders are at this time seemingly more open to considering regional entities, this is not reinforced with political strength or societal acceptance.

Secondly, the region's social, cultural and geographic intricacies presently function as dividing elements rather than connectors. CARICOM Member States were conquered by various sovereigns, speak different languages and have distinctive communities. Furthermore, the sea that separates our territories is another intricacy which distinguishes the Caribbean's position from that of the EU. These thousands of miles of water are viewed as the biggest limitation to economic integration[10] but are in reality a prime highway for exchange.

Factually, the Caribbean islands are smaller than the EU, which has masterfully embraced the common market, providing their consumers with cheaper, higher qualities of good and services without tariff restrictions and checks. Thus, establishing and maintaining unity is not impossible. The high level of commonality between the territories through the shared experiences of slavery and colonisation underscore this position. It is accepted that establishing a stable relationship between sovereign states is more difficult from a trade perspective than within a singular landmass such as the EU. A cohesive move of this nature requires political willpower and support. Consequentially, the region must to some extent accept responsibility for these challenging but not insurmountable internal difficulties.

External challenges

External challenges such as shifts in the global market, the reduction of preferential trading agreements, the predisposition of the region to natural disasters and most recently Brexit possibilities also threaten CARICOM's present and future realities.

7 These territories are Barbados, Belize, Dominica and Guyana.

8 Caribbean Media Corporation, 'CCJ President Respects the Outcome of the Referenda in Antigua, Grenada' *Nation News* (Bridgetown, 7 November 2018) <www.nationnews.com/nationnews/news/211743/ccj-president-respects-outcome-referenda-antigua-grenada>.

9 George Alleyne, 'Barbados PM Wants Out of Carib Court of Justice' (2018) 29(21) Caribbean Life News 6.

10 Richard L Abbott, 'The Caribbean Free Trade Association' (1969) 1(3) Lawyer of the Americas 1, 3.

CARICOM Member States rely on trading agreements to sustain their economies and facilitate further trade.[11] To increase bargaining power and global profile, CARICOM has negotiated as a unified group entering into several one-way preferential agreements and reciprocal agreements. A prominent example is the 2008 CARIFORUM-EU Economic Partnership Agreement (EPA), which creates a preferential trading relationship with the EU.[12] This agreement allows for foreign investments and financial support for the Caribbean to set up commercial practice within the EU, ensuring predictable market access.[13] The difficulty with this and many of the region's formal trading relationships[14] is that there has not been 'movement up the value chain'.[15] Instead of generating surplus trade, figures have plateaued or declined. [16] CARICOM recorded trade deficits moving from USD 3.1 billion in 2011 to USD 9.1 billion in 2016.[17] In fact, 2017 was the first year that foreign trade showed marginal signs of recovery after years of negative performance.[18] Since the trends do not reflect the initial aspiration, there has been great concern about the cost-benefit ratio of preferential trading agreements.

There have also been unfavourable changes in the global trading market; for example, the erosion of the region's preferential arrangements for exporting sugar and bananas to the EU.[19] This shift was most detrimental to Member States such as Saint Lucia and Dominica, which export these goods. Moreover, CARICOM's long-standing trading relationship with Canada has been eroded by Canada's increased market liberalisation, making preferential margins less effective.[20] The

11 Sheldon Mc Lean and Jeetendra Khadan, *An Assessment of the Performance of CARICOM Extraregional Trade Agreements: An Initial Scoping Exercise* (Studies and Perspectives Series – The Caribbean No. 41, United Nations ECLAC Subregional Headquarters for the Caribbean 2015) ch 1, 8.

12 CARIFORUM is made up of the CARICOM Member States except Montserrat along with Cuba and the Dominican Republic. However, Cuba and Haiti did not sign the Economic Partnership Agreement. See Economic Partnership Agreement between the CARIFORUM States of the one part, and the European Community and its Member States of the other Part [2008] OJ L289/I/10 pt 2 ch 1 art 19.

13 Economic Partnership Agreement between the CARIFORUM States of the one part, and the European Community and its Member States of the other Part [2008] OJ L289/I/10 pt 2 ch 1 art 1.

14 See text to (n 10).

15 Mc Lean and Khadan (n 11) 18.

16 ibid. 15. CARIFORUM Exports to the UK and the EU have contracted since 2008. CARIFORUM Exports to the EU halved from about USD 6.2 billion in 2008 to USD 3.1 billion in 2015.

17 The Regional Statistics Programme, *Snapshot of CARICOM's Trade: CARICOM's Total Trade Summary by Trading Partners 2011–2016* (Series 2, The CARICOM Secretariat 2018) 1.

18 Economic Commission for Latin America and the Caribbean (ECLAC), *International Trade Outlook for Latin America and the Caribbean: Recovery in an Uncertain Context* (LC/PUB.2017/22-P, 2017), Santiago, 14.

19 Paul Goodison, 'The ACP Experience of Preference Erosion in the Banana and Sugar Sectors' (*International Centre for Trade and Sustainable Development*, Issue Paper 7, May 2007).

20 CARICOM Secretariat, 'Background to CARICOM's Trade Relationship with Canada' (*Caribbean Community*, 26 February 1979) <https://caricom.org/Document-Library/view-document/background-to-caricom-s-trade-relationship-with-canada>.

agreement with Canada is also limited to trade in goods, which is significantly less important to most CARICOM Member States than trade in services.[21] In many instances, though the sub-region negotiates as a block, this has not compensated for the small markets and 'weak supply side capacity'. This coupled with the different priority markets of individual islands has negated the benefits from these relationships.[22]

Another factor is the global financial crisis of 2008–09. While developed nations are recovering from the downturn, many developing nations, including CARICOM Member States, have remained vulnerable to changes in the international economy. This crisis compounded nationalistic interests leading to increased national debts and dependency on foreign borrowing and foreign aid.

The uncertainties of Brexit, as discussed in chapters 2, 3 and 9, are also a major challenge for the EU-CARICOM trading relationship. This is because the EU remains one of CARICOM's major trading partners, surpassed only by the United States.[23] Within the EU trading block, the UK is CARICOM's closest ally due to the strong historical connections and ever-growing trade.[24] However, the precise ramifications remain unclear as negotiations on implementation strategies continue. CARICOM's concern is that the UK's withdrawal from the EU will weaken the EU trading block, leaving fewer resources for foreign aid and creating disruptions of the trade links affecting remittances, tourism and investments. [25]

21 ibid.

22 Mohammad Razzaque and Brendan Vickers, 'Post-Brexit UK – ACP Trading Arrangements: Some Reflections' (*The Commonwealth Trade Hot Topics*, 2016) issue 137, 3 <http://thecommonwealth.org/sites/default/files/news-items/documents/5jln9q109bmr-en.pdf>.

23 CARICOM Secretariat, 'CARICOM's Total Trade with Principle Trading Partners and the Rest of the World' (*CARICOM Regional Online Trading System*, 2001) pt 1, 4 <www.caricomstats.org/Files/Publications/Quick%20Ref%20Files/Updated%20files/Part%20I-%20Total%20Trade.pdf>.

24 CARICOM Secretariat, 'CARICOM's Top 10 Trading Partners' (*CARICOM Regional Trade Information System*, 2014) <http://caricomstats.info/tradsysonline/PDF_Reports/report8.pdf>. The total UK Bi-lateral Trade with CARIFORUM group of nations totalled 2.1 billion pounds in 2016. United Kingdom Department for International Trade, 'Joint Statement on Trade between UK and the CARIFORUM States' (*Gov. UK*, 16 November 2017) <www.gov.uk/government/news/joint-statement-on-trade-between-uk-and-the-cariforum-states>. CARICOM's imports in 2017 amounted to USD 30,801,946, and of that figure the EU 28 accounted for $3,376,652 (10.96%), and of that percentage USD 423,913 (1.38%) was imported from the United Kingdom. The 2017 exports picture was similar, CARICOM's exports had a value of USD 14,270,901; 2,677,262 (18.76%) of which went to the EU 28 and USD 352,498 (2.47%) to the UK. International Trade Centre, 'Bilateral Trade between Caribbean Community (CARICOM) and United Kingdom All Products' (*International Trade Centre*, 2017) <www.trademap.org/Bilateral_TS.aspx?nvpm=1||37|826||TOTAL|||2|1|1|1|2|1|1|1|1>.

25 As a result of Brexit, the EU will be losing its second largest economy, the UK, which accounts for approximately 17% of its GDP. Edwin Laurent, Lorand Bartels, Paul Goodison, Paula Hippolyte and Sindra Sharma, *After Brexit . . . Securing ECP Economic Interests* (Rila Publications Ltd 2017) 11.

In response, the UK proposed maintaining the terms of the current CARIFORUM-EU EPA post-Brexit.[26] In fact, in March 2019, members of the CARIFORUM grouping signed an Agreement[27] with the UK, which replicates the ongoing EPA and 'will govern their trade after the UK leaves the European Union'.[28] Prior to the 2019 EPA, the UK had suggested that 'a technical exercise to ensure continuity in their preferential trading relationship, rather than an opportunity to renegotiate exiting terms' was what was required.[29] However, the sustainability and feasibility of implementing this Agreement is questionable. While CARICOM's negotiating position and signature of the EPA make it unlikely CARICOM would discontinue the CARICOM-UK relationship, the performance of the UK market as a sole entity and the pound sterling is yet to be seen. Until this becomes a reality, the true effects of this continuity agreement remain to be seen.[30] Any formal engagement in trade negotiations by the UK as a solitary entity would be contrary to the EU's objectives[31] and implicitly prohibited until the UK has left the Union.

Some forecasts predict that arrangements such as those in the EPA could become unsuitable for the region when replicated with the UK alone. The Caribbean's major exports to the UK such as bananas, rum and tobacco are currently governed by treaties and could incur new requirements, removing the competitive nature of the region's goods. To combat this possibility, the 2019 EPA[32] seeks to 'eliminate tariffs on all goods imported from signing CARIFORUM States into the UK',[33] making the products more competitive. On the other side, these 'Caribbean states will continue gradually to cut import tariffs on most of the region's imports from the UK'.[34] Even with this 'safeguard', it is imperative that CARICOM's trade negotiators firmly place regional interests at the forefront when implementing this new Agreement. While the UK features prominently in

26 United Kingdom Department for International Trade (n 24).
27 Economic Partnership Agreement between the CARIFORUM States, of the one part, and the United Kingdom of Great Britain and Northern Ireland, of the other part (Castries, 22 March 2019).
28 CARICOM Secretariat, 'CARIFORUM Member States Sign Agreement to Preserve Trade with the United Kingdom after Brexit' <www.caricom.org/media-center/communications/press-releases/cariforum-member-states-sign-agreement-to-preserve-trade-with-the-united-kingdom-after-brexit>.
29 United Kingdom Department for International Trade (n 24).
30 Jeetendra Khadan and Inder J Ruprah, *Brexit and the Caribbean: Much Ado About Nothing?* (Inter-American Development Bank, October 2016) 5. The CARIFORUM-UK EPA is expected to come into effect in January 2021 or in the case of a no-deal Brexit, as soon as possible after the UK leaves the EU.
31 United Kingdom Department for International Trade (n 26).
32 Economic Partnership Agreement between the CARIFORUM States, of the one part, and the United Kingdom of Great Britain and Northern Ireland, of the other part (Castries, 22 March 2019).
33 United Kingdom Department for International Trade, 'UK Signs Trade Continuity Agreement with Caribbean Countries' (*Gov. UK*, 22 March 2019) <www.gov.uk/government/news/uk-signs-trade-continuity-agreement-with-caribbean-countries>.
34 ibid.

EU-CARICOM trade and absorbs a large portion of the region's exports, the contributions of the remaining 27 EU Member States cannot be negated, and this relationship must also be respected.

In the last few decades, environmental and climate change concerns have reached new global proportions. They have become prevalent enough to be included in the Sustainable Development Goals.[35] For the Caribbean region this has been particularly meaningful. The physical location and small sizes of these islands create a vulnerability to natural disasters such as hurricanes, floods and earthquakes. These phenomena have great destructive potential for the economic strongholds: tourism and agricultural goods. Within the last five years, weather patterns have become more erratic with an increase in more devastating natural disasters. In 2017 alone, Hurricanes Maria, Irma and Tropical Storm Erika have ravaged islands such as Dominica and Antigua and Barbuda among others. The occurrences have diminished the export capacity of the region in agricultural goods and the inward flow of tourists.[36] By extension, this has impacted foreign trade and weakened or destroyed economies. The cost of these 2017 natural disasters is estimated to have exceeded the national gross domestic products (GDPs) of the affected islands.[37]

All these challenges indicate that there must be significant change for the growth and development of CARICOM. What is unclear is the path for reform. Should the Caribbean chart our own path first proposing our own interests, or should we continue along the journey of partnerships, being possibly forced into a defensive position? To maintain any relevance CARICOM as a sub-regional grouping must be self-sustaining in the globalised world. The Sustainable Development Goals and their impact on global relationships will now be discussed as a mechanism to remain globally 'relevant'.

A global look at development

Development is a concept which has proven difficult to define but has been understood as 'a process of expanding the real freedoms that people enjoy'.[38] The process requires removing the barriers to freedom, including poverty, tyranny, poor economic opportunities, systemic social deprivation and state intolerance or over-activity.[39] Successful development involves the participation and progression

35 United Nations General Assembly, *Transforming Our World: The 2030 Agenda for Sustainable Development*, UNGA Res 70/1 (21 October 2015) UN Doc A/RES/70/1, Goal 13.

36 In the British Virgin Islands, damages and loses in the tourism sector are estimated to be USD 1.2 billion. United Nations Development Programme Barbados and the OECS, *From Early Recovery to Long-Term Resilience in the Caribbean: Hurricanes Irma and Maria: One Year On* (UNDP, September 2018) 7.

37 Recovery needs for Dominica amounted to USD 1.37 billion and for Antigua and Barbuda they amounted to USD 222 million. United Nations Development Programme Barbados and the OECS (n 36) 6.

38 Amartya Sen, *Development as Freedom* (Anchor Books 2000) 3.

39 ibid.

of all people and is necessary for all States. To achieve a worldwide standard of development 191 UN Member States signed onto the United Nations Millennium Declaration[40] in September 2000.

The resulting eight interdependent Millennium Development Goals (MDGs) created an unprecedented approach to development. Eradicating poverty was the primary focus of the MDGs, but there was a shift from the unilateral focus on economic growth. The MDGs also included concrete targets and indicators for measuring progress. This concept became known as sustainable development and encompassed several major development issues, including health, the environment, education and global partnerships. It was acknowledged from an early stage that sustainable development requires 'the participation of diverse stakeholders and perspectives' that have different and at times opposing views and goals.[41] These stakeholders work collectively to achieve simultaneous goals categorised into three pillars: economic, social and environmental sustainable development.

However, these goals were very thin on participation and partnership and took on an unsuitable one-size-fits-all approach. For example, Goal 8, 'Global Partnership for Development' was intended to be funded by developed countries investing 0.7% of their Gross National Income to this effort. However, most of the donor countries fell below this target assistance rate thought necessary to achieve the MDGs. Moreover, the MDGs failed to recognise the different needs of individual countries.

Therefore, in 2015 it came as no great surprise that the Goals were not met, giving way to the Sustainable Development Goals (SDGs) and the 2030 Agenda for Sustainable Development.[42] These 17 goals have advanced the causes of their predecessors, now including issues such as climate change.[43] These goals are intended to apply to all countries equally with the central premise of global collaboration towards shared challenges.

The EU has committed to being a forerunner in the implementation of the SDGs, integrating them into its development policy. In an effort to support SDG 1, 'End poverty in all its forms everywhere',[44] the EU has lent assistance to the least developed countries and lower income countries where poverty is most concentrated.[45] One instrument facilitating this funding is the European Development Fund, from which many CARICOM Member States are direct beneficiaries. As previously mentioned, Brexit could have implications for the Caribbean

40 United Nations Millennium Declaration, UNGA Res 55/2 (18 September 2000) UN Doc A/RES/55/2.

41 Robert W Kates, Thomas M Parris and Anthony A Leiserowitz, 'What Is Sustainable Development? Goals, Indicators, Values, and Practice' (*Environment Magazine*)10. <www.cepn-paris13.fr/epog/wp-content/uploads/2016/01/CONSOLO_Kates-et-al.pdf>.

42 United Nations General Assembly (n 35).

43 See text to (n 35).

44 United Nations General Assembly (n 42).

45 European Commission, 'Sustainable Development Goals' <https://ec.europa.eu/europeaid/policies/sustainable-development-goals_en>.

through this fund as Britain's substantial contribution might cease leaving fewer resources available for foreign aid.

Conversely, in the Caribbean, the SDGs have been a constant source of discussion, and the need for development and innovation is non-contentious. However, the relevance, both intellectually and practically, of the specific SDGs in their present formulation has arguably been neglected. [46] In presenting frameworks for CARICOM's future, the SDGs applicability to the region will be considered.

Frameworks for the future of CARICOM

It has been concluded that, 'without fundamental change, CARICOM could expire slowly over the next few years'.[47] This position of uncertainty makes the Caribbean a prime catchment area for sustainable development. Therefore, rather than advancing an infallible solution to the region's difficulties, this chapter will suggest a number of possibilities.

Arguably, the most practical way to ensure progress is to build upon the already-established Caribbean Community in a way similar to the EU's approach. As previously mentioned, CARICOM's success is hindered by the nationalistic attitudes plaguing the nations. As early as 1943, West Indian scholars recognised that if the region fails to 'think and plan in terms of a federated West Indian group', [48] there will always be single island units 'entirely at the economic mercy of the more advanced and more powerful countries of the world'.[49] Thus, the first step to a new approach is to solidify internal perspectives and objectives into a unified action plan. One of the major goals of the action plan should be examining current institutions to confirm their appropriateness for contemporary society. Next, the weaknesses of these institutions must be addressed. CARICOM's governance structure could benefit from a restructuring. The current periodic rotations reduce perceptions of bias or 'favouritism' but do little to mitigate nationalistic attitudes. The EU system presents a possible model for reform.

Within that system Commissioners are nominated by their Member States in consultation with the President of the European Commission. The entire team requires approval subject to hearings by the European Parliament, after which the Commission is formally put into office. Once the Commission takes office, the Commissioners must act in accordance with the best European interests rather than as representatives of their states. This system heightens the level of independence and transparency but has its own prevailing faults such as a gender imbalance and a lack of ethnic minorities.

46 Nigel O M Brissett, 'Sustainable Development Goals (SDGs) and the Caribbean: Unrealizable Promises?' (2017) 18(1) Progress in Development Studies 18, 18.

47 'Centrifugal Force: Caribbean Integration' (*The Economist*, London, 2 June 2012) <www.economist.com/node/21556277>.

48 Colin A Palmer, *Eric Williams and the Making of the Modern Caribbean* (University of North Carolina Press 2006) ch 2, 38.

49 ibid.

As a prerequisite to the 'new CARICOM', Member States should be required to make certain commitments, financial and otherwise to the institutions. This could diminish any animosity between the islands that are reluctant to give 'supranational authority to any of CARICOM's organs'.[50] Externally perceived unity remains one of the EU's strengths. They created and codified a structure influenced by their agreed principles, which has guided them through both internal and external challenges.[51] An added advantage to this proposal is that it could stimulate buy-in from those Member States which are hesitant to embrace some regional institutions. While this would not be an exact replica of the EU, we could use this entity for guidance. For example, SDG 16, which promotes peace, justice and strong institutions, is pertinent to the Caribbean due to ongoing challenges with child rights, human trafficking and domestic violence. CARICOM already embraces democratic principles such as the respect for human rights and non-discrimination and uses the Caribbean Court of Justice (CCJ) to promote these ideas. Making the suggested reforms and expanding this portfolio could lead to capacity building and promotion and enforcement of non-discriminatory laws and policies for sustainable development as the EU has done with the European Courts.

One challenge to these amendments is the economic constraints which the region is currently facing. Institutional capacity-building requires finances for training, payment of personnel and physical infrastructure but simultaneously presents an opportunity for the international community to engage the SDGs. Goal 17 mentions the need to 'revitalise the global partnership for sustainable development'. CARICOM already relies on foreign aid and investment to keep its economies afloat. Now would be the time to expand these established relationships and create new agreements, which include and use the technical resources of developed countries, such as those in the EU.

Additionally, establishing a modern-day 'federation' would require placing more emphasis on economic cooperation through the CARICOM Single Market and Economy (CSME).[52] Currently, the CSME has not been fully implemented but aims to build economic resilience by ensuring free intra-regional trade.[53] In the past, issues including the common currency have remained contentious but must now be decided conclusively. Adopting a common currency similar to the EU's euro would bind the nations as a fully integrated movement and is considered by some as 'vital to economic unity'. This move would also benefit the

50 David S Berry, *Caribbean Integration Law* (OUP 2014) 440.

51 'The Caribbean and the European Union' (*European Commission*, May 2002) 4.

52 His Excellency Brigadier David Granger, President of the Cooperative Republic of Guyana, 'The Spirit of Chaguaramas' (28th Inter-Sessional Meeting of the Conference of Heads of Governments of the Caribbean Community, Guyana, 16 February 2017) <https://caricom.org/media-center/communications/speeches/the-spirit-of-chaguaramas>.

53 Dr the Rt. Honourable Keith Mitchell, 'Opening Address' (29th Intercessional Meeting of the Conference of Heads of Government of CARICOM, Port-au-Prince, 01 March 2018) <https://caricom.org/media-center/communications/communiques/communiqu-29th-intersessional-meeting-of-the-conference-of-heads-of-government-of-caricom>.

market through reduced trade barriers, less risks and a more competitive market environment.[54] Removing exchange rates via a common currency would enable quicker and more efficient trade within the region and raise the dollar value in some territories. This method of collaboration would correct the internal concerns while equipping the region to drive existing and future trading relationships more effectively. Internal strength would provide the fortitude to weather external challenges like economic downturns and changes in the trade community better than in the past.

Moreover, the prospect of a fully functioning single market could propel changes in the agricultural sector, which accounts for a significant percentage of the exports of many Caribbean nations. [55] CARICOM's goods exports go mainly to extra regional markets[56] with goods exports within the sub-regional group accounting for approximately 15 percent of goods exports.[57] On the other hand, taking an approach modelled after Europe could be risky considering that Europe's seemingly impenetrable unity is slowly disintegrating.[58] Even the adoption of the euro was not unanimous, indicating that total integration was simply an illusion and Brexit was a long-standing possibility.[59] Alternatively, the EU's consistent performance without a single currency could suggest that this is not a necessity for success. Moreover, the current practical difficulties for the sub-region in implementing a single currency such as the presence of the IMF, downgrades and the fluctuation of currency in some of its islands highlight that a single currency might not be as progressive for the Caribbean as once thought.

The EU's usefulness as a model or the region is limited to being a good example for the necessary level of economic integration rather than being an ordinary federation.[60] Thus, the approach taken in the Caribbean must be different. After addressing the weaknesses of CARICOM's present institutions, their contemporary appropriateness must be analysed to determine whether they remain too ambitious and if the necessary political will and courage to continue the progress exists.[61] Caribbean leaders have recently stepped forward, re-affirming their support for regional institutions and commencing further works. Stakeholder consultations have been held on the CARICOM Single Market and Economy (CSME) to examine its current organisation and implementation and to make

54 (n 51) 3.
55 Mitchell (n 53).
56 Mc Lean and Khadan (n 11) 8.
57 ibid. 8.
58 France and Germany are drifting apart, and other territories are moving in a different direction, disengaging from the EU project. See Miroslav N Jovanovic, 'Was European Integration Nice while It Lasted? (2013) 28(1) Journal of Economic Integration 1, 2.
59 Edwin Laurent and others, *After Brexit . . . Securing ECP Economic Interests* (Rila Publications Ltd 2017) 19.
60 Miroslay N Jovanovic, 'Was European Integration Nice while It Lasted?' (2013) 28(1) Journal of Economic Integration 1, 17.
61 CARICOM Secretariat, 'Stakeholders Zero in on Implementation as CSME Consultation Gets Underway' (Guyana, 8 June 2018).

recommendations on enhancing effectiveness. The findings from these consultations are designed for consideration by the Council for Trade and Economic Development (COTED) and informing the review of the CSME, being undertaken by the CARICOM Conference of Heads of Government.[62]

Moreover, CARICOM has begun to strengthen its current international relationships with blueprints based on the SDGs and the 2030 Agenda. With this new knowledge and the suggestions outlined, the region could be poised to move forward with a third federation attempt.

Diversification of products and markets

Only a few CARICOM Member States can be categorised as goods producers, and most are dominated by the service industry, specifically tourism.[63] In those states that do export goods, the top ten products account for over 75% of exports. This low number of primary products makes the economies vulnerable to external shocks, particularly changes in commodity prices. Additionally, internal complexities such as natural disasters contribute to the precarious situation, making Caribbean economies susceptible to challenges such as economic recessions mentioned earlier.[64] To mitigate the effects of these difficulties CARICOM countries have increasingly relied on external financing. This external reliance exacerbates the debt crisis and could be a colossal failure as the conditions in Europe change post-Brexit. Added to this, the UK has been a primary export market. Effectively, many of the current issues associated with this limitation would be remedied by more diversifications in markets and trade.

It has been suggested that the Caribbean region can offer to the world unique services such as historical and cultural tourism. Indigenous resources including marijuana and other plant-based substances could increase the primary goods, providing additional foreign revenue. Global perspectives are shifting as markets open up to items that would once have been thought taboo, notably, the recent legalisation of marijuana in many countries for both medical and recreational purposes. If properly utilised, this could open up research and intellectual property options, provide jobs in manufacturing, product development and marketing, among others. This seemingly controversial and complex choice is not impossible. Alcohol, which is now a commonly traded commodity, has itself faced a similar past of prohibition and criminalisation.

This diversification should go beyond products and must include new trading partners to reduce the reliance on the EU and more specifically the UK. In diversifying our trading partners, we must also reshape our approach to trade totally. CARICOM's trading relationships require it to open its borders in a way that wasn't previously required. On one hand, open trade and cheap imports benefit

62 ibid.

63 Sheldon Mc Lean et al, 'Regional Integration in the Caribbean: The Role of Trade Agreements and Structural Transformation' LC/CAR/L.448. Santiago, Chile. ECLAC sub-regional headquarters for the Caribbean (ECLAC).

64 ibid.

consumers through lower prices. However, this is detrimental to the domestic industries and can have severe implications for the balance of trade, as has been the case with CARICOM. Thus, some critics of liberalisation have suggested that CARICOM institute a level of protectionism allowing the region to grow as a trading block before re-opening the market. Following the 2008 economic crisis, the EU members implemented these types of mechanisms with some level of success to aid the recovery of their economies. [65] The concern of many economists, policymakers and scholars is that protectionist measures do more harm than good by limiting consumer choices while enforcing higher prices and inciting trade wars. Considering the small size of our markets, it is doubtful that the region possesses the resources necessary to be completely self-sustaining. Any close-market protectionist mechanisms could also open the region to disputes as a result of various international obligations. This would be counter-productive as any negative international attention could damage our reputation and by extension our economic success.

The Caribbean experience highlights that trade liberalisation is not enough for development, and there must be an integrated approach.[66] Though policy is important as it guides the functioning of bureaucratic institutions, this reformation must venture beyond written policies. Practically, CARICOM's sustainable development would require internal industrial policies, which inform trade policies.[67] Reformulating existing policy is necessary, and trade must play a central role in conjunction with all other policies. The full integration of all roles and capacities of both the governmental and non-governmental sectors are very important from an institutional standpoint.[68] The concept of partnerships is also prominent on the global level as SDG 17 makes reference to the building of global partnerships to achieve the other goals and foster collaboration rather than completion. The idea is that developing countries will do more to ensure their own development, and developed countries support them through, aid, debt relief and better opportunities for trade. Thus, partnerships, both domestic and international are seen as vital to 'enabling trade policy', which by extension contributes to resolving development problems.[69] These partnerships would further efforts to ensure that the practices of various stakeholders properly fulfil the sub-region's mandates. Efforts to achieve these objectives have begun, as sustainable development has been included in Article 3 of the CARIFORUM-EU EPA in furtherance of SDG 17. This is a momentous move as trade can be one of the most instrumental mechanisms to achieve sustainable development. There can be

65 Marta Wajda-Lichy, 'Trade Protectionism versus Behind-the-Border Barriers in the Post-crisis Era: Experience of Three Groups of Countries: The EU, NAFTA and BRICS' (2014) 7(2) Journal of International Studies 145.

66 JR Deep Ford, Crescenzo dell'Aquila and Piero Conforti, *Agricultural Trade Policy and Food Security in the Caribbean: Structural Issues, Multilateral Negotiations and Competitiveness* (Trade and Markets Division of the Food and Agriculture Organisation of the United Nations 2007) 31.

67 Mc Lean and Khadan (n 11) 15.

68 Deep Ford, dell'Aquila and Conforti (n 66) 32.

69 ibid. 8.

an indirect connection to the eradication of poverty, hunger and so on since trade is a vehicle for economic growth and development.

Building on this framework and recognising that CARICOM consists of developing countries, there should be a push to increase their global exports. As the major goods and services market of the UK becomes exposed to the ramifications of Brexit, there needs to be the opening of more markets in a timely manner. It must also be noted that this approach is not the fastest nor easiest. Its implementation would require significant research, planning, and collaboration between several sectors. At present, it is unclear just how much domestic reform will be needed, but once properly planned and implemented this could be the key to CARICOM not only developing and becoming self-sustainable but also emerging as a hub for innovation.

Conclusions

Now is the time for an adjustment of national attitudes to the implementation of regional norms. Rather than reject regional notions we need to hold tight to each other. It is the time to look at change to avoid a 'Caribbean Brexit'.

Regional integration is based on the premise of equality and equitable distribution of prosperity and regional stability. This philosophy is a powerful tool to combat the economic and social challenges of globalisation. As one of the EU's founders, Jean Monnet highlighted in August 1952, 'our nations today must learn to live together under common rules and institutions freely arrived at'. While said many years ago and with reference to the EU, this is perhaps the strongest lesson the Caribbean region must adopt today in order to resolve its pending challenges.

As this chapter has shown, the challenges are not insurmountable, and options do exist for CARICOM to achieve its ultimate goal of regional integration and sustainability. It first considered a path closely aligned with the EU's visions, which could manifest as a 21st-century federation. This option offered the distinct advantage of building upon existing structures and critically analysing the EU, who have overcome similar obstacles. However, the caution highlighted was that though invaluable, the EU's contribution must be limited due to the Caribbean's unique realities and the ongoing uncertainties of the EU framework.

Further is the proposal for the diversification of CARICOM markets and trading relationships. This suggestion would afford the region a new level of independence and remedy its heavy reliance on external economies. However, it was clearly shown that to achieve these goals, partnerships on the regional and international scale would be key. No matter which path the region takes, what emerged was that now is the time to make the shift. The region is at a crossroads of crisis but also with a renewed level of political support. These factors could be the catalyst to combine the two aforementioned approaches to create an indigenous mechanism. This chapter will not instantaneously 'cure' CARICOM. However, if we can emancipate ourselves from the current mental slavery, the hope and future of CARICOM on the regional and international scale is bright.

Conclusions

14 Reflections for the future

Alicia Elias-Roberts, Stephen Hardy and Winfried Huck

Over a decade since EU-CARICOM was formed, it can be stated that this partnership has demonstrated both resilience and breadth. The relations between the EU and the Caribbean countries are based on different fundaments promoting political relations, trade and development. In the youngest past both the EU and the CARICOM shared the cognition for the need to reach out for the SDGs of the UN Global Agenda 2030, in particular to tackle climate change but also to address security. A greater framework and a deep impact for both the Caribbean countries, the CARICOM and the EU can be recognised in the ACP-EU Cotonou Agreement 2000, signed by 15 Caribbean nations. It has been expressed from the EU and the Caribbean States that the future ACP-EU Partnership from 2020 on will strengthen the ties between the EU and ACP countries on the world stage.

The Economic Partnership Agreement (EPA) with CARIFORUM and the 2012 Joint Caribbean EU Partnership Strategy reflect further in-depth relations with the EU. In October 2008 Antigua and Barbuda, The Bahamas, Barbados, Belize, Dominica, Grenada, Guyana, Jamaica, Saint Lucia, Saint Vincent and the Grenadines, Saint Kitts and Nevis, Suriname, Trinidad and Tobago, and the Dominican Republic signed the CARIFORUM-EU Economic Partnership Agreement. The Caribbean region also includes 16 territories with direct links to EU Member States (four French 'outermost regions'; and 12 'overseas territories' – five British, six Dutch and one French territory).[1] Another EU's counterpart for the bi-regional partnership process between the EU and the Caribbean States are the Community of Latin American and Caribbean States (CELAC), launched in 2010, which is a regional mechanism for political dialogue and cooperation involving the 33 countries of Latin America and the Caribbean (LAC).

As the previous chapters of this book have shown, the EU-CARICOM has enabled much trade, as well as diversification and promoting regionalism. The EU is CARIFORUM's second-largest trading partner, after the US.[2] Plainly, the EU-CARICOM share a commitment to equality, clearly resulting in increased

1 EU Commission International Cooperation and Development <https://ec.europa.eu/europeaid/regions/caribbean-0_en>.

2 EU Caribbean <https://ec.europa.eu/trade/policy/countries-and-regions/regions/caribbean/>.

and improved trade as a fortunate by-product. As Caribbean integration began its continuous evolution into the current CARICOM system during the 1970s, it has embraced the drivers of globalisation, such as trade, tax, investment and SDGs which now provide a vibrant development framework.

Having evaluated how EU-CARICOM relations have fostered trade and security and other development measures, through key case studies on key issues such as immigration, tax and energy, this book has widened awareness of the growing international significance of the EU-CARICOM. Notably, as this book has charted, with the pending Brexit of the UK, which also affects CARICOM, the EU-CARICOM relationship will have to ultimately remould itself. Above all, this book has highlighted how the EU-CARICOM epitomises multilateralism in terms of a model that provides the basis for many successful initiatives and agreements. Of growing importance is that all these new agreements and negotiations accept the SDGs and thus make inequality, climate change and other goals of the SDGs the basis of an order that puts people at the centre, as will the global agenda 2030 and its impact on EU-CARICOM.

In its survey of the key and diverse range of issues, including trade, tax, environment, sustainable development and migration, this book's survey, now complete, provided intuitive comparative evidence of how the EU-CARICOM model provides a new legal order, an alternative new strategic approach to EU-CARICOM issues. Notwithstanding Brexit (Chapter 2), as Hardy advocates, the UK is in search of a new legal order post-Brexit and one where the EU-CARICOM model offers an interesting trade as a legal tool. Further, in Part 1, Liu (Chapter 3) demonstrates how EU jurisprudence can be used to problem solve in anti-suit injunctive matters. It also served to warn against reverting back to the full practice of anti-suit injunctions and departing from established EU legal principles post-Brexit, a warning which equally applies to the EU-CARICOM relationship.

In Part II, Rogmann (Chapter 4) in assessing the WTO model, demonstrated that various standards of the EPA already form part of other multilateral instruments in the area of customs legislation. Prochno (Chapter 5) re-emphasised this key message in terms of the trends in digitalisation. The two major challenges in the context of trade facilitation were the implementation of a so-called Single Window concept and the introduction of blockchain technology into the digital infrastructure of shipping, discovering its potential beyond crypto currency. This contribution showed that EU-CARICOM was at the forefront of innovation and sustainable development. As was evidenced by Kurkin (Chapter 6), the implementation of Sustainable Development Goals (SDGs) in the energy and investment sectors showed EU-CARICOM effective interactions in the context of transnational law-making.

Gafoor et al. in Part III critically evaluated the key issues of taxation and immigration and their regulation in the EU-CARICOM and identified the development and evolution of the relationship between EU-CARICOM in relation to trade and development. This demonstrated how these two trading blocs grew through emerging developments in regional integration and the application and importation of trade-related principles through case law from both the Court of

Justice of the European communities, as well as the Caribbean Court of Justice in relation to treaty interpretation. Such scrutiny showed the growing global significance and importance to EU-CARICOM cooperation on tax avoidance. To that end, as MacLennan (Chapter 8) highlighted, for almost two decades institutions including the OECD, the EU, and, more recently, the G20 have sought to develop measures to curtail tax avoidance and failed, whilst the EU-CARICOM has triumphed in this legal arena. More significantly, this scrutiny highlighted that coordinated action against tax havens proves a more prudent and effective way of tackling tax avoidance. Further, it evidenced that the prevailing global trend is towards stricter rules on tax avoidance and that further action against tax havens, including those in the Caribbean, are needed in the future.

However, this book has also illuminated upon the social dimension to the EU-CARICOM. As Clarke-Mendes (Chapter 9) advocates, the new concept of self-deportation within the CARICOM region offers lessons for EU and wider-ranging reforms. Such a challenge must be met most pertinently if the EU-CARICOM State is to address the continuing fallout of the Venezuelan Refugee Crisis. In Part IV of this monograph, Elias-Roberts (Chapter 10) identified the challenges to maritime law as a means of illustrating that the EU-CARICOM shows how regional organisation provides an opportunity for development of new frontiers in the oil and gas industry. However, the current *Guyana v Venezuela* border dispute also exposes the potential weaknesses, or at least the sensitivities, in embracing regional integration.

Of more importance is how this book assesses the impact of globalisation. As Huck (Chapter 11) contended, the EU-CARICOM case study shows how embracing soft law, as opposed to well-established hard law approaches, enables more rapid and effective eradication of historical injustice and inequality through the application and implementation of SDGs. Such active corporate social responsibility has enabled the development of legal principles on sustainable development. Consequently, through adoption in international, inter-regional, European, national and transnational law, SDGs transform into directly applicable law and have a legally binding effect. Consequently, the future for EU-CARICOM, implementing the United Nations' Sustainable Development Goals and Global Agenda 2030, has enabled a human rights-based approach to development. As Stancke (Chapter 12) further elaborated, the usage of National Champions for SDGs is now well placed as an important tool for industrial politics, which means the potential for longer-term goals to tackle future structural problems. In the context of trade, Francis (Chapter 13) has explored the viability of the EU-CARICOM's current approach to development in light of recent global challenges. That analysis evidenced that the option of creating a totally indigenous proposal is welcomed and supported.

This book has covered several areas of law and provided evaluation and analysis of the jurisprudence in EU and CARICOM regional systems. However, this is only the start of an important discussion which highlights the relationship between the development of EU and CARICOM jurisprudence. Areas such as international environmental law, including climate change and biodiversity protection, integrating sustainable development into investment and development policies, corporate social responsibility and cyber security issues are dynamic areas that represent a growing jurisprudence in both the EU and CARICOM. While not covering all the disparate areas under the wide-ranging relationship between EU and Caribbean relations, this book sheds light on many areas that the EU CARICOM systems can learn from each other and forge the way forward to develop and strengthen the regional economic integration movements in both regional systems.

Overall, this concluding chapter shone a light towards the future in terms of producing a home-grown structure. Such a revolutionary approach could also encounter several challenges at the implementation level, such as maintaining CARICOM's competitiveness without foreign aid. Yet its forward-thinking approach has the potential to strengthen the future of transnational law and governance as well as sustainable development in EU-CARICOM relations. As this book has shown thorough the lens of development, law and economics, the EU-CARICOM model, as with all other legal models, is facing challenges of globalisation. However, such diversification, as shown throughout this evidence-based monograph, underlines that the diversification of the EU-CARICOM model, where the strength of renewal is seen through the prism of regionalism, an often-neglected legal area, is one which tackles dilemmas and can turn them into opportunities.

Index

For Product Safety Concerns and Information please contact our EU
representative GPSR@taylorandfrancis.com
Taylor & Francis Verlag GmbH, Kaufingerstraße 24, 80331 München, Germany

www.ingramcontent.com/pod-product-compliance
Ingram Content Group UK Ltd.
Pitfield, Milton Keynes, MK11 3LW, UK
UKHW022130190926
475702UK00013B/1720
9780367562335